DIY Divorce and Separation

The Expert Guide to Representing Yourself

DIY Divorce and Separation

The Expert Guide to Representing Yourself

By a Team of Barristers
from 1 Garden Court Family Law Chambers

Family Law

Published by Family Law
A publishing imprint of Jordan Publishing Limited
21 St Thomas Street
Bristol BS1 6JS

Whilst the publishers and the author have taken every care in preparing the material included in this work, any statements made as to the legal or other implications of particular transactions are made in good faith purely for general guidance and cannot be regarded as a substitute for professional advice. Consequently, no liability can be accepted for loss or expense incurred as a result of relying in particular circumstances on statements made in this work.

© Jordan Publishing Limited 2014

© 2014, cover image, Jessica Roberts at https://www.facebook.com/bbcreations24

All rights reserved. No part of this publication may be reproduced, stored in a retrieval system, or transmitted in any way or by any means, including photocopying or recording, without the written permission of the copyright holder, application for which should be addressed to the publisher.

Crown Copyright material is reproduced with kind permission of the Controller of Her Majesty's Stationery Office.

British Library Cataloguing-in-Publication Data

A catalogue record for this book is available from the British Library.

ISBN 978 1 84661 923 6

Typeset by Letterpart Limited, Caterham on the Hill, Surrey CR3 5XL

Printed in Great Britain by Hobbs the Printers Limited, Totton, Hampshire SO40 3WX

Contributors

From 1 Garden Court, Family Law Chambers
Andrew Bagchi
David Burles
Penelope Clapham
Julien Foster
Claire Heppenstall
Darren Howe
Nasstassia Hylton
Eleri Jones
Richard Jones
Kate Mather
Alison Moore
John Stocker
Simon Sugar

From 1 King's Bench Walk
Stephen Jarmain

From 36 Bedford Row
Stuart Nichols and Ian Robbins

Contents

Chapter 1
Introduction 1

Chapter 2
Initial Considerations 5
What you will learn 5
Is this the end of your relationship? 7
    Relationship counselling 8
    Couple therapy 9
The practical side of break ups – children and finances 10
    Children 10
    Finances 12
Resolving things without going court – collaboration, mediation
    and arbitration 14
    Collaboration 15
    Mediation 17
    Family arbitration 20
Going to court 21
How and when to obtain legal advice 21
Public or direct access barristers 25
Bar pro bono unit 26
Costs and funding 27
    Internet divorces 28
Resources 29
Dos and don'ts 29

Chapter 3
How to Think Like a Family Lawyer — 31
What you will learn — 31
Disputes involving children — 33
   Section 1 of the Children Act 1989 — 34
   Delay — 35
   Factors taken into account — 35
   The no order principle — 37
Disputes about your finances — 38
   Financial applications made by married couples or civil partners — 39
   Division of the assets and needs of the parties — 41
   Contributions, discrimination and the sharing principle — 42
   The compensation principle — 43
   A broad-brush approach — 44
   Full, frank and clear disclosure — 44
   Cohabitation claims — 45
Issues that need to be resolved on separation — 47
   If married/in a civil partnership — 47
   If unmarried — 49
   Issues connected with the children — 50
Preparations you need to make: information and evidence gathering — 52
   If there are issues connected with children — 52
   If there are financial issues that need to be resolved — 53
Case-law — 54
   Useful Websites — 58
Dos and don'ts — 59

Chapter 4
Bringing the Marriage/Civil Partnership to an End — 61
What you will learn — 61
Introduction — 61
The process of divorce — 68
   Statement of arrangements for children — 70

What do I have to send to the court with the petition?	70
Where do I send it to and how do I send the petition to my husband or wife?	71
Responding to a petition	73
Having received the acknowledgment of service there are three routes	74
A summary of an undefended application	74
A summary of a defended application	76
Ending a civil partnership	79
The grounds for ending the partnership	80
The process of dissolution of a civil partnership	80
An undefended dissolution	81
A defended dissolution	83
Annulment of a marriage/civil partnership	84
Judicial separation	85
Dos and don'ts	85

Chapter 5
Pre-proceedings Conduct and Case Preparation

	87
What you will learn	87
Introduction	87
Pre-proceedings negotiations and attempts at settlement	89
Without prejudice correspondence	89
Keeping a file	92
Mediation	93
Letters before action	95
Letter before action in financial remedy claims	96
Letter before action in cases concerning children	96
Preparation for court and the issue of proceedings	97
Where to issue your application?	97
What is required to issue your application?	98
Applications concerning children	98
Making an application	98
Urgent applications in cases concerning children	102

Responding to an application for an order concerning children	103
Applications for divorce of a marriage, dissolution of civil partnership or judicial separation	104
Applications for a financial remedy	104
Making an application	104
Responding to an application for a financial remedy	105
Applications for a non-molestation order or occupation order	105
Making an application	105
Responding to an application for a non-molestation or occupation order	106
Case preparation for interim hearings	107
Preparing the papers for the court hearing	107
Case summaries	109
Position statements	109
Is a bundle required for every hearing?	110
Case preparation for fact-finding and final hearings	110
Scott-Schedules and fact-finding hearings	110
Final hearings	112
Financial remedy proceedings	113
Preparation for hearings under Schedule 1 of the Children Act	113
Preparation for final hearings in applications for non-molestation and occupation orders	113
Preparing a statement for court	114
Enforcement	117
Dos and don'ts	117

Chapter 6
Advocacy – How Best to Make your Case at Court

	119
What you will learn	119
Introduction	119
Before you get to court – what to prepare	120
What do you want the court to do?	120
Case management documents	121
Telling the judge on paper what you want and why	121

Getting ready for the hearing	125
On the day	126
Types of hearing	128
Cases involving children	128
First hearing dispute resolution appointment	128
Interim/directions hearing	128
Fact-finding hearing	129
Final hearing	129
Financial cases	129
First directions appointment	129
Financial dispute resolution hearing (FDR)	129
Final hearing	130
Addressing the judge	130
Dealing with oral evidence and closing submissions	133
Questioning	135
Examination-in-chief	135
Cross-examination	136
Re-examination	137
How to prepare for being questioned	137
Closing submissions	138
Judgment	139
Permission to appeal	139
Dos and don'ts	139

Chapter 7
Domestic Violence	141
What you will learn	141
Introduction	141
Non-molestation orders	142
Examples of things that can be prohibited by non-molestation orders	143
Occupation orders	145
How to make an application for a non-molestation or occupation order	146
The application	146

The 'without notice' hearing	149
Serving the application (and order)	150
What happens if you are served with a non-molestation or occupation order	151
Factors the court takes into account	154
Without notice hearings	155
Orders and undertakings	156
Further provisions	158
Directions	158
Duration	159
Evidence and contested hearings	160
The statement in support	160
Schedule of allegations	161
Respondent's statement	162
The hearing	163
Appeal	165
Enforcement	166
Further information and guidance	168
Dos and don'ts	169

Chapter 8
Children — 171
What you will learn	171
Introduction	171
How to start proceedings	174
The Child Arrangements Programme (CAP)	174
Should I prepare a position statement for the FHDRA?	176
Review hearings	181
Dispute resolution appointments	181
Fact-finding and final hearings	185
Expert evidence	186
Enforcement	187
Costs	187
Appeals	188
Further research	189

Tips and traps	189
Having parental responsibility: sections 2 and 3 of the Children Act 1989	190
What does it mean?	190
Who has automatic parental responsibility for a child?	191
How does it work if more than one person has it?	191
Acquiring parental responsibility: section 4 of the Children Act 1989	192
Do fathers named on the birth certificate have parental responsibility?	192
What if the wrong person is named on the birth certificate?	193
Does a father who subsequently marries the mother acquire parental responsibility?	194
Can parents otherwise agree that the father should have parental responsibility?	194
If an unmarried father is not on the birth certificate and the mother does not agree to his having parental responsibility, can the court order it?	195
What should the court consider when deciding whether to grant parental responsibility to a father?	196
How does acquiring parental responsibility relate to seeking to spend time with a child?	196
Can a mother apply to court to impose parental responsibility upon the father?	197
Can a step-parent apply for parental responsibility?	197
Child arrangements and other orders in respect of children: section 8 of the Children Act 1989	197
Prohibited steps orders	199
Specific issue orders	199
Decisions about children: section 1 of the Children Act 1989	200
Dos and don'ts	204

Chapter 9
Finances	**207**
What you will learn	207

What are financial remedy proceedings?	207
What type of orders can a court make?	210
Principles governing the way in which the court decides what order to make	212
Section 25 factors	215
Starting the ball rolling – Form A	217
The financial information form – Form E	218
Gathering your own information about your spouse's financial means	220
Other documents that you must produce prior to the first appointment	221
Other documents that you might choose to produce prior to the first appointment	222
The first appointment	225
Service on mortgage companies/trustees etc	230
The first appointment hearing	230
Expert evidence	230
Questionnaires	232
Ordering the FDR appointment	233
Preparing for the first appointment	233
Steps following the first appointment	234
Using the first appointment as an FDR appointment	235
The financial dispute resolution appointment ('FDR')	236
How does an FDR work?	236
FDR – key points	238
Preparing for an FDR appointment – before the hearing	240
Preparation – the rules	240
Preparation – other steps	240
The FDR hearing	244
If you reach agreement – drawing up a final order	245
If you fail to reach agreement – directions order	246
The final hearing	247
Before the final hearing – general updating	247
Before the final hearing – exchanging 'open proposals'	248

Preparing 'the court bundle'	249
The final hearing itself	252
Judgment – drawing up the order	254
After the order has been made	254
Costs orders	254
Permission to appeal	255
Implementing the final order/'liberty to apply'	255
Appeal	255
Permission to appeal – time limits	256
Appealing 'out of time'	257
The appeal – a review and not a rehearing	257
New evidence	258
Respondent's notice	258
Stay	258
Variation	259
Interim hearings – maintenance pending suit, costs allowances and injunctions	260
Dos and don'ts	263

Chapter 10
Cohabitation

Cohabitation	265
What you will learn	265
What issues arise on cohabitation coming to an end?	265
Introduction to TOLATA claims	271
Basic principles	272
'Joint names' cases	274
'Sole name' cases	276
Procedural overview	279
Starting proceedings	281
Statements of case	282
Case management	283
Trial	284
Costs	285
Appeals	286
Further research	287

Do's and don'ts	287

Chapter 11
Obtaining Money for your Children from the Court

Obtaining Money for your Children from the Court	289
What you will learn	289
Introduction	289
Who qualifies?	290
What else do you need to know before making an application under Schedule 1?	292
How to make an application	293
The application process	293
Three possible court hearings to determine the outcome of your case	295
What the court will take into account when deciding your case	296
Factors set out in Schedule 1 of the Children Act 1989	297
Factors set out in the case-law	299
Some specific examples	300
Settlement of property and lump sum orders	300
Capital costs incurred in connection with the birth of the child or in maintaining the child and reasonably incurred before an order can be made	303
Income provision – generally	304
Income provision – where the child or non primary carer live abroad	306
School fees, university fees and training	306
Disabled children	307
Costs	307
The costs of running your case	307
Procedure	308
Costs orders at the end of proceedings	311
Checklist of things to think about if making or responding to a claim	313
If you are the person making the claim for the benefit of the child	313
If you are the person responding to a claim	315

Chapter 12
Enforcement of Court Orders — 317
What you will learn — 317
Introduction: what to do if the other side fails to comply with a court order – 'enforcement' — 317
Enforcement of orders relating to children (including child arrangements orders and other orders under the Children Act 1989) — 318
    The starting point – the importance of the warning notice — 319
    What happens if you do not comply with a child arrangements order or other Children Act 1989 court order? — 320
    What factors does the court consider when deciding whether or not to make an activity direction? — 321
    Are there any limits on making an activity direction? — 321
    What types of activities may be included? — 322
    Who can have an activity direction or an activity condition imposed upon them? — 323
    When can the court make an activity direction or activity condition regarding enforcement? — 324
    When can the court make an activity direction or activity condition? — 324
    When is the court prevented from making an activity direction or activity condition? — 325
    What if your ex partner is breaching the terms of the child arrangements order (or the previous contact order) and there is no warning notice attached? — 325
Enforcement orders — 326
    What must the court be satisfied about in order to grant an enforcement order? — 326
    Is there a defence to an enforcement order application? — 328
    Who has to prove 'reasonable excuse'? — 328
    Some important facts about enforcement orders — 328
    Committal to prison for contempt — 329

Are there any limitations on the court's ability to make an enforcement order?	329
Compensation for financial loss	330
Is there a defence to an application for compensation for financial loss?	330
Who has to prove reasonable excuse?	330
If the application is successful, how much compensation will be received?	331
How will the court determine how much compensation should be paid?	331
How to make an application for an enforcement order or an application for an order for financial compensation	331
Costs	332
Contempt of court (including the powers to impose a fine / committal to prison)	332
Order transferring who the child lives with	333
Useful resources	333
Enforcement of orders relating to finances	334
Methods of enforcement	334
Starting point – essential words	335
Does the person in breach of the order have any assets? – Obtaining information from judgment debtors	335
Which enforcement method should I use and how do I make my application?	336
Can I claim interest?	336
How can I remove an uncooperative party from the equation?	337
Can you raise money by selling or transferring the other party's assets or income?	337
How do you make an application?	338
What action will the court take?	338
What about the costs of the application?	339
Attachment of earnings order	340
If money is received via an attachment of earnings order, where does it go?	341

How does an attachment of earnings order work in practice?	341
How to make an application for an attachment of earnings order	342
The costs	343
Third party debt orders	343
How to make an application for a third party debt order	343
What action will the court take?	344
Execution against goods	345
How to make an application for an order for execution against goods	345
The costs	347
Fines and imprisonment (punitive / coercive)	347
What must the court be satisfied about in order to grant an order for a fine or imprisonment?	347
Judgment summons	348
How to make an application for an order for judgment summons	348
What action will the court take?	349
Committal for contempt of court	350
How to make an application for an order for committal to prison	352
Less common methods of enforcement	353
Enforcement of undertakings	354
Enforcement and variation	355
Further research	355
Dos and don'ts	356
Appendix	
Glossary	359
Index	369

Chapter 1

Introduction

Not so many years ago this book would have had a very limited market. Few people chose to represent themselves in family proceedings – and for good reason. Representing yourself in legal proceedings when you are not a lawyer is hard enough; representing yourself in family proceedings is even more difficult as a consequence of the inevitable emotional dimension to every case. However times change. More and more people are representing themselves. What was previously unusual is now commonplace.

There are two main reasons for the rise in self-representation. Public funding has been effectively abolished and many people are left with no option but to represent themselves following family breakdown. The provision of legal services has also changed beyond recognition and is now far more consumer driven. There are many who now choose to self represent, and take legal advice and obtain representation as and when necessary. A person representing themselves is known as a 'litigant in person' (LIP). Continuous legal representation from cradle to grave is fast becoming an unaffordable luxury and a thing of the past for many.

It is said that a journey of a thousand miles begins with a single step. This book is your first step in understanding the options available to you and the themes and issues that you will encounter as you embark upon the resolution of your family dispute. Consequently, the book is intentionally 'law lite' and conversational in tone. If you choose to represent yourself from the start to the end of the process, whether you have decided to use lawyers intermittently for advice or representation, or whether you just want to know more about the process of the resolution of family disputes to better understand what is driving your lawyers to act as they are, we hope this is the book for you.

One of our goals has been to produce a book that is relatively easy to read for non-lawyers. Nevertheless some areas of the subjects that we deal with are complex and difficult to understand and some chapters will need to be read more carefully than others. We have also not sought to provide you with a comprehensive statement of the law. Such a book would run to many volumes. Consequently we hope that our recommendation to read the book from cover to cover so that you get an overview of the entire process of dispute resolution following family breakdown is not too arduous. In order to make it easier to read, the book's key terms are explained in boxes. We have similarly used boxes within the text to highlight informative websites, and to deal with extracts from statutes which you may find useful to refer to.

The chapters in the book follow chronologically in broad terms the issues that you will encounter as your family break-up evolves. The first question asked in chapter 2 is whether in fact your relationship is at an end. The remainder of the chapter deals with the initial considerations that you will have to take into account as you move towards the resolution of the issues that arise following the breakdown of your relationship. On the basis that you have decided to separate, chapter 3 helps you to get inside the mind of a family lawyer in order to understand the key concepts that inform their judgment and their work in every case.

Chapter 4 provides assistance with the process that you are required to follow to formally bring your relationship to an end. Having started the legal process, the book moves on to shed some light on two crucial aspects of a lawyer's role in securing a favourable outcome for their client: effective case management and the art of advocacy. Case management is dealt with in chapter 5 and advocacy in chapter 6.

Domestic abuse will need to be dealt with as a matter of priority, and this is covered in chapter 7. Having resolved any potential domestic violence issues, you will need to resolve matters relating to the children before dealing with the financial issues that arise at the end of a marriage. Chapter 8 deals with children and chapter 9 with finances.

Of course, many couples choose to live together without getting married. On the breakdown of cohabitation different problems are required to be resolved. These issues are identified in chapter 10 and chapter 11, which deals with applications for financial relief on behalf of children, usually in cases where the parents were not married at separation.

Finally, for an unfortunate few, obtaining an order from the Family Court may not be the end of the process if your former partner fails to comply with an order of the court. The enforcement of orders is dealt with in chapter 12.

There are many legal terms which may at first appear to be difficult to understand, but this book aims to clarify and explain these (with the help of a glossary at the end of the book) and help you on your way to a successful outcome.

Chapter 2

Initial Considerations

What you will learn

- How to decide if this is the end of the relationship
- Your options for saving your relationship – counselling and therapy
- How to approach the practical side of break ups – children and finances
- How to resolve issues without going to court
- Collaboration, mediation and arbitration – what these terms mean
- What steps are involved if you go to court
- How and when to obtain legal advice

The process

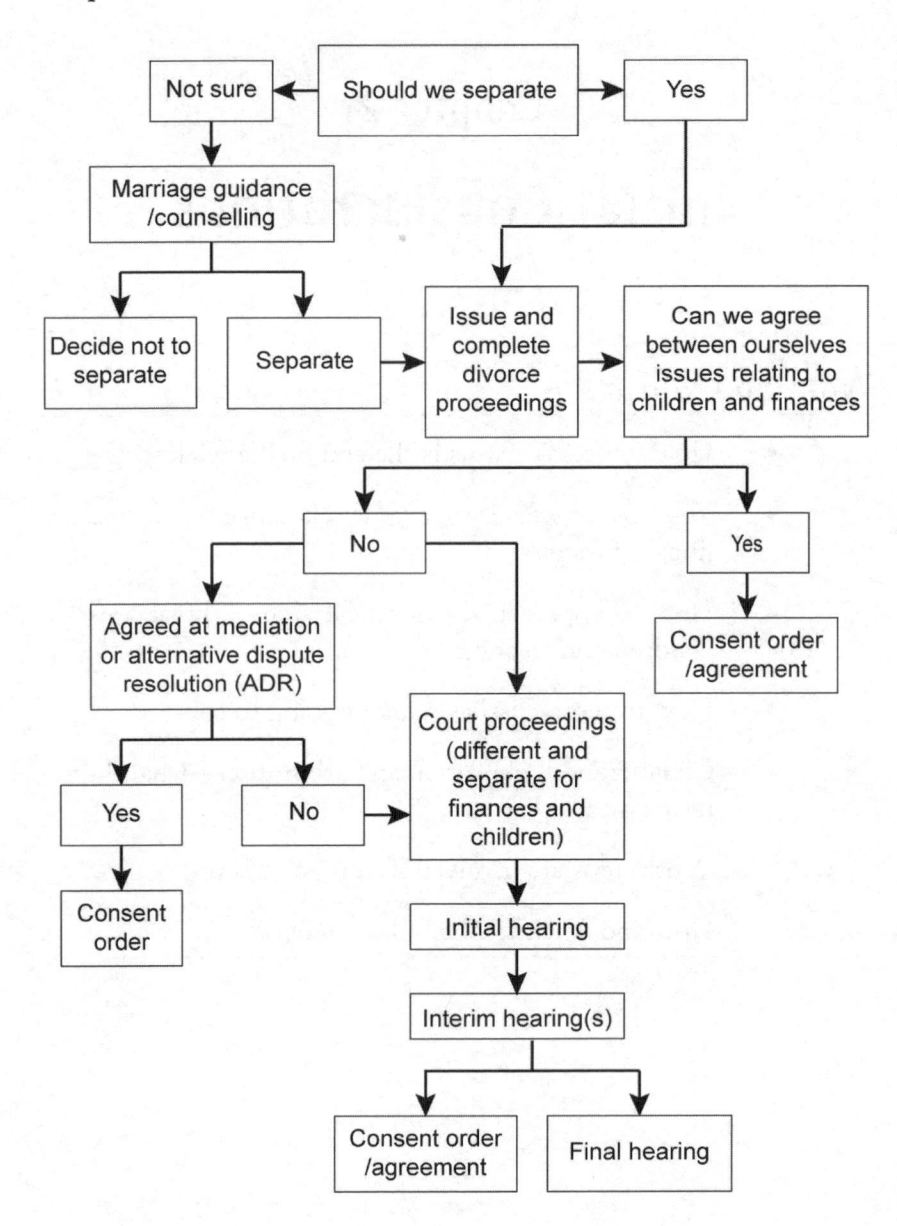

```
                    ┌─────────────────┐
      ┌─Not sure──  │Should we separate│  ──Yes──┐
      │             └─────────────────┘         │
      ▼                                         │
┌──────────────┐                                │
│Marriage      │                                │
│guidance      │                                │
│/counselling  │                                │
└──────────────┘                                │
    │      │                                    │
    ▼      ▼                                    ▼
┌────────┐ ┌────────┐    ┌──────────┐    ┌──────────────┐
│Decide  │ │Separate│───▶│Issue and │───▶│Can we agree  │
│not to  │ │        │    │complete  │    │between       │
│separate│ │        │    │divorce   │    │ourselves     │
└────────┘ └────────┘    │proceedings│    │issues relating│
                         └──────────┘    │to children   │
                                         │and finances  │
                                         └──────────────┘
                              │                  │
                              ▼                  ▼
                            ┌────┐             ┌───┐
                            │ No │             │Yes│
                            └────┘             └───┘
                          │      │                │
                          ▼      ▼                ▼
                 ┌────────────┐              ┌──────────┐
                 │Agreed at   │              │Consent   │
                 │mediation or│              │order     │
                 │alternative │              │/agreement│
                 │dispute     │              └──────────┘
                 │resolution  │
                 │(ADR)       │
                 └────────────┘
                    │     │
                    ▼     ▼
                 ┌───┐ ┌────┐    ┌─────────────┐
                 │Yes│ │ No │───▶│Court         │
                 └───┘ └────┘    │proceedings   │
                   │             │(different and│
                   ▼             │separate for  │
                 ┌───────┐       │finances and  │
                 │Consent│       │children)     │
                 │order  │       └─────────────┘
                 └───────┘             │
                                       ▼
                                ┌──────────────┐
                                │Initial hearing│
                                └──────────────┘
                                       │
                                       ▼
                                ┌──────────────┐
                                │Interim hearing(s)│
                                └──────────────┘
                                    │      │
                                    ▼      ▼
                           ┌──────────┐ ┌──────────┐
                           │Consent   │ │Final     │
                           │order     │ │hearing   │
                           │/agreement│ │          │
                           └──────────┘ └──────────┘
```

Is this the end of your relationship?

One of the biggest decisions anyone has to make even before contemplating the minefield of separation is in fact whether the relationship is really at an end. As emotions are understandably running high, it can be extremely difficult to make a rational decision without becoming clouded by feelings of hurt, bitterness or fright. For this reason, decisions about your future should not be knee-jerk reactions but need to be thought out clearly and from all angles with all the alternatives being identified.

It is normal for marriages to go through good and bad times but if things have not been working for some time then it may be the case that they are not going to improve. Very often, people continue to stay in a relationship for months even after it has, to all intents and purposes 'ended'.

Whether the problems come from money troubles or coping with the aftermath of an affair one useful tip given to people contemplating a break up is to sit down and make a list of the pros and cons of staying in the relationship/ending it. This can be a good way to focus on what you are getting or not getting from the relationship, on whether your needs are being met and whether on balance it is worth another try.

If the relationship is not at an end or you think it is worth trying to solve the problems, the most important thing is communication. By not talking to your partner the problems will simply fester and grow. Can you talk to one another about the problems in your relationship or does that simply result in more arguments? Is there a family friend or member of the family who could act as a kind of unofficial mediator for either you as an individual or for the two of you?

It may be worthwhile trying marriage guidance or relationship therapy.

> **(i) What is relationship therapy?**
>
> Relationship therapy is a method of counselling a couple to try and identify, manage and reconcile upsetting differences between them that have caused an ongoing cycle of distress.

Counselling can take place either face-to-face or can be done by email or telephone. It may be that counselling changes nothing, that the relationship cannot be transformed or the problem solved, but often it can help. If it does not, it is likely to enable you to look at things from a different perspective, to approach the problem from a new angle. Sometimes it can just help to have someone give advice who has the advantage of being an outsider looking in and is not wrapped up in the emotional turmoil that you are both experiencing.

Whilst there is a whole array of services available for couples they broadly fall into either *'relationship counselling'* or *'couple therapy'*.

Relationship counselling

Relationship counselling refers to a process of a few sessions (1–3 for instance) to help people, often a couple, recognise and better manage or even reconcile their differences; breaking the constant pattern of anguish. This model is not exclusive to couples and has been used to assist where family members have fallen out.

The basic principles behind such counselling include:

- aiming to improve communication between the two of you;

- providing a confidential space for constructive dialogue between you;

- permitting both you and your partner to speak freely and to be able to listen to one another;

- providing a 'mirror' to reflect where the relationship is and assist in moving the direction of that relationship;

- empowering you both to take charge of your relationship; to help you both feel there is 'a way out' of the cycle.

Couple therapy

In contrast, couple therapy is frequently a longer process than counselling and can be for upwards of 12 to 24 sessions. This addresses more deep rooted intractable problems and uses emotions as the key to solving these problems. In couple therapy the therapist will try and help you to:

- identify the repetitive and damaging elements in your relationship as a cycle;

- understand the emotions that drive that cycle;

- rethink emotional responses;

- move your communication to a new and more positive form;

- enable new and more positive bonding within the relationship; and

- develop a sustained sense of intimacy.

It is well worth looking at Relate's website if you both want to try and make the relationship work. It may not succeed in the end in keeping you together but it may well be worth a try. It may also be worthwhile contacting your GP who can recommend local services to assist you keeping your relationship together.

> For information and support about your relationship and for your nearest Relate go to:
>
> www.relate.org.uk

The practical side of break ups – children and finances

If the relationship really is irretrievable, then you will need to think about how best to bring your marriage or civil partnership to a formal end. The steps you need to take are dealt with in chapter 4.

The first thing to stress is that after a divorce or separation the focus has to be on the future. The two big areas of shared arrangements and responsibility are typically children and finances, so how these will be handled is of particular importance. These are also the areas that can cause the greatest arguments and distress.

Dealing with practical issues sucessfully requires a dispassionate approach – not easy when the relationship is breaking down. Very often people become fixed on analysing the past, and often focus on the break down itself, be it 'Whose fault was it?' 'Where did I go wrong?' or 'How could s/he or she do this to me?' As understandable as this is, all this does is lock you into a cycle of bitterness and anger, and will not help you plan for the future. Whilst emotionally upsetting, a more positive approach to handling these thoughts may be to think about what was lacking in the relationship or in what areas it failed to meet both your own needs and those of your partner.

Children

One very practical issue that may need to be addressed is the welfare and needs of your children. There are a number of initial considerations that you ought to bear in mind. You both need to give careful thought as to where the children are going to live and how often you will both see them. Some couples divide the week up in a manageable form whereas for others there is one clear resident parent with whom the children live and they see the non-resident parent every weekend or alternate weekends. Arrangements change from family to family but some form of routine needs to be established quickly so that the children do not feel more unsettled than they need to.

Whilst children do not need to know all the details of what is going on in their parents' divorce, they should not be lied to or misled. All they need to know is that the arrangements for the family are changing and that you and your partner are trying to sort it out. You both need to ensure that children are not exposed to sudden changes in arrangements unless they are absolutely unavoidable.

Children need to be reassured that what is happening is not their fault and that though as parents you will be living apart that does not mean that they cannot have a full relationship with both of you. Even if one parent lives far away, communication can be maintained, be it by text, telephone, cards and emails, Skype etc.

Whilst most of the focus may be on you as a couple, be clear that any children of the relationship will be enormously affected by the break up. Children must be reassured that whatever is happening in terms of their parents' relationship, they are still very much loved by both of you and will continue to be. A key point to keep in mind is that children have the right to a relationship with both their parents. During the time that you are both sorting out arrangements it is important to ensure children are able to keep in touch with wider family and friends who have always been involved in their lives so that there is continuity for them. Likewise, any new partners either of you have need to be supportive of new arrangements and have good relationships with the children.

Finances

The other major practical issues are finances. You will need to sort these out both in the long term and of course in the short term to meet your immediate needs. Whilst the prospect may seem like a maze you must remember that you are one of thousands of everyday people who have been through this process – and survived. Obviously no one comes out at the end of the divorce process talking of a great experience but it can be an amicable process. Many people can become fixed on the emotional hurt of divorce which results in them focusing on more minor petty matters like who gets the car. The key thing is for both couples to focus on being practical and sensible in respect of resolving short and longer-term financial issues.

Understandably, when divorcing the temptation is to think mostly about what you want here and now but what you also need to do is focus on your longer-term needs. For example, if you live in Coventry with no family in the area and think you may want to move to Swansea to be close to your family in three years time when your child begins secondary school, this is something that needs to be thought about now. Many people can end up back in court even after a settlement because they have not looked ahead as to their future needs.

You will need to have a think about your income and what money the family will need to live separately as two houses. There may be areas where you will have to 'cut back'. Ensure that existing bills and debts are not ignored but are dealt with in terms of who will pay them and when. It is not possible to say with any accuracy how long it will take to resolve any financial dispute. If the matter is not resolved by agreement between you; it may be that it takes around a year to resolve a dispute through the courts. In the event that no agreement is reached, it is possible to apply to the court for an interim order but be careful not to run up unnecessary costs. An alternative is to make enquiries with your bank to see if they can assist.

> **What is an interim order?**
>
> An interim order is a hearing to deal with matters that arise before a final hearing.

> A useful website to visit to assist with managing your financial affairs is:
>
> www.moneyadviceservice.org.uk

If you have a high level of assets or your money is set up in a particularly complex way, it might be sensible to get some advice on the tax implications of divorce/separation from an accountant or a lawyer who is used to dealing with such issues.

> The government also produces a 'helpsheet' which will give guidance – for example:
>
> www.hmrc.gov.uk/helpsheets/hs281.pdf

One practical tip. If it is possible, try and time any separation so that it does not occur just prior to the end of a tax year as it will give you little time to think about the most tax efficient arrangements for you. In general terms, transfers between spouses of capital assets do not give rise to a charge of capital gains tax if the transfer takes place in the tax year of separation. In an appropriate case early consultation with a tax adviser would be sensible.

Always keep in mind that your bank accounts will be scrutinised by your partner and potentially their lawyer – so don't take out any anger by way of a wild spending spree by running up money on credit cards. Remember, the court has the power to add back money wasted in such a way.

Child maintenance needs to be addressed where relevant. This needs to be paid regularly and reliably to assist in the upkeep of the children.

> **What is child maintenance?**
>
> Child maintenance is paid by a parent to provide help with a child's everyday living costs which include things like food, clothes, and helping to provide a home for them.

Resolving things without going court – collaboration, mediation and arbitration

If it is possible, sensible co-operation is the best way to resolve a divorce and the arrangements that need to be made in respect of finances and children. This is of course very often easier said than done but it is worth keeping in mind the reality that if the process of deciding who gets what or how much time the children should spend with either parent becomes a lengthy drawn out process then no one will come out of it feeling that something has been achieved; not to mention the cost in emotional and financial terms. It is worth focusing on the fact that though you may not wish to give money to your other half, neither of you will want to give more money to lawyers than is strictly necessary.

There are a number of different ways to resolve disputes without going to court and they will be dealt with below. Collaborative law, mediation and arbitration (all explained below) are methods of alternative dispute resolution. Think long and hard about which of the processes you feel most comfortable with.

> (*i*) **What is alternative dispute resolution?**
>
> Also known as ADR, this is a process that tries to enable parties with differences to come to an agreement instead of engaging in litigation and going to court.

You cannot force your former partner to engage in any of these alternative methods of dispute resolution. The final method of dispute resolution is litigation in the courts.

If you can have a constructive and calm discussion with your former partner this will assist. It is important to keep in mind that blame for the breakdown of the marriage is not a relevant consideration for the future.

> **Some incredibly useful tips about how to take the heat out of discussions and generally on how to deal with some of the issues that arise on separation can be found at:**
>
> www.cmoptions.org

Collaboration

Collaborative law is a way for a couple to work together with trained professionals so as to resolve disputes without going to court. Both sides can have the assistance of their own legal team who can call in experts, such as accountants, to assist at any point.

The only elements of the court process in this context involve dealing with the legal formalities of the divorce itself and of approving the settlement that is agreed. Many people opt for a collaborative approach as it has the following advantages over engaging in the court process:

- it is cheaper as you avoid the significant expenses involved in court hearings;

- it is quicker as it can often take months to wait for a court hearing;

- the process is open and transparent with you both taking control of the issues you wish to be resolved and the pace at which that is done;

- it removes the need for often very lengthy and expensive correspondence between the parties respective legal teams;

- it increases your chances of obtaining an outcome that you can both live with which is much more preferable than having a decision imposed on you by a judge; and

- it is non aggressive.

The collaborative format is a series of meetings with the couple and their respective solicitors – which means it is a four way face-to-face discussion. To prepare for this you will of course have a private meeting with your own solicitor beforehand.

As with mediation, there is full and open disclosure in terms of finances so that an informed agreement can be reached.

In the event that no agreement is ultimately reached, the solicitors who participated in the process will not be able to represent you at court and new ones will need to be appointed. In itself this very factor can be a powerful incentive to settle.

> ⓘ **What is the difference between the collaborative process and mediation?**
>
> There is a fundamental difference between the collaborative process and mediation. In the collaborative process you are guided as a couple to reach an agreement with everyone working as a team. This contrasts with mediation as in that process, the mediator cannot advise or represent anyone.

Mediation

Mediation is a process that enables couples to negotiate a way forwards face to face with the help of a neutral third party (a mediator).

There are 4 main principles of mediation:

- It is a **voluntary** process where you will not be pressurised into either participating or making a particular decision. Mediators will however be cautious about undertaking cases where there have been instances of abuse or violence or where there is a clear imbalance of power between the parties.

- The mediator or mediators are **impartial** and will not express an opinion or try and persuade you into any particular course of action. They will not be able to provide you with any advice on the merits of a settlement, although they can give you legal information.

- Mediation is a **confidential process** with the only exceptions being if issues of child protection, severe domestic violence, or issues relating to money laundering arise. Any proposals that the parties agree on can be drawn up in a confidential summary called 'a memorandum of understanding'. This document will not be legally binding until it is drawn up as a legal document or reviewed by the court. It is important to remember that the confidential summaries cannot be referred to within court proceedings, so they cannot be used if you do need to go to court. As part of the mediation process there must be full and frank disclosure between the parties so that each has a complete picture of the financial assets available.

- The couple are themselves the **decision makers**, not the mediator. The mediation process is all about enabling you both to be able to work out what is best for you and your family moving forwards.

Mediation can fall into three categories: children mediation, finance mediation and all issues mediation. The important thing about all mediation is that before you start exploring options for the future, you both have a clear financial picture of each other. The other crucial thing is that once you have this picture, time is given to consider the various options that are available.

Usually mediations follow the following format:

- to set the agenda of what it is you both want to discuss in the process and set out the issues that you need to address;

- to work out the order in which the issues you have identified need to be addressed, for instance, does maintenance and where the children are going to live need to be sorted out first before the long term issues such as division of assets;

- to put in place time scales to deal with particular issues such as when maintenance is to begin, how frequently it is to be paid and into what account;

- look at the various options open to you for the long term for instance, whether the matrimonial home should be sold; and

- once you have reached a resolution that you are both content with ensure it is put in documentary form before the parties are sent to take legal advice on the agreement reached.

Mediation can be an emotionally draining process and will be difficult. It is by no means a 'soft option'.

It is worth you being aware that if you are considering going to court then you are required in the first instance to attend a Mediation Information and Assessment Meeting (MIAM) with a mediator (either with or without your partner) to assess whether your dispute is suitable for mediation (it may not be suitable if one of you has been subject to domestic violence, for example).

> **What is a Mediation Information and Assessment Meeting?**
>
> A Mediation Information and Assessment Meeting (or MIAM) is a meeting between you (with or without your partner) and a mediator which you must attend before you can make an application to the court. The purpose of the MIAM is to see if you can resolve your difficulties through mediation rather than going to court.

One thing to keep in mind is that you should not enter the mediation room with a fixed view about what should happen or what you think a court would decide. Keep an open mind about exploring and finding a way forward that works for you both.

> For further information about how mediation can help you sort out arrangements for your children and your finances and help you find a mediator in your local area go to:
>
> www.familymediationcouncil.org.uk

Family arbitration

Family arbitration is a process whereby you both appoint one specialist family arbitrator to settle the issues between you. Like mediation, it is confidential and is a voluntary process but the purpose of it is to deliver a decision that is intended to bind both of you. Also like mediation, it is not dependent on court dates and you will not have to wait several months for a date. The arbitrator will only make decisions on issues identified by you both as requiring resolution and the identified arbitrator can be the same individual throughout the process.

At the outset, the arbitrator will provide you both with written information outlining what the process will be. This will then be followed by a formal first meeting to identify the information that will need to be obtained to ensure that the arbitration can proceed effectively.

Whereas mediation is a process that enables you both to reach your own decision, the arbitrator will impose an outcome on you both. It is an option for you to be represented at the arbitration meetings by either a solicitor or a barrister but it is not a must and you are perfectly entitled to represent yourself.

> You can find out more about arbitration and search for a local arbitrator at:
>
> http://ifla.org.uk

Going to court

Litigation through the courts is the traditional method of coming to a resolution in family proceedings. This can be expensive, confrontational and slow; however it does not have to be. In both children and financial cases the court rules, known as the Family Procedure Rules (the 'FPR'), are devised with a view to achieving speedy resolution and saving costs. Indeed the early stages of the court process are designed very much with the idea of trying to move the parties to reach their own settlement as quickly as possible with the assistance of a judge. If you are unable to reach a settlement the role of the judge is to decide the outcome of a case following a trial. There is no doubt that trials are expensive, confrontational and emotionally draining.

> **What is litigation?**
>
> This is the process of taking a case through the court where the decision is made by the judge.

How and when to obtain legal advice

You may well choose to do a substantial part or perhaps all of the work involved in your divorce by yourself, or you may choose to use a lawyer occasionally or for a specific purpose, depending on the cost.

If you have limited funds you should plan ahead and try to think in advance about the kind of help you might need with your case.

Set goals of the top things you really think you need to achieve. Be realistic when setting goals, for instance if you work long hours throughout the week and your spouse has always been the full time carer of the children it may well be an up-hill struggle to have the children live with you half of the time. Calmly think about what is realistic when setting your goals for the future.

Choosing a lawyer is a matter of personal choice. Try to choose a solicitor/barrister who wants to resolve the case amicably but who is prepared to stand up for your rights and take the case to court if needs be. Be wary of overly aggressive lawyers. An overly aggressive stance is likely to back your former partner into a corner leaving them with no option but to fight back – which is a recipe for increased and frequently unnecessarily high legal costs.

> **What is a barrister?**
>
> Barristers can also be known as 'counsel'. They are lawyers instructed by solicitors to represent you in court. You can also go directly to a barrister to discuss your case and for representation (known as public or direct access).

Find out clearly and in advance how much you will be charged for the provision of legal services. When looking to choose a lawyer, ensure that you are fully aware of what services each lawyer is offering and what their charges are. There are some lawyers that offer a fixed quote but make sure you are aware of exactly what is and is not included in this together with what the costs would be if something unexpected happened in the case. Shop around. Ensure that you compare like for like with a clear understanding of what the lawyers' fees are together with VAT charges and all disbursements.

> **What are disbursements?**
>
> The term disbursements refers to money paid by your lawyer to third parties and cover such expenses as court fees and fees for barristers.

Make sure that you know what disbursements are covered and ask for clarity about any such charges that have not been mentioned. Given that the cost of a divorce will vary case to case most lawyers will not be in a position to tell you exactly how much the process will cost and will instead provide you with an estimate of the amount of work they are likely to undertake together with their costs. At each stage in the process, ask for updates as to costs and ensure you have an agreement as to how you are to be informed as to these costs, be it email or letter for instance.

Deciding to use the services of a lawyer is one thing. Finding one is another. Personal recommendations are obviously helpful and you should ask friends and family for any recommendations.

> **If you wish to instruct a solicitor a good resource is the 'find a members' tab on the Resolution website at:**
>
> **www.resolution.org.uk**

Resolution is an organisation of family lawyers and other professionals who believe in a constructive, non-confrontational approach to family law matters. A solicitor who is a member of Resolution has to stick to a strict code of conduct. If you wish to instruct a direct access barrister, the Bar Council is an organisation that represents barristers.

> **To instruct a direct access barrister look at the public access directory on the Bar Council website at:**
>
> **www.barcouncil.org.uk**

If you chose to represent yourself in court proceedings you will be referred to as a 'litigant in person'. Whilst you may represent yourself you may also decide to have someone accompany you to assist you at court. Such a person is known as a 'McKenzie friend'.

> **What is a McKenzie Friend?**
>
> A non-legally qualified person who helps a litigant in person at court by providing support.

The term McKenzie friend comes from a famous case in 1970 and whilst it is not an automatic right to have a McKenzie friend, the judge would only refuse for you to have one for a good reason. A McKenzie friend is not able to act on your behalf or as an agent in relation to matters outside of court, for example they cannot negotiate on your behalf or sign documents on your behalf. Also, they cannot address the court on your behalf or examine any of the witnesses. In truly exceptional circumstances, a McKenzie friend may be granted by the court 'rights of audience' and then they will be able to speak on your behalf in court; however such a right is unlikely to be granted other than in truly exceptional circumstances.

What a McKenzie friend can do is:

- provide you with moral support;
- take notes for you in court;
- assist you with the court papers;
- quietly and privately provide you with advice and observations as to law and procedure;
- remind you of issues that you wish to raise in court; and
- assist you with questions you may wish to ask in court.

You may not have had a good marriage; but aim for a good divorce.

Public or direct access barristers

You are probably aware of the existence of two legal professions: barristers and solicitors. Traditionally the public would instruct a solicitor who would provide initial advice and handle the legal matters, but could not appear in court. Barristers had that right, so the solicitor would in turn instruct a barrister to handle representation in court. However, the division in function between the two professionals has all but broken down. Solicitors can and do represent clients in court. Barristers can and do provide initial advice, draft letters and conduct litigation on your behalf. It used to be the case that it was not possible for a member of the public to instruct a barrister directly without going to a solicitor first. This rule is no longer in existence. It comes as a surprise to many to learn that it is now possible to approach a barrister directly without having to first involve a solicitor. This is known as public or sometimes direct access. In many respects the role of the barrister does not change from what they would do if instructed through a solicitor. They are able to draft and send documents for you and represent you in court or in a mediation for instance. They will also be able to advise you on your legal status or on your rights. In many cases instructing a barrister directly can lead to significant costs savings.

Importantly, however, not all barristers accept public access work so have a look at the public access directory where you can search for barristers by town, city, name or area of practice. The Bar Council has set up a telephone number and email address for enquiries as to public and licensed access:

Telephone: 0207 611 1472

Email: PAenquiry@BarCouncil.org.uk

Look also at the various family chambers on the internet to see whether they do direct or public access work. Remember, there may still be some very complex instances where you will need to instruct a solicitor in addition to a barrister.

Bar pro bono unit

This is a charity that assists you in finding pro bono (free) legal help from volunteer barristers. They can help with advice and representation at court and for mediations both where proceedings are underway and where they have yet to begin. Please be aware that pro bono assistance is available only to those who cannot afford to pay and who are not eligible to public funding.

Finally, there are some general tips that you should be aware about when it comes to instructing lawyers:

- Communication is key and this works both ways. Your lawyer must consult you as to decisions to be made in the case and likewise you must ensure that your lawyer is fully informed of what exactly you want, for instance, if there is some jewellery which is of such sentimental value to you that you feel you could not part with it, ensure that this is communicated so that it can form part of an agreement.

- Do try to listen to advice given as you are employing these experts for a reason. They will tell you if you have unrealistic expectations and help you 'reality check' the situation along the way. If you are unhappy with the advice given, you could consider a second opinion.

- Lawyers have other cases apart from yours and when dealing with solicitors try and think about the units of charge so as to ensure you spend no more than is absolutely necessary. Remember, whilst your lawyer is there to assist you through the process they are not there as a friend or as a counsellor. Lawyers are expensive and it is important to remember what their role is.

- If there is anything you are not certain about – ask!

Costs and funding

The general rule in both financial disputes and those relating to children is that each side pays its own costs. Only in unusual cases where misconduct is established will one party have to pay the other side's costs. In most cases however, you need to be concerned only about how you pay for your own legal costs. There are a number of options to consider.

Perhaps the first thing that you need to consider are your own resources. Do you have excess income over your monthly needs to assist you to fund legal costs? Do you have any savings or policies that you might reasonably surrender? Are there any family members or indeed friends who would be prepared to give or loan you money to assist with legal costs? Remember that in cases where the assets are modest, there is a risk that a loan from family members might be considered a soft loan (ie not immediately repayable). Having identified the level of your own resources that are available to fund legal expenses you will then need to think about how best to use those resources. Your options include an initial advice on possible outcome but perhaps more importantly on the evidence required to assist your case. An advice on merits after all the evidence is obtained is obviously useful. Finally you will need to think about representation.

> **It is unlikely that you will receive legal aid to assist you with your case. You can find out if you are entitled to legal aid from the Legal Aid Calculator at:**
>
> www.communitylegaladvice.org.uk/en/legalaid/calculator.jsp

Banks may assist you with a loan and some will seek to link the loan with an agreement to be repaid out of the final settlement in the case. There is also the possibility to 'roll up' the interest payments due into the final payment so that no repayment will be made before the end of the case.

In certain circumstances it is possible to apply to the court for an order for money to be made available out of your other half's income or for some capital contribution from them to enable you to meet the costs of legal fees. However, for this to occur there must be the money available there in the first place and all other options must have been explored which includes the option of a 'Sears Tooth' agreement.

> **What is a Sears Tooth agreement?**
>
> A Sears Tooth agreement is named after a famous London firm of solicitors. It takes the form of a deed in which the client is agrees to assign his or her rights in any financial orders to the instructing solicitor which enables them to cover the costs incurred in representing the client. Once the case is finished, the solicitor pays himself in full from the fund, before giving the client their entitlement. The court will uphold this type of agreement if it is entered into, signed by you in front of a witness and after obtaining independent legal advice. It is possible for a lump sum to be assigned in this way in court proceedings. Once entered into, the fact of the agreement must be disclosed both to the other party and to the court. Not all solicitors accept this form of payment as it is a risk for them given that during the course of the proceedings, they will be left with the cost of the case.

Internet divorces

You may have heard about 'internet divorces' and whilst the internet can be a useful place for information beware of sites that charge you money for document packages. Remember, all divorce documents can be obtained for free either from your local court or can be downloaded from the Court Service website. These forms are accompanied with helpful guidance and are completed online.

> **To download these forms from the Court Service website go to:**
>
> **https://www.justice.gov.uk/forms/hmcts**

Resources

- http://www.relate.org.uk/
- www.moneyadviceservice.org.uk
- http://www.hmrc.gov.uk/helpsheets/hs281.pdf
- www.cmoptions.org
- www.familymediationcouncil.org.uk
- http://ifla.org.uk
- www.resolution.org.uk
- www.barcouncil.org.uk
- www.communitylegaladvice.org.uk/en/legalaid/calculator.jsp
- https://www.justice.gov.uk/forms/hm

Dos and don'ts

DOS

✔ **DO** consider carefully if separation really is the road you want to go down

- ✔ **DO** weigh up the pros and cons of separation
- ✔ **DO** consider if counselling is possible to help your relationship
- ✔ **DO** look at what the arrangements will be for the children – where will they live and when are they going to see their other parent
- ✔ **DO** think about what your financial needs are both in the short and long term
- ✔ **DO** investigate the various forms of alternate dispute resolution before turning to the courts

DON'TS

- ✘ **DON'T** look only to your short term needs without consideration of your long term future
- ✘ **DON'T** ignore the likely impact of separation on your children; consider who will tell them what is happening and how you are going to reassure them
- ✘ **DON'T** rush to court without exploring more cost effective and less aggressive ways of resolving matters

Chapter 3

How to Think Like a Family Lawyer

What you will learn

- An introduction to the key legal concepts involved in disputes connected with children

- An introduction to the key legal concepts involved in disputes connected with married couples and civil partners

- An introduction to the key legal concepts involving cohabitants

- The steps that you need to consider when considering separation

- The approach to be adopted in preparing for court

- Useful information that you might need to access in readiness for court

The aim of this chapter is to give you an introduction and overview of the key legal concepts that govern a court's approach to dealing with family law issues. Understanding these key concepts will enable you to be better placed to understand how your dispute is likely to be resolved. Once you know how to think like a family lawyer, you will be better equipped to read and understand some of the more detailed chapters in this book.

Throughout this chapter (and in other parts of the book) you will see references to 'Acts' also called 'statutes' for example the Children Act 1989 which provide the overall framework for the court in family law matters. But every case – like every family – is different. Situations are rarely black and white, and often both sides in a dispute have good points. So courts operate under a principle of 'broad discretion' which means that the court will apply the principles behind the law in a flexible way, to best accommodate the needs of the particular case before it.

There is a difference in the court's approach depending on whether children are involved, the case only involves the financial impact of the separation of a couple, or, in some cases, whether the couple are married or unmarried. As we go through the book we will tell you which part of the law is relevant for the situation we are discussing. Although you (as a non-lawyer), will not be expected to know the law in detail, the law will always form the basis of the court's decision, and is what lawyers refer to, so it is useful to know their sources.

Statutes are the primary source of law that governs the court's approach. The main statutes for family lawyers to consider are:

(1) The Children Act 1989 (for all children related issues).

(2) The Child Support Act 1991 (for all maintenance issues connected with children).

(3) The Civil Partnership Act 2004 (for the law applicable to civil partners and the law applicable to issues connected with the relationship breakdown).

(4) The Matrimonial Causes Act 1973 (the law applicable to married persons and the law applicable to issues connected with the marriage breakdown).

Statutes are often broken down into numbered sections, sub-sections, paragraphs and sub-paragraphs which lawyers refer to in a shortened form, eg s 1(3)(c) of the Children Act 1989 (meaning section 1, sub-section 3, paragraph c).

> **The statutes can be downloaded from the official website at:**
>
> **www.legislation.gov.uk**

Disputes involving children

This section will cover the legal concepts involved when the court deals with disputes between parents over the care of their children. A child is defined as someone who is under the age of 18, but for children over 16 the court will usually only deal with living arrangements (unless there are exceptional circumstances).

At the outset, it must be stressed that it makes no difference to the court's approach whether the parents are married or unmarried. Both married parents of a child share parental responsibility and have equal standing before the court. If the child's parents are unmarried, as long as the unmarried father was named on the child's birth certificate (for children born after 2003) – both will share parental responsibility.

However, even if an unmarried father is not named on the birth certificate (or the children were born before 2003), he would still have the right to make applications to the court and the court will recognise him as the father. The main difference for an unmarried father without parental responsibility is that the mother is not obliged to consult with him or seek his agreement in advance of certain decisions eg choice of name for the child, choice of religion, choice of school etc. However, the court will still allow him to make applications for these disputed issues to be determined by the court if there is no agreement.

When making an application in relation to a child, the key statute that you will need to consider is the Children Act 1989. If you are a parent (or other relative or involved person) making or defending an application in relation to a child, you should read certain key sections, which establish and underpin the court's approach.

For more detailed guidance on the procedure regarding making or defending an application in connection with your child see chapter 8 and also chapter 11 (for financial issues connected with your child).

Section 1 of the Children Act 1989

The most important concept you need to know is that, when dealing with children, the court must follow the principle of putting the child's welfare first (the law uses the phrase 'paramount consideration').

This means that when coming to a decision, the court must independently consider in every case how the child's welfare is going to be best served. This is a fundamental principle, and lies at the heart of every judicial decision where a child is concerned.

The court is essentially charged to reach a decision, which it considers to be in the child's best interests. In determining what is in the child's best interests, it must be made clear that the court is not interested in the notion of safeguarding the parent's 'rights' or indeed the child's 'rights' – the court will only consider what the best interests of the child require.

A court reaches a decision as to what is in a child's best interests by considering and taking into account all the relevant facts, relationships, claims and wishes, the risks, the competing choices and any other relevant circumstances. Once information on all those factors has been gathered, they are then taken into account and weighed in what will be a balancing exercise for the court. The course that the court finally follows will be that which the court has determined is most in the interests of the child's welfare.

Delay

Section 1(2) of the Children Act 1989 makes it clear that, in general, any delay in determining the issues in question is likely to prejudice the welfare of the child.

Unfortunately, pressure on the courts caused by the volume of cases has tended to lengthen the time that can be taken for a case to come to a final decision. Senior judges are working hard to overcome this and have introduced case management protocols or directives in an effort to ensure that as little time as possible is wasted.

Finally, sometimes delay can be described as serving a purpose, eg if further enquiries or particular assessments need to be carried out. These further enquiries may actually be in the child's best interests and in such circumstances the delay would not be viewed as prejudicial to the welfare of the child.

Factors taken into account

When making decisions about children (such as with whom they will live or spend time, and what parents should or should not do), the law specifies some factors the court must take into account. This is commonly known as the 'welfare check-list'. It would be better for the child than making no order at all. It will always ask 'Will it be better for the child to make the order than making no order at all'.

That said, in most cases where the court has to intervene to resolve a dispute, it is likely to be in the child's best interests for an order to be made. Clear instructions about arrangements can help give certainty and structure, and will potentially reduce the likelihood of damaging arguments and further disputes going forward. Even where parties reach agreement at court as to the way forward, the fact that there has been a dispute previously (and hence the application to the court) means it may well be sensible for an order to be put in place to assist in regulating future behaviour.

Disputes about your finances

When it comes to money and finances, the courts treat married and unmarried couples differently. Couples in civil partnerships are treated the same way as married couples.

You may have heard that being a common law husband or wife (unmarried cohabitants) somehow gives you legal rights and status. This is a myth. **It does not**. The court currently has much more limited powers to assist unmarried couples than it does married couples in the event of separation.

The court has to judge how your previously intertwined finances can be fairly split up following the breakdown of the relationship. To help it achieve a fair decision, there are some factors and principles that it will use. We will cover the basics below. For more detailed advice on this issue see chapter 9 (in relation to married couples/civil partners) and chapter 10 (for cohabitants).

Financial applications made by married couples or civil partners

The primary piece of legislation giving the court power to make financial arrangements in the event of a divorce/civil partnership dissolution is found in the Matrimonial Causes Act 1973 (similar terms are found in the Civil Partnership Act 2004). Sections 23 and 24 of the Matrimonial Causes Act 1973 give the court power to make orders for:

(1) periodical payments (ie maintenance) for a spouse and child of the marriage;

(2) lump sum awards for a spouse and child of the marriage;

(3) property adjustment orders requiring the transfer of ownership of property as between parties to the marriage and also orders for sale of property; and

(4) pension sharing.

> **What is pension sharing?**
>
> Pension sharing is a division of the capital value of a pension, so that each party emerges from the case with pension funds of their own.

The court will consider all of the circumstances of the case when making its decision. The court is also required to give first consideration to the welfare of any child of the family who is under the age of 18. This does not mean that the child's welfare is the most important matter and should therefore override all other factors that the court has to consider – simply that it has to be considered by the court first. In practice the court will tend to focus on ensuring that the children are appropriately housed (even if this is to be at a lower standard than they have been used to during the marriage).

There are a number of factors that the court is also required to taken into account when deciding what orders it should make (see Matrimonial Causes Act 1973, section 25 below). They need to be considered individually and there is no order of importance. The court will look at the facts behind each, and some factors will be of more significance than others in any given case. The court needs to balance all the factors in order to achieve a just and fair result:

(1) The finance resources that each person has access to now, or is likely to have access to in the future. This includes earning capacity (salaries), property and other financial resources. The court will also think about possible increases to earning capacity in the future.

(2) The financial needs of each person. This includes their obligations and responsibilities now, or that are likely in the foreseeable future.

(3) The standard of living enjoyed by the family before the breakdown of the marriage.

(4) The age of each person in the marriage and the duration of the marriage.

(5) Any physical or mental disability of either of the people in the marriage.

(6) The contributions which each person has made to the welfare of the family, or is likely in the foreseeable future to make. This includes any contribution by looking after the home and caring for the family.

(7) The conduct of each of the parties, which the court thinks is relevant to arriving at a fair decision.

(8) The values of things that either person may have lost because the marriage ended.

As the court will follow them, it is worth using this list of factors as a checklist when preparing your case and presenting it to the court. If you speak to the court about each factor, it will provide a good structure and will help you to persuade it that the outcome you are proposing is a sensible and fair result.

Remember that the court will use the factors to decide a fair outcome. There are three main principles that are the aim of the court when it comes to sorting out the distribution of a family's assets where the relationship ends. They are: 'needs', 'sharing' and 'compensation'.

Courts will start from the position that both people in the marriage or civil partnership are entitled to expect an equal share of the assets generated during the course of the relationship, unless there is good reason to the contrary. This is because, in most cases, each person has made an equal contribution to the building up of the assets of their marriage or civil partnership, and so an equal division at the end of the relationship must therefore be a fair outcome. There is no strict legal requirement for this, but the idea of an equal division is simply to help the court to find a fair outcome.

Division of the assets and needs of the parties

However, in most cases before the court, an equal sharing of the assets would not provide a fair outcome. This is usually because there are simply not enough assets to actually meet everyone's needs, if they were to be shared equally. The court has to prioritise the most important needs within the limited assets available.

In the majority of cases, the court will be considering the practical realities of how both spouses and their children will have their housing needs met, and how their respective incomes can meet their day-to-day needs, both now and in the future.

This is normally the end of matter as there is not enough to share equally. So meeting the needs of the parties may well result in an unequal distribution of the assets of the marriage simply because there is only a limited amount to go round. Such an outcome ought to be carefully justified by the court on the basis of the available evidence before it and the factors that it is required to consider under section 25 of the Matrimonial Causes Act 1973. The court will also need to consider whether an unequal distribution of the assets is required only during the time that the children's needs absolutely require it. In some situations, the court may provide that one party receives capital back once the children are over 18 and financially independent.

The court is flexible in the range of outcomes it can consider in seeking to achieve a fair outcome for the parties both in the short and long-term. If there is to be a departure from equality, the court should normally give good reasons for doing so. The court has a broad discretion as to the manner in which it will make financial provision for the parties to a marriage/civil partnership. This flexibility is needed because each case is different, and one size does not fit all.

Contributions, discrimination and the sharing principle

The sharing principle is justified on the basis that there has been an equal contribution to the building up of assets during the relationship, irrespective of who did what. It is very important to understand that the court does not discriminate between different types of contribution made during the marriage/civil partnership, so the person who stayed at home to look after the children and run the family home work is considered to have made the same contribution as the person who went to work to earn the money.

During a marriage/civil partnership, the partners reach joint decisions about how their lives are to be organised and the court will generally respect those decisions and the consequences that it brings after the ending of the relationship. So if someone stayed at home to focus on meeting the needs of the children, they may then find it harder to find a job and earn money once the relationship has broken down. This will be a factor that the court is required to weigh in the balance when sorting out the future financial arrangements once there is a separation.

The fact that the children need a roof over their head will mean that a priority is given to the establishment of one main home if there are insufficient funds available. That said, in every case the court will try to ensure that both parties have the ability to meet their future housing needs, even if it means a drastic reduction in their respective standards of living. Sometimes there is sufficient to meet everyone's needs by an equal division of the assets – this is likely to be an attractive outcome for the court.

The compensation principle

This rarely features as an individual principle in the majority of cases before the court, due to the fact that the focus on 'needs' actually covers aspects of compensation. The notion of compensation has arisen in circumstances where one party has as a result of their actions suffered a relationship-generated disadvantage. For example, by staying at home to care for the children after having given up a significant career, a party will probably suffer a reduction in their potential earning capacity compared to what they might have had available had they continued in the workplace. The reality is however that this economic disadvantage will result in financial needs that the court has already considered and made provision for. In some rare cases, however, it is considered that the economic disadvantages should be compensated over and above the needs requirement.

A broad-brush approach

A judge will tend to look at the 'big picture' rather than the rights and wrongs of bad behaviour that might have occurred on the pathway to the courts. All too often, because people are immersed in the detail of their lives together and then the fall out after their separation, they are tempted to try to put everything of concern before the court. This will not find favour with the judge. The best advice is not to get bogged down in the detail (especially over historical issues) but to focus on the headline factors of housing need, budgetary needs and incomes and resources that are available to meet those needs.

Full, frank and clear disclosure

The court will make its decision on the basis that each party to the case has provided all information about their financial position.

It must be stressed that there is an on-going duty of disclosure (of providing information). It does not end once the financial statement in Form E has been filled out. Any change in circumstances that might potentially have an impact on the way in which the court exercises its discretion needs to be notified to the other side and the court.

The best approach is to remember that the court expects 'all cards to be placed on the table'. If a decision is reached on the basis of incomplete or inaccurate disclosure it risks being over-turned. Having gone through a potentially lengthy and expensive process (both financially and emotionally) the last thing you might want to risk doing is to have the whole case re-heard all over again because you failed to tell the other side and the court something that was financially relevant.

You should also remember that if the court thinks that someone was not being entirely open during the course of the final hearing, then this might work against them. The court might decide that, as something is being hidden, the other side should receive more of the available assets. It can also be punished by an order to pay part or all of the other side's costs due to perceived litigation misconduct.

Sorting out financial claims on divorce or civil partnership dissolution can be extremely complicated. Even if you feel it is straightforward, in most situations it may be helpful to obtain some expert advice as to the likely outcome and strategies for the litigation. Specialists in family law – whether barrister or solicitor – would be able to give you advice and guidance as to the particular features that a court is likely to consider important in the unique set of facts of your case. Even where finances are stretched, obtaining some initial or structured advice may well serve you well financially and be a good investment.

Cohabitation claims

The only claims that unmarried cohabitants can bring against each other are in relation to the resolution of ownership interests in property. The most common claim that is made in this context is a claim to an interest in property. Where for example the title to the former home is in the name of one party only, the other party may seek to assert that they have a 'beneficial interest' in the property, due to the particular circumstances in which the property was purchased or occupied. Or, where the property is jointly owned, one party may seek to claim that they have a greater than equal share of the equity.

Unlike the court's power in divorce/civil partnership dissolution cases, in property disputes involving ex-cohabitants, the court has no power to change the basis of ownership. It can only interpret the ownership deeds (if there is a declaration of trust defining the basis of ownership) or infer from the parties' conduct their intentions in relation to the purchase and ownership of the property.

The leading case to consider is the House of Lords case of *Stack v Dowden* [2007] UKHL 17. It sets out detailed guidance on the court's proper approach in such cases. *Stack v Dowden* establishes that if a property is in the sole name of one party – the starting point for the court is that this party owns it solely. If a property is in joint legal ownership, the starting point for the court is that the property is owned jointly.

The onus and burden of proof will be on the person who seeks to argue that the beneficial ownership differs from the legal ownership.

> **What is meant by 'legal ownership' and 'beneficial ownership'**
>
> Legal ownership means that ownership of property is recognised by law, for example, because a person's name is on the title to land. Beneficial ownership means that a person may still have possession or beneficial interests in a property even though the legal title of that property belongs to another person.

This will be more difficult to establish in cases where the property is in joint names, where the presumption is 50/50 ownership. If a party does succeed in establishing that the starting point of 50/50 should be departed from – the court will then search for what the parties must be taken to have intended in the light of all their conduct. Unlike matrimonial/civil partnership cases, the court is not entitled to substitute its own view of what is fair, based on the exercise of discretion.

Other than a claim for child support, there is no right to claim on-going financial support or maintenance for a former cohabitant. This is in contrast to the situation with married or civil partnership couples.

See chapter 10 for more detailed information on cohabitation disputes.

Issues that need to be resolved on separation

Once it is felt that the relationship has finally come to an end, you will need to consider the steps that should be taken.

If married/in a civil partnership

(1) Is the relationship really at an end or can a further attempt be made to improve the relationship eg by attending for relationship counselling or family therapy? We cover this further in chapter 2.

(2) If the relationship has finally broken down – is divorce appropriate or should there be a judicial separation?

(3) If you are looking for a divorce, one of you will need to submit a form listing the grounds (reason) for it. It is worth trying to agree between you which option you will choose. Even where unreasonable behaviour is being cited, it is possible to water down the allegations of bad behaviour so that they are acceptable to the other side, but would still be acceptable to satisfy the court that the marriage had irretrievably broken down. Family lawyers tend to be extremely pragmatic when it comes to advising clients, and you really want to avoid the expense and emotional strain of defended divorce proceedings (ie going to court), if at

(4) If there are issues of domestic abuse, think about applying to the court for personal protection orders. The court can also issue instructions about who is allowed into the family home, and it has power to order that a person continues to pay the mortgage due. Chapter 7 covers more about how to get protection from the courts if you are suffering or at risk of domestic abuse.

(5) Apply to the Child Maintenance Service for child support if this cannot be agreed with the non-resident parent.

Issues connected with the children

(1) The same considerations apply whether you are married or unmarried. Once the relationship ends, consideration will need to be given to:

- with whom the child is going to live or have their main home;

- the arrangements whereby the child will be encouraged to maintain a relationship with the other parent – both during term time and in school holidays;

- whether there will be any likely change to the child's living arrangements in the short, medium or long-term.

(2) There is no right answer or stock arrangement. Although people may talk about a pattern of alternate weekends and half of holidays with the parent who does not live in the child's main home, this is not compulsory. It is about what is right for your particular child – based on their age and stage of development. Further, this will not remain 'set in stone' or static. What may be right for a 2-year-old is not

going to be appropriate for an 8-year-old or a 14-year-old. Changes to the arrangements will have to happen, as the child grows older.

(3) Family lawyers will often adopt a broad common-sense approach based on their world experience. The best advice we can give you is that it pays not to be too rigid in your approach. This applies equally whether you are a mother or a father. Remember courts are not interested in any sense of entitlement or rights – the court is only interested in what is going to be in the child's best interests (as we discussed above).

(4) Both parents will need in the early stages of the relationship breakdown to think about how the child will be told:

- about the separation;

- about what the future arrangements will be for their living arrangements and seeing the other parent.

(5) Consider mediation to help resolve these issues. Sometimes members of the wider family can be helpful intermediaries to assist in resolving issues connected with children.

(6) If no agreement is possible then an application can be made to the court to define these issues – this will be made under section 8 of the Children Act 1989. See chapter 8 for more detailed information.

(7) Are there any risks or threats of abduction? If there are, an urgent interim application will need to be made for a prohibited steps order to prevent removal; or an application for delivery up of passports/port alert.

Preparations you need to make: information and evidence gathering

Good family lawyers are organised and have gathered the information they need to persuade the court about the merits of their case. The court needs evidence upon which it can make a decision. If there is no evidence upon a particular issue it may be more difficult to persuade a judge to make a decision that you are asking for. If you are in any doubt, or the situation appears to be complicated, it may be sensible to get some initial legal advice on your particular situation either by seeing a specialist family law solicitor or a family law barrister on a direct access basis (as covered in chapter 2).

See chapter 5 for more detailed information on case preparation.

If there are issues connected with children

- It may help with general preparation to write a narrative account of the history of your relationship with your ex-partner.

- Consider the involvement each of you have had with the children.

- Consider the particular characteristics of the children and what they particularly need referable to their age, development and experiences.

- This narrative account (imagine you were meeting with a friend whom you hadn't seen for years and who wanted to hear all about what had been going on) may not need to be used in a statement for court proceedings but it will help you focus on the issues and think about what further evidence may need to be gathered to prove your point.

- Consider whether you have documentary evidence that is helpful – eg emails or texts can be produced in evidence.

- Are there other people who have witnessed events and who might be able to provide corroborating evidence?

- Are there school reports or medical reports that may be helpful to the issues – if so make sure you have copies.

- Has there been any involvement with Social Services due to the family problems – if so consider what supporting evidence you have of this eg reports/assessments.

If there are financial issues that need to be resolved

- Consider obtaining some recent evidence of the value of the jointly owned house and any outstanding mortgage.

- Consider obtaining a quote as to your own mortgage capacity.

- Consider obtaining evidence of alternative property costs.

- Consider how you might justify the location of alternative properties (eg proximity to schools, work, social support networks etc).

- Gather together your own financial evidence eg 12 months bank statements, policy details and values, credit card statements, details of any assets owned solely or jointly with your partner, details of any debts.

- Prepare a budget breakdown of your current expenditure needs – find one online or go through your own bank statements and work out what the available income is actually being spent on. Try to predict how these might change if you are in a separate household to your partner.

- Investigate any potential claim for working tax credits or child tax credits for you or your partner.

- If you or your partner is not working – consider what employment options that there might be to generate additional income.

- Consider whether any of the family assets were owned prior to marriage/civil partnership or have come into the marriage/civil partnership as a result of inheritance or gift. Documentary evidence may need to be produced of this.

- Are there any social or medical needs of any members of the family that need to be taken into account – documentary evidence eg medical reports may be required.

- Get a copy of a draft Form E (available online) as this will provide clear guidance as to the information you will need to produce to the court.

If you are unmarried but there is a property, additionally consider whether there is documentary evidence of any agreements as to how the property would be owned; or evidence of financial and other contributions made to the property.

Case-law

Previously decided cases can be used to provide guidance to the court as to the approach that the higher courts have taken in relation to a particular issue – whether on the interpretation of statute law or in the exercise of the court's discretion in a particular set of factual circumstances.

This is because the family courts determine cases on a case-by-case basis. If you find a reported case that is very similar to your case (due to the factual circumstances being comparable or because it deals with similar legal issues) it might be useful for you to quote this case to the judge hearing your case.

If you intend to do so, then you will need to provide a copy of the case to the court (and to the other side). Equally you may want to be able to argue that your factual circumstances are different and that you don't want your judge to follow the approach adopted in the reported case for that reason.

Generally speaking the higher the court that dealt with a reported case, the more note a lower court will take of the approach that was adopted in the reported case. The courts in descending order of importance are:

- The Supreme Court (formerly the House of Lords), (written shorthand is: UKSC)

- The Court of Appeal (written shorthand is: EWCA)

- The High Court (written shorthand is: EWHC)

- The county court

- The family proceedings court.

Although all levels of court are now unified under the umbrella of the Family Court – the levels of seniority are still important. A case that was decided in the Supreme Court will bind all courts below it in terms of the interpretation given to the particular statute that was being considered and in relation to what the Supreme Court had to say about their views on the particular issue that was being determined.

Similarly, a case decided in the Court of Appeal will bind all courts below it and so on.

It is possible to refer the judge hearing your case to a case decided at a similar level – eg you can refer a reported county

- 'Children Act Private Law Proceedings – A Handbook' by HH Judge John Mitchell

Useful Websites

www.Resolution.org.uk/familymatters

www.relate.org.uk

www.divorceaid.co.uk

www.yourrights.org.uk

www.moneyadviceservice.org.uk

www.advicenow.org.uk

www.justice.gov.uk

www.hmrc.gov.uk/taxcredits

www.gov.uk/child-maintenance/overview

www.cmoptions.org.uk (child maintenance options)

www.familymediationhelpline.co.uk (advice on mediation)

www.gov.uk/legal-aid (advice on legal aid)

www.nfm.org.uk (national family mediation service)

www.cafcass.gov.uk

www.naccc.org.uk (national association of contact centres)

www.childline.org.uk

www.actionforadvocacy.org.uk (national youth advocacy service)

www.fathers-4-justice.org or www.mothers4justice.co.uk

Dos and don'ts

DOS

- **DO** be prepared to think flexibly about the issues that are in dispute
- **DO** think of ways in which a solution can be found to the issues in dispute
- **DO** be prepared to adopt a pragmatic approach, if necessary
- **DO** be realistic about what the court can and cannot do on a practical basis
- **DO** think about what is in the child's best interests
- **DO** think about how the finances available can meet the separated family's needs, in terms of income and housing
- **DO** think carefully about what evidence you need to present your case to its best advantage

DON'TS

- **DON'T** be rigid in your approach
- **DON'T** adopt an approach which relies on your perceived rights or entitlements
- **DON'T** criticise the other party unnecessarily, unless their behaviour is particularly relevant to the issues that the court needs to determine

- ✗ **DON'T** dwell unnecessarily on matters of ancient history

- ✗ **DON'T** be unrealistic about the likely outcome and be prepared to move matters on slowly

- ✗ **DON'T** expect the court to make a decision without the available evidence to support that decision

Chapter 4

Bringing the Marriage/Civil Partnership to an End

What you will learn

- The facts and grounds required to end a marriage or civil partnership
- The practical steps to take to start the process: the petition
- What to do if you receive a petition
- The practical steps to take to complete the process
- To defend or not to defend – the differences

Introduction

When your marriage or partnership comes to an end, the steps you need to take to bring it to an end legally need not be overly complicated. If you are divorcing or separating it is worth attempting to reach agreement with your husband, wife or partner as to how this is best going to be achieved. Allegations of affairs and bad behaviour can make it difficult to deal with the arrangements for your children and your finances.

It can avoid conflict if a copy of the petition (the form you use to start the process) is shown to the other party to attempt to agree the facts before it is filed with the court. This is not always possible but is worth keeping in the forefront of your mind.

The main facts allowing you to apply for a divorce are relatively straightforward.

(1) You have to have been married for one year.

(2) Either husband or wife can apply for a divorce if the marriage has permanently broken down. The words used in section 1 of the Matrimonial Causes Act 1973, which is your main point of reference to start with, are 'the marriage has broken down irretrievably'.

(3) You must legally have been married to apply for a divorce. This is particularly relevant if you were married abroad as sometimes a ceremony on a beach is not actually a legal marriage.

(4) The court will only let you apply for a divorce if:

> EITHER one of you has been living in England or Wales (Scotland has its own legal rules) for a period of one year ending with the date on which the proceeding started;
> OR if neither of you are living in England or Wales, one of you is 'domiciled' in England or Wales for a period of a year prior to the proceedings starting. Domicile is a legal term and has a particular definition but basically means that either you or your spouse has a connection with a country. So you may have been born here even if you have spent time abroad, or you may have been born in a different country but have chosen to live in England or Wales.

The process of divorce has three stages:

Bringing the Marriage/Civil Partnership to an End 63

- Filing the divorce petition. The person applying is called the petitioner and the other spouse or partner is called the respondent.

- Applying for decree nisi (a sort of 'nearly there' stage where the court decides if you are allowed to divorce).

- Applying for decree absolute (this is the final order which terminates the marriage).

There are **five grounds** for divorce; that is to say, the court must conclude that a party actually has a reason for ending the marriage:

Ground	Full wording	Meaning	Comments
Adultery	The respondent committed adultery and you find it intolerable to live with the respondent.	Your husband or wife has had sex with another and you cannot bear to live with them.	Note there are restrictions on relying on adultery if you live together for 6 months after you know of the adultery. Give the date and place where the adultery took place.
Unreasonable behaviour	The respondent behaved in such a way that you cannot be reasonably expected to live with the respondent.	This is perhaps the most cited ground and can include relationships with other people.	Half a dozen examples are sufficient, including the most recent.

Ground	Full wording	Meaning	Comments
		Examples of unreasonable behaviour include: financial irresponsibility, domestic violence, verbal abuse as well as physical, a refusal to engage in a loving relationship, abuse of drink.	
Desertion	The respondent deserted you for a continuous period of at least 2 years prior to your petition.	The main points are that desertion is not consensual, it ends the relationship and has been for more than 2 years.	Give the date of desertion, brief details and confirmation that you have lived separately since.
2 years separation by consent	Lived apart for a continuous period of 2 years before the petition and the respondent agrees to a decree.	The agreement has to be in writing and state that the separation has been for two years.	Give the date, brief details of how you separated and the consent.
5 years separation	Lived apart for a continuous period of 5 years.	No agreement required and it is hard to think of a circumstance in which you could say that after 5 years apart the marriage was fine!	Date and details of separation and that you have not lived together since.

When you fill in the facts of the ground for the divorce bear in mind that in England and Wales, despite retaining the grounds such as adultery and unreasonable behaviour, our divorce system is essentially a 'no fault' system.

> **(i) What is meant by 'no fault' system?**
>
> This means that the spouse or partner that is asking for the divorce does not have to prove that the other spouse or partner did something wrong.

You may feel upset and angry about your ex partner's behaviour but the court does not want you to use your divorce petition to go over past issues in depth. It simply wants the facts on which you rely. Conversely if you file a petition which states that he doesn't let you watch Eastenders or listen to The Archers (whichever you prefer) and that he (or she) snores then the court is likely to reject your petition.

For example if you are relying on adultery, you do not need to list each and every occasion that you believe that your ex partner was committing adultery. A reasonable paragraph might read as follows:

> The respondent embarked upon an adulterous relationship when he started his new job at Smith's causing the parties to separate on the 01.01.10.

Putting allegations in the petition that are likely to be extremely upsetting is rarely helpful as it may cause the respondent to defend the petition – that is not agree to the divorce and want to contest the matter before a judge. This is likely to be time-consuming and stressful. People usually want to focus on agreeing the arrangements for the children or sorting out the finances rather than spending time in court arguing the allegations in a divorce petition.

Simplified divorce procedure

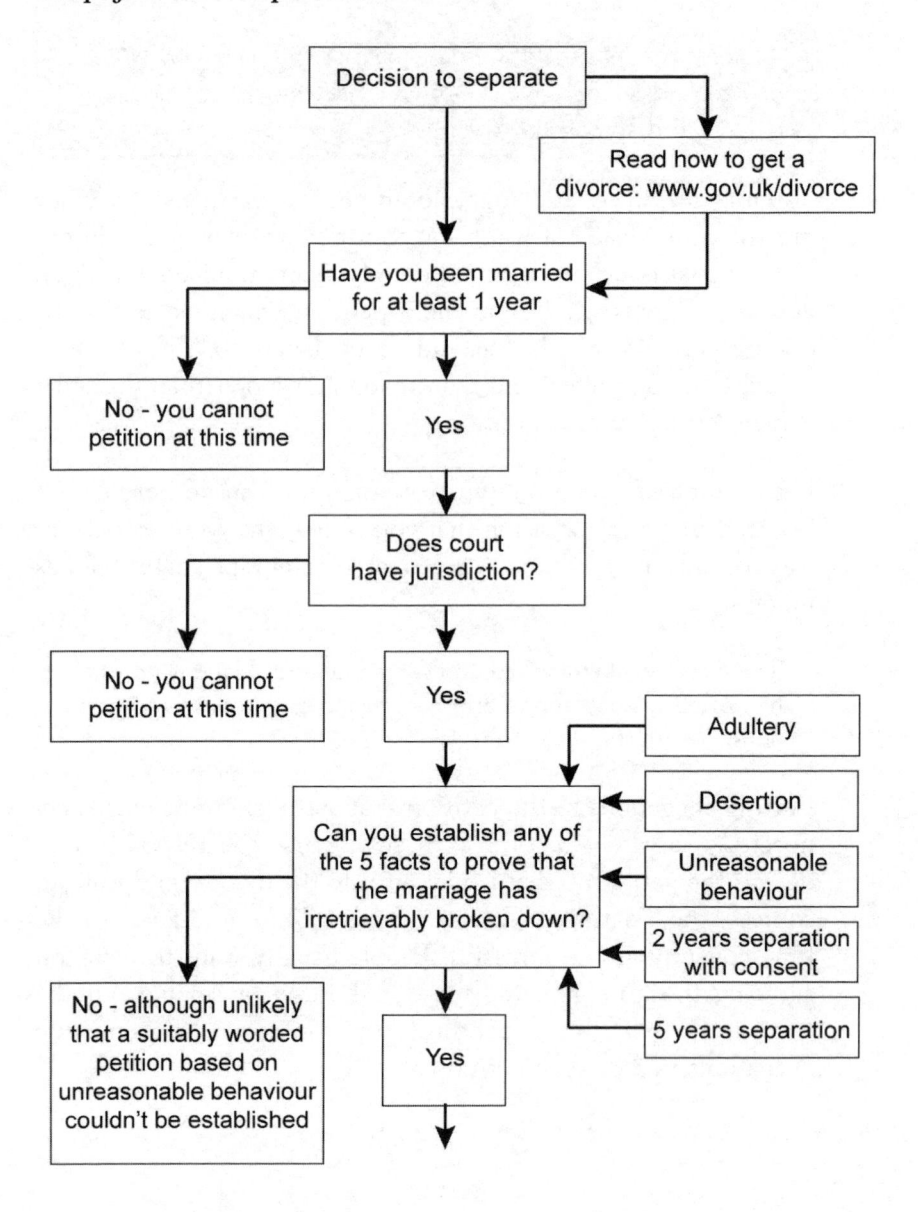

```
Decision to separate
    │
    ├──────────────► Read how to get a
    │                divorce: www.gov.uk/divorce
    ▼
Have you been married ◄─────┘
for at least 1 year
    │
    ├──► No - you cannot petition at this time
    │
    ▼ Yes
Does court have jurisdiction?
    │
    ├──► No - you cannot petition at this time
    │
    ▼ Yes
Can you establish any of      ◄──── Adultery
the 5 facts to prove that     ◄──── Desertion
the marriage has              ◄──── Unreasonable behaviour
irretrievably broken down?    ◄──── 2 years separation with consent
    │                         ◄──── 5 years separation
    ├──► No - although unlikely that a suitably worded
    │    petition based on unreasonable behaviour
    │    couldn't be established
    ▼
   Yes
```

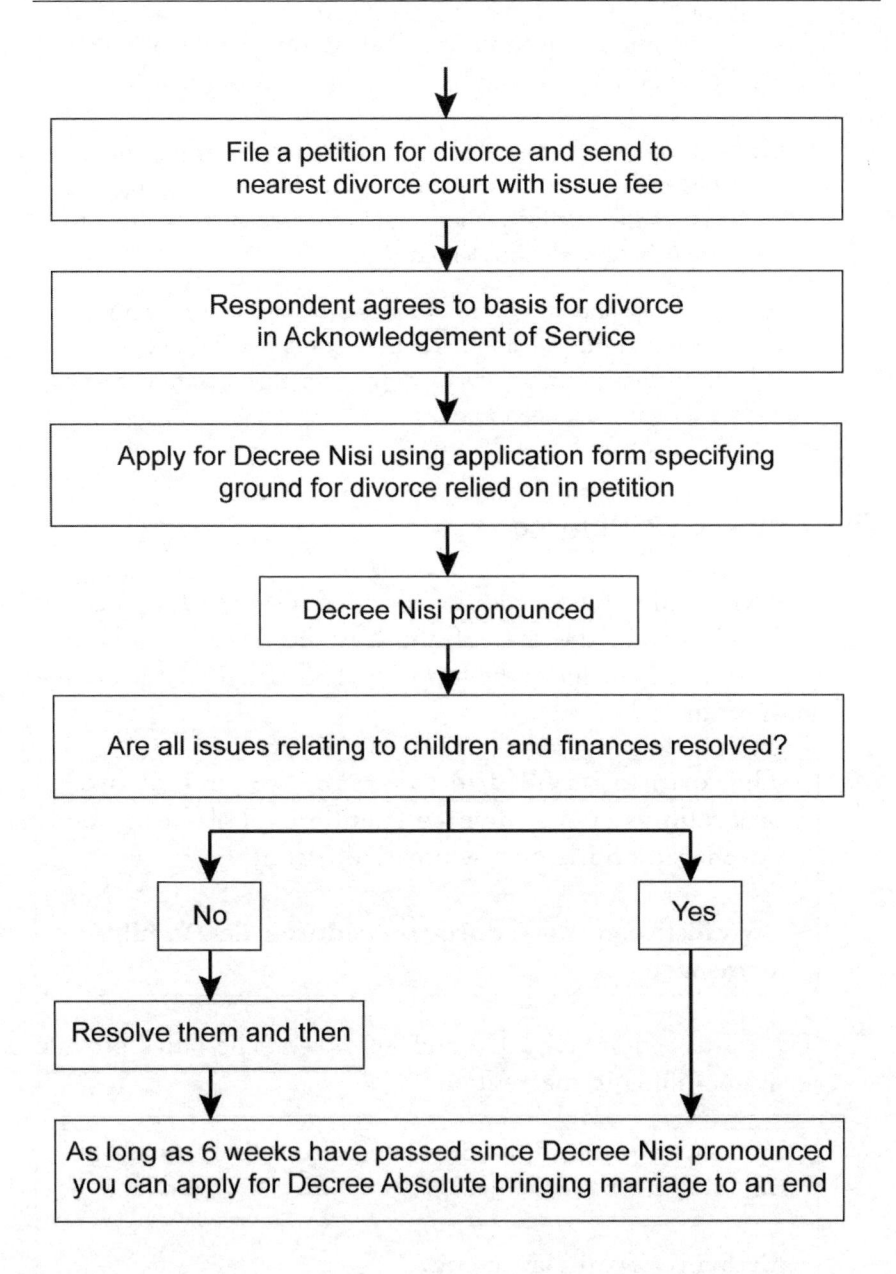

```
                    ↓
┌─────────────────────────────────────────────┐
│       File a petition for divorce and send to│
│       nearest divorce court with issue fee   │
└─────────────────────────────────────────────┘
                    ↓
┌─────────────────────────────────────────────┐
│     Respondent agrees to basis for divorce   │
│        in Acknowledgement of Service         │
└─────────────────────────────────────────────┘
                    ↓
┌─────────────────────────────────────────────┐
│  Apply for Decree Nisi using application form specifying │
│     ground for divorce relied on in petition │
└─────────────────────────────────────────────┘
                    ↓
         ┌──────────────────────────┐
         │   Decree Nisi pronounced │
         └──────────────────────────┘
                    ↓
┌─────────────────────────────────────────────┐
│  Are all issues relating to children and finances resolved? │
└─────────────────────────────────────────────┘
             ↓                      ↓
        ┌────────┐             ┌────────┐
        │   No   │             │  Yes   │
        └────────┘             └────────┘
             ↓                      │
    ┌──────────────────────┐        │
    │ Resolve them and then│        │
    └──────────────────────┘        │
             ↓                      ↓
┌─────────────────────────────────────────────────────────┐
│ As long as 6 weeks have passed since Decree Nisi pronounced │
│ you can apply for Decree Absolute bringing marriage to an end│
└─────────────────────────────────────────────────────────┘
```

The most common ground is called 'unreasonable behaviour'. Below are example paragraphs:

(a) The respondent has failed throughout the later part of the marriage to show the petitioner any love or affection and constantly belittles her and criticises her ability to contribute to the household.

(b) The respondent chooses to spend his spare time with his friends at the pub and the petitioner often will spend nights in the house on her own with the respondent coming home after she has gone to bed.

The process of divorce

You will need to follow additional procedures regarding finances and children. In the eyes of the law, the divorce/dissolution procedure only includes the formal ending of a marriage or civil partnership.

> **The form to be filled in to commence your divorce proceedings is a divorce petition. This can be purchased online or downloaded free at:**
>
> **www.justice.gov.uk/courts/procedure-rules/family/formspage**

The forms required are D8 and D8 notes. The notes provide advice on filling in the petition.

> **For an example of a completed Form D8, please go to:**
>
> **diydivorce.familylaw.co.uk/**

The petition requires you to provide the following:

Bringing the Marriage/Civil Partnership to an End

- Your name and address.

- The names and ages of your children.

- Your husband or wife's name and address.

- Your marriage certificate (if you do not have the original you must get a proper copy from the General Register Office (www.gro.gov.uk) as a photocopy will not be accepted).

- Details of when and where you were married.

- Details as to why the court has the legal right to deal with your divorce – this is usually because either you or your husband or wife currently live in England and Wales.

- Whether you are involved with your husband or wife in any other legal proceedings to do with your marriage/your children or the property that you and your husband or wife own.

- The grounds upon which you seek the divorce and the 'statement of your case' – these are the particular facts which you say make out the ground for divorce on which you rely.

- If you have relied on adultery and named the person with whom your husband or wife has had an affair you will need to fill in Box 4 naming them as a co-respondent and they will need to be given a copy of the petition. It is not necessary to name a person if you are relying on adultery and it is sufficient to simply say that your husband or wife has had an affair.

On the final page of the petition is the prayer. On this page you will identify what you are applying for (ie marriage to be dissolved). Paragraph 2 allows you to ask the court to order that your husband or wife pay your costs. As a litigant in person the costs you will have will be limited to the court fees and the court will usually order costs or some contribution to your costs. It will not normally make any order on a 5-year separation petition, and if you claim for costs it should be made in the petition, as it is not possible to make a claim after a decree has been granted. When deciding whether to make a claim for costs be practical, and if your husband or wife has little or no ability to pay such an order think about whether it is really worth applying or whether you should share the costs.

Paragraph 3 of Part 10 of the petition concerns what financial order you may ask the court to make as a consequence of your divorce. On divorce, the court has power to make orders resolving disputes over finances called an application for 'financial remedy'. You should tick all the boxes as failure to do so may cause difficulties at a later stage if you need to ask the court for an order. By ticking the boxes you are not setting in motion separate proceedings. If you decide that you need to ask the court to make a financial order you will need to fill in a Form A at a later stage.

Statement of arrangements for children

There is no longer any requirement to complete Form D8A (setting out the proposals for arrangements for the children) which was required before the changes in April 2014.

What do I have to send to the court with the petition?

Completed petition	One copy for the court, a copy to be given to your husband or wife ('served on the respondent') and keep a copy for yourself.

Bringing the Marriage/Civil Partnership to an End

Original married certificate or certified copy	A photocopy will not be accepted. In cases of urgency you may be able to give the court a promise to provide this at a later date but this is unusual
Issue fee	This is the fee you will have to pay to the court to issue the petition, ie to send it out and get the whole process underway. As at 2 Jan 2014 this was £410 – but leaflet EX50 Civil and Family Court Fees has up-to-date information. If you are on benefits or a low income you may be able to get assistance www.gov.uk/court-fees-what-they-are/

Where do I send it to and how do I send the petition to my husband or wife?

- The petition must be formally delivered to your husband or wife. Lawyers call this 'service' or say that the petition is 'served on the respondent'.

- Your petition should be sent to your local divorce court – this will be your local Family Court.

> **To find your local Family Court go to:**
>
> https://courttribunalfinder.service.gov.uk

- The rules for the service of the petition provide that the petition should be served personally on your husband or wife but this can be done by sending the petition to them in the post. On receiving the petition the court will send a copy of the petition to your husband or wife. That is why it is so important to complete Part 9 of the petition accurately.

> **What is service?**
>
> Service means the delivery of a legal document to the person who is required to respond to it.

- If the address is wrong or he or she has moved the Post Office will return the forms to the court. The court will tell you if this happens.

- If your husband or wife has a solicitor who is acting for them the petition will be served on the solicitor at his or her office.

- In some circumstances, where for instance the respondent is trying to avoid service or where the respondent does not reply to the petition, you can ask the court to serve the respondent via the court bailiff or, if you have evidence that the respondent has the petition, you can ask the court to 'deem' service, ie to declare that it is satisfied that service has taken place.

- If you do not know where your husband or wife is living and have tried to find out you can ask the court to 'dispense' with service of the petition. This means the court will accept that the party cannot be served personally but understands that it is important to let the application for divorce proceed.

- There are specific rules which deal with serving documents abroad and the time limits for replying to the application, if it has been 'served out of the jurisdiction'. This will depend on whether the country is in the European Union which essentially allows service by post or whether the country is party to a convention signed by England and Wales. Further information can be obtained from Foreign Process Section, Room E02, Royal Courts of Justice, Strand, London, WC2A 2 LL (Tel: 020 7947 6691).

Responding to a petition

If you receive a petition for divorce you will also receive two further important forms:

(1) Notice of proceedings – this tells you the 'case number' given to the divorce by the court and what steps to take next.

(2) Acknowledgment of service – it is important that you complete this and return it to the court.

The acknowledgment of service asks you to reply to several questions and to sign and return the document to the court. This is your opportunity to indicate whether you agree or not to the divorce. You cannot stop the divorce by simply failing to return the acknowledgment of service.

The acknowledgment of service deals with the following matters:

(1) Have you received the petition, and the date and address at which you received it?

(2) Are you the respondent?

(3) Do you agree the court has jurisdiction as identified in Part 3 of the petition? This is the question about whether you live or are domiciled in England and Wales.

(4) Are you going to defend the divorce?

(5) Do you agree to the ground for divorce relied on in the petition (unreasonable behaviour, desertion, adultery etc)?

(6) Costs.

Before considering the points raised in the acknowledgement of service, here is a general word on defending a divorce. Having indicated your intention to defend you will have to file an answer. An answer is simply a denial of the facts in the petition. Defended divorces are costly and very rare these days. The court will take the view that the fact one party has presented a petition is strong evidence of the permanent breakdown of a marriage. If you accept that the marriage is over but you are unhappy about the facts in the petition then it is worth speaking to the petitioner or their solicitor to see if the facts can be amended to avoid a defended divorce. This has to be done quickly, as after the filing of an answer it can only be done with leave of the court.

Having received the acknowledgment of service there are three routes

(1) Do nothing – this is not a sensible response. You cannot stop the divorce by simply failing to return the acknowledgment of service, and things could proceed in your absence.

(2) Return the acknowledgment of service stating no intention to defend.

(3) Within 7 days of receipt, give notice of intention to defend.

A summary of an undefended application

An undefended divorce proceeds without the need for the attendance at court of either of the parties	Once the respondent has sent the acknowledgment of service stating no intention to defend …
Apply for a decree nisi	The first step is for the applicant to apply for a decree nisi: this can be done at any time after the time for filing the acknowledgment of service has expired; if your husband or wife has stated they do not intend to defend then you can apply!

To get a decree nisi	Fill in the application for a decree nisi (Form D84) plus a supporting form. There are five different supporting forms (D80A – D80E), one for each ground of divorce. Select the form which matches the ground of divorce you have relied upon. (http://hmctsformfinder.justice.gov.uk/) Do not fill in section B as this is for Defended Divorces but fill in the statement confirming that the facts in your divorce petition are true. Attach a copy of the acknowledgment of service.
What the court will do	The judge then has to consider if you are entitled to your decree nisi. The nisi is the stepping stone to the final dissolution of your marriage, the decree absolute. If the judge is satisfied that all is in order he will certify this as being the case and direct that the decree be made by a judge at the next hearing date: you do not need to attend. If for any reason the court is not satisfied that the procedure in respect of the divorce has been followed it can refuse to certify the application for decree and ask for further evidence or ask for you both to come to court to explain the situation. The certification of the application and listing for decree is a serious step and if you are a respondent and have any reason to change your mind you should apply to the court prior to the certification. You can apply to set aside a certificate but you need very good reasons.
Costs	The court on decree nisi can make your order for costs if you have asked for this in the petition. If you are the respondent and you want to contest the costs application this can be done but you should inform the court of your attendance for this reason and give notice to the other party.
Pronouncement of decree nisi	This means that you can now apply for decree absolute.

Applying for decree absolute	If you are the petitioner you can apply for your final order – decree absolute – 6 weeks after decree nisi. Notice of application is in writing. The cost is included in the divorce application. If you are the respondent you can apply 3 months after the 6 week period has elapsed, subject to an additional fee. Generally if you are involved in financial remedy proceedings (a dispute about finances) you may wish to delay the application for the decree absolute until the finances have been agreed or decided by the court. This usually applies to a wife who needs to resolve pension arrangements. However, the fact that there are unresolved financial issues is not a reason in itself to refuse an application for decree absolute.
Applying more than 12 months after decree nisi	Apply in writing to the court stating: – why the application was not made before – whether you have lived with your husband or wife during this period and if so the dates. – if you are a female applicant or respondent whether you have given birth to a child and, if so, whether the child is a 'child of the family', namely the child's father is your husband; The court can order you to file an affidavit or statement of truth to confirm the explanation.
Applying before 6 weeks	There are limited circumstances in which you can apply before – for instance a permanent move abroad (Legal reference: PDA 7A, paras 8.1 – 8.4).

A summary of a defended application

A defended divorce	As the respondent you will ...
Receive acknowledgment of service	File acknowledgment of service – must be signed – must include your address – must indicate if you intend to defend

Time limit	7 days commencing with the day that the petition was served. This does not include weekends. The court will calculate service as having taken place two working days after posting by first class post if there has been no reply.
What next? An 'answer'	A respondent must file an 'answer' (more detail on this below) with the court and the petitioner. This must be done within 21 calendar days after the 7 working day deadline for the acknowledgement of service. If you simply object to paying costs do not file an answer, but give notice to the court and the other party in writing of this specific issue. This will avoid the confusion of whether you wish to defend the divorce or simply object to this issue. If you miss the time limit and still want to file an 'answer' to the divorce you will have to apply to the court for permission.

What is an answer?	The answer is Form D8B and it states as follows: Complete if you wish to defend the divorce – because you do not agree the marriage has broken down or you wish to defend the facts alleged against you. On the 5 year separation ground only you can oppose a decree if the result will be grave financial or other hardship. Give your reasons for defending the application/allegations. You can seek costs at Part 5. If you accept that the marriage has broken down but believe it is because the petitioner has caused it you can apply for an order on this basis. This must be done within 21 days of the date of the acknowledgment of service, like an answer. In this type of application the party can ask for a decree on the facts he or she is alleging and ask for the original petition to be dismissed. If this situation arises it is wise to speak to your husband or wife or their solicitor to see if you can agree to only one application being before the court and that being an undefended one.
Example of time limits	If I receive a petition on Friday the 3rd I will have until Tuesday the 14th to file the acknowledgment of service and then 21 days from the 14th to file my answer. This date is calculated in a different manner as the 7 days does not include weekends or public holidays but the 21 days is regardless of whatever weekends or holidays intervene.

Bringing the Marriage/Civil Partnership to an End 79

What does the court do next?	The case will be listed for 'directions' or a 'case management hearing'. This will allow the parties to attend court so the judge can make the necessary orders for the filing of evidence, attendance of witnesses and the trial. This will include asking the parties to produce evidence in a timetable set by the court and file a statement of their case. The court will at this hearing also expect the parties to continue to attempt to settle the dispute and not have a final hearing.
Hearing	This will generally be in 'open' court meaning that it can be attended by members of the public if they so choose. The judge will hear evidence and decide whether to grant a decree nisi or dismiss the application.
Where will the hearing be held?	If it is a divorce, any Family Court.
What next?	Once the court has made the decree nisi the rules in respect of time limits set out above for the application for a decree absolute apply.

Ending a civil partnership

In the same manner as a divorce you will need to show that the partnership has irretrievably broken down and one of the grounds for ending the partnership exist. If this is the case then, as with marriage, there is a three stage process of:

- Filing the petition. The person applying is called the petitioner and the other spouse or partner is called the respondent.

- Applying for a conditional order (a sort of 'nearly there' stage where the court decides if you are allowed to end the partnership).

- Applying for a final order (this is the final order which terminates the civil partnership).

The court has a duty throughout to consider with you whether there is a possibility of reconciliation.

The grounds for ending the partnership

There are **four grounds** for dissolution of a civil partnership; that is to say, the court must conclude that a party actually has a reason for ending the civil partnership.

Unreasonable behaviour	This will include behaviour such as being sexually unfaithful, domestic violence, verbal abuse, financial irresponsibility or simply no longer engaging in the relationship over a period of time.
Desertion	You will need to have a recorded date of separation and not recommenced cohabitation.
2 years separation by consent	Written agreement and separation for a period in excess of two years.
5 years separation	Separation for a period in excess of 5 years: no agreement required.

The process of dissolution of a civil partnership

The procedure for ending a civil partnership is basically the same as that for a divorce, so please see above for the full details of filing and responding to a petition. The forms you use are the same, although of course you will need to choose the civil partnership options on the forms where indicated. In summary, the steps are:

(1) File petition.

(2) Pay the court fee.

(3) The court will serve the petition on your former partner. You will need to send two copies of the petition to the court and to keep one for yourself.

(4) Your local Family Court will be the appropriate court, the address of which can be found online.

> **To find documents relevant to your dissolution go to:**
>
> http://hmctsformfinder.justice.gov.uk

An undefended dissolution

An undefended petition proceeds without the need for the attendance at court of either of the parties	The respondent will receive an acknowledgment of service. You have 7 days from the date of service to return this to the court. On this you must indicate whether you will defend or consent to the dissolution.
Apply for a conditional order	The first step is for the applicant to apply for a conditional order. This can be done at any time after the time for filing the acknowledgment of service has expired. If the respondent has not replied, you must wait at least 9 days after the petition was sent before applying.
To get a conditional order	Fill in the application for a conditional order. There are 4 forms, each of which matches the various grounds of dissolution. Select the form that matches the ground upon which you have relied. (http://hmctsformfinder.justice.gov.uk) Do not fill in section B as this is for defended dissolutions but do fill in a statement confirming the facts in your petition are true. Attach a copy of the acknowledgment of service.

What the court will do	The judge then has to consider if you are entitled to your conditional order. The conditional order is the stepping stone to the final dissolution. If the judge is satisfied that all is in order he will certify this as being the case and direct that the conditional order be made by a judge at the next hearing date – you do not need to attend. If for any reason the court is not satisfied it can refuse to the application and ask for further evidence or ask for you both to come to court to explain the situation. The certification of the application and listing for a conditional order is a serious step and if you are a respondent and have any reason to change your mind you should apply to the court prior to the certification.
Costs	The court on making a conditional order can make your order for costs if you have asked for this in the petition. If you are the respondent and you want to contest the costs application this can be done but you should inform the court of your attendance for this reason and give notice to the other party.
Pronouncement of a conditional order	This means that you can now apply for a final order.
Applying for final order	If you are the petitioner you can apply for your final order 6 weeks after the conditional order. If you are the respondent, you can apply 3 months after the 6 week period has elapsed. Notice of application is in writing. The cost is included in the dissolution application. A respondent has an additional fee. If you apply after 12 months you will have to apply in writing with a sworn statement stating to the court that you have not cohabited, nor had a child.

Bringing the Marriage/Civil Partnership to an End 83

| Applying before 6 weeks | There are limited circumstances in which you can apply before – for instance a permanent move abroad (Legal reference: PDA 7A paras 8.1–8.4). |

A defended dissolution

Receive acknowledgment of service	File acknowledgment of service – must be signed – must include your address – must indicate if you intend to defend
Time limit	7 days commencing with the day that the petition was served. This does not include weekends: see above. The court will calculate service as having taken place 2 days after posting by first class post avoiding non-business days.
What next? An 'answer'	A respondent must file an 'answer' (more detail on this below) with the court and the petitioner. This must be done within 21 calendar stays after the 7 working day deadline for the acknowledgement of service. If you simply object to paying costs do not file an answer but give notice to the court and the other party in writing of this specific issue. This will avoid the confusion of whether you wish to defend the divorce or simply object to this issue. If you miss the time limit and still want to file an answer to the dissolution you will have to apply to the court for permission.
What is an answer?	The answer is Form D8B and it states as follows: Complete if you wish to defend the dissolution – because you do not agree the partnership has broken down or you wish to defend the facts alleged against you. Give your reasons for defending the application/allegations You can seek costs at Part 5.

Example of time limits	If I receive a petition on Friday the 3rd I will have until Tuesday the 14th to file the acknowledgment of service and then 21 days from the 14th to file my answer. This date is calculated in a different manner as the 7 days does not include weekends or public holidays but the 21 days is regardless of whatever weekends or holidays intervene.
What does the court do next?	The matter will be listed for 'directions' or a 'case management hearing' – this will allow the parties to attend court so the judge can make the necessary orders for the filing of evidence, attendance of witnesses and the trial of the case.
Hearing	This will generally be in 'open' court meaning that it can be attended by members of the public if they so choose. The judge will hear evidence and decide whether to dismiss the application or grant a conditional order.
Where will the hearing be held	The Family Court.
What next?	Once the court has made the conditional order the rules in respect of time limits set out above for the application for a final order apply.

Annulment of a marriage/civil partnership

In certain limited circumstances a court may 'annul' your marriage. This is like saying that rather than it having taken place and broken down, from a lawyer's point of view your marriage was never a proper legally recognised relationship.

The reasons for annulling a marriage include matters like either of the parties being under age, being too closely related, already being married (or having a civil partner), being under duress or not having been capable of understanding what they were agreeing to.

The use of these provisions is quite rare. The petition to commence an annulment is Form D8N and is extremely similar to a divorce petition. The petitioner will identify the facts he or she relies upon, whether it is a marriage or a civil partnership (Part 5), and set out at Part 6 the reasons supporting the facts relied upon. The prayer and provision for costs and financial remedy are at Part 10 of the petition and should be completed in the same way as a divorce petition.

On an undefended and defended case the procedure is the same as for the divorce procedure described above.

Judicial separation

If you wish to formalise a separation from your husband or wife but you do not wish to divorce or terminate your civil partnership, you can apply for a judicial separation. The procedure follows that of a divorce as described above; however you do not have to show that your marriage has irretrievably broken down. These proceedings are rare. One or both of you can seek financial provision as if you had undergone a divorce or termination of a civil partnership.

Dos and don'ts

DOS

- **DO** aim to avoid conflict – it is almost always cheaper in the long run
- **DO** try to reach agreement where possible
- **DO** make sure you follow the court rules

DON'TS

- **DON'T** underestimate the emotional impact of divorce/dissolution proceedings

- ✘ **DON'T** waste time on seeking to prove pointless allegations – or seeking to defend them
- ✘ **DON'T** ignore court documents

Chapter 5

Pre-proceedings Conduct and Case Preparation

What you will learn

- What type of pre-proceedings letters you need to write and tips on how to do so
- How to approach the expectation to attend mediation before applying to the court
- How to keep your files of documents
- How to prepare the papers for court
- How to write a statement
- How to issue you application to the court
- How to prepare for attending hearings at court

Introduction

The purpose of this chapter is to provide a practical guide to help you prepare for the possibility of appearing in the Family Court. This chapter will provide practical advice on what you need to do for some of the most common applications and will refer you to later chapters of the book where you can find more detailed information.

If thinking like a family lawyer, you will always be trying to reach an agreement and avoid the need to issue court proceedings. However, you will be keeping one eye on the possibility that going to court will be necessary. You need to ensure that your pre-proceedings work will help your case before the judge rather than harm it.

All Family Court applications have the same five phases, whether it is arrangements for the children or the financial issues that are at the heart of the dispute.

The five phases of the process are:

(1) Pre-proceedings negotiations and attempts at settlement.

(2) Preparation for court and the issue of proceedings.

(3) Interim hearings (ie all court hearings that take place after the proceedings are issued but before the trial when a final decision is made).

(4) The final hearing and judgment.

(5) Enforcement.

Each phase of the process requires different administrative functions. Good preparation and record keeping in phase 1 will make it easier for you in phase 2. Good administration of phase 2 will help you in phase 3 etc, etc. Court proceedings can become dominated by paperwork and the control of that paperwork is a very important skill to master to ensure that you are able to effectively convey your case to the judge.

Pre-proceedings negotiations and attempts at settlement

First contact after separation is usually very difficult. Emotions are running high and it is not easy to discuss matters in the business-like fashion that is required. Always remember that modern forms of communication (text, email, Facebook, Twitter etc) are all capable of being accessed at some later time and used as evidence in court proceedings. It is a very good idea not to respond to emails and texts 'in the heat of the moment'. Compose a response but do not send it. Let some time pass before re-reading and, often, changing your original draft. You do not want to say something in an email that you will later regret. The use of emotive or inflammatory language will only antagonise the other party and will do nothing to help in resolving the situation.

It is likely that the correspondence that takes place immediately post separation will be informal and by email, text or phone call. Hopefully, arrangements for seeing the children can be made informally in this way. Addressing financial issues are likely to require more formality.

Once it becomes clear that agreements will not be reached easily, you should consider taking advice from a family lawyer. Even a short appointment with an experienced family law barrister or solicitor will be very helpful. You may then decide to manage all of the negotiations and litigation yourself or, as is becoming increasingly common, take legal advice at certain points of the process while managing the administration of the case yourself to keep costs down.

Without prejudice correspondence

You may well have heard of 'without prejudice' negotiations and may have seen this written at the top of solicitors' letters. The effect of negotiations being 'without prejudice' is that, subject to certain exceptions, what is called 'privilege' will attach to the content of those negotiations, be they written or oral, and this will render the content of the negotiations inadmissible in court.

There are important exceptions that are set out below but the general rule is that written or oral communications which are made for the purpose of genuinely attempting to resolve a dispute between the parties may not be admitted in evidence. Privilege will attach to direct discussions between the parties, provided that it would have applied if the negotiations had been conducted by their solicitors.

In cases concerning children, the same 'without prejudice' principles do not apply. The court is charged with a duty to investigate what is in the best interests of the child. 'Without prejudice' cannot be relied upon on in cases about the arrangements for children and it is common practice for some litigants and their solicitors to include large amounts of correspondence in the court bundle.

> **What is a court bundle?**
>
> A court bundle is essentially papers that are needed by the court for your case. It makes sure that all the information and evidence relevant to your case can be found in one place so that it is easy to refer to during your hearing.

Many judges do not agree that large quantities of letters between the parties should be included within the court bundle and it is likely, with the advent of the new Family Court, that the approach on this will be tightened-up. However, always have in mind that what you write to the other side, during a case that concerns children, may find its way before the judge at an interim or final hearing.

If the case has not been concluded informally, you will need to write letters to your ex-partner or to his or her representatives. As your letters may appear before the court, particularly if concerning arrangements for the children, you should have in mind the following guiding principles:

(1) Use plain and simple language. Do not use provocative expressions and do not make remarks that are unnecessarily personal and likely to cause offence. Remember – you are thinking like a family lawyer so be factual and direct but not emotional.

(2) State clearly and very early in the letter what you are seeking. For example, the letter can have a heading such as 'Arrangements for Seeing the Children on 17 September' or 'Proposals for the Payment of Child Maintenance' so that it is clear immediately what the letter is concerning. If the letter is about a number of different issues, use numbered paragraphs so that any reply to your letter can say, for example 'regarding your offer in paragraph 7'. This helps to keep correspondence concise.

(3) If replying to a letter you have received from a solicitor, include at the top of your letter the reference number for the case used by the solicitor and state 'in reply to your letter dated [insert date]'.

(4) Refer to the other party by name ie Mrs Smith or Mr Smith. Never say 'my ex' or 'the respondent' or 'your client'. Treat the letter as a business letter and use appropriate forms of address for the persons referred to within it. If you receive a letter addressed to you using your first name only, then you should reply in the same way. If you are referenced more formally, then adopt the same mode of address.

(5) Never be drawn into personal criticism of the solicitor

acting for the other party. Remember, they are just doing their job and they take their instructions from their client.

(6) It is always best to keep correspondence short where possible. It is not necessary to write a long letter raking over past events and what you feel the other party has done wrong. Simply state your proposal for a way forward and only refer to past events where necessary. Both you and your ex-partner will know the history, or your individual versions of it. If the other party is represented, the representative will have been told about the history.

(7) You are likely to receive responses to letters that decline to accept your proposals and give reasons why your offer has been declined. Remember that you are in a period of negotiation. It may be that you can make a counter offer that addresses the concerns raised. Of course, there are cases when negotiation by letter does not work, which is why mediation or court proceedings become necessary, but do not abandon attempts to settle by correspondence at the first hurdle.

There is guidance available that should be followed by family law solicitors when drafting letters and emails to their own clients and to the other party to a dispute. You can read this guidance and adopt the same principles when preparing your pre-action letters.

> This guidance can be found at:
>
> http://www.resolution.org.uk/site_content_files/files/guides_to_good_practice_2012_lo_res_merged.pdf

Keeping a file

You will need to keep a record of all the correspondence that you send and all the correspondence that you receive. Keeping a file in a useful way will assist you to manage your litigation. You can keep your file electronically or in paper copy but you will always need to produce paper copies of anything you wish to rely upon in court.

The Family Court does not operate on a paperless basis.

You can keep your file how you choose but a useful tried and tested arrangement is to keep your file in sections so as to separate out different types of documents:

(1) Section 1 should be the court applications (main and interim) and acknowledgements of service.

(2) Section 2 should be court orders.

(3) Section 3 should be statements.

(4) Section 4 should be correspondence. Keep the correspondence in chronological order. Solicitors do this by using a clip with the oldest correspondence at the back and just adding new correspondence on the front as it comes in. You may wish to print out emails and add them on the correspondence clip or just keep them electronically *but* do remember that judges require hard copies of anything you want them to read.

Mediation

The purpose of 'without prejudice' correspondence is to attempt to reach an agreement without the need to go to court. As part of that process, you should always consider trying mediation as an alternative to going to court. It may be that you can agree all the issues between you in correspondence. However, if this is not achievable, before you are permitted to issue a court application, you have to consider mediation.

There is a requirement to attend a Mediation Information and Assessment (MIAM) for most proceedings in respect of children and for financial remedies. The court requires prospective applicants for orders will have attended a Mediation Information and Assessment Meeting prior to lodging an application with the court.

> **What is a Mediation Information and Assessment Meeting?**
>
> A Mediation Information and Assessment Meeting (or MIAM) is a meeting between you (with or without your partner) and a mediator which you must attend before you can make an application to the court. The purpose of the MIAM is to see if you can resolve your difficulties through mediation rather than going to court.

The court office will not issue a court application concerning children or finances unless a Form FM1 is filed with the application or the relevant section of the C100 application form signed. These forms have to be signed by a solicitor or litigant in person giving reasons why that party should not attend mediation, or, the form must be signed by a mediator approved by the Ministry of Justice who has met with the prospective applicant at a MIAM.

The requirement to attend for a MIAM does not apply where the case involves allegations of domestic abuse, the application to the court is urgent (as it involves a risk to life or physical safety of the application or a risk of significant harm to a child) and some other situations including where one party is known to be unwilling to attend mediation. If these exceptions do not apply, a prospective applicant is *required* to attend a Mediation Information and Assessment Meeting to explore the alternatives to court proceedings. If following the meeting the case does not appear suitable for mediation, the mediator will complete Form

FM1 that must then be submitted to the court with the application form or complete the appropriate section in the Form C100.

For further information concerning the requirement to attend a MIAM prior to applications concerning children, please refer to chapter 8. The Family Procedure Rules (the court rules that apply in the Family Court) also require you to attend a MIAM if you are applying for a financial order. If you do not attend a MIAM the court has the power to adjourn the court proceedings until the parties have attended. It is, therefore, very important that you attend a MIAM before issuing your court application.

> **A list of mediators authorised to undertake MIAMs can be found at:**
>
> **www.familymediationcouncil.org.uk**

As mediation is an attempt to resolve the dispute between the parties, what is discussed (concerning money) and the settlements that may have been proposed during mediation are not admissible in any court proceedings that follow. The mediation itself is a 'without prejudice' process. Generally speaking, the court will not permit evidence to be called as to what occurred during mediation unless it is asserted by one party that a concluded agreement was reached and that this agreement should be enforced by the court.

Letters before action

A letter before action is a letter that you will write to the other side before you issue an application to the court. Your attempts to settle the dispute by correspondence or by mediation will have failed and you have decided that you have no alternative except to issue court proceedings.

Letter before action in financial remedy claims

The Family Procedure Rules 2010 include, at Practice Direction 9A, a pre-action protocol that must be followed in financial remedy cases. You should read the protocol but you will find that this is written with solicitors in mind and not litigants representing themselves.

> **This protocol can be found at:**
>
> http://www.justice.gov.uk/courts/procedure-rules/family/practice_directions/pd_part_09a#IDADD5S

The principles to draw from the protocol if you are representing yourself are the following:

(1) You should always be seeking to resolve the case by agreement.

(2) If asked, you should provide voluntary full and frank financial disclosure.

(3) All letters should be sent with the aim of seeking to clarify what claims are being made and how issues between the parties can be resolved or narrowed but there should not be an excessive period of correspondence if achieving agreement looks unlikely.

Letter before action in cases concerning children

In disputes concerning children, there can often be very little pre-action correspondence. Issues can be urgent and require a quick decision by the court. Remember, in any case where there is a risk of harm to a child, the normal formalities required by the rules have to come second to ensuring the child is protected.

The rules applied in the Family Court for cases concerning children are called the Child Arrangements Programme (CAP). For more detail on the requirements of the CAP, please refer to chapter 8.

There are no specific rules concerning the content of letters before action in cases concerning children. However, you should follow the guidance given later in this chapter and your letter can end with a statement that says 'unless I hear from you within 7 days of the date of this letter that my proposals concerning the children are agreed, I will be issuing an application for a child arrangements order'. If agreement is not reached or you receive no response to your letter, then you have given sufficient notice of your intention to issue a court application. You will have to attend a MIAM before the court will accept your application so it may be that you are unable to issue your application in the time frame that you provide in your letter.

Preparation for court and the issue of proceedings

Where to issue your application?

All areas of England and Wales have a designated central Family Court where you should go to issue you application to the court.

> **To find your local central Family Court, you can search at:**
>
> https://courttribunalfinder.service.gov.uk

What is required to issue your application?

To make any application to the court, you must use the form provided by the Court Service. The type of case dictates the form that must be used to issue the application.

> **All the court forms required can be found at:**
>
> http://www.justice.gov.uk/courts/procedure-rules/family/formspage

Applications concerning children

Making an application

For cases concerning children, you will need to complete a Form C100. This can be found using the link above. It is extremely important that you complete all sections of the application form. If you are making an application within proceedings that are already before the court, you should use Form C2.

> **For an example of a completed Form C100, please go to:**
>
> **diydivorce.familylaw.co.uk/**

When completing the section of the form concerning the order that you are applying for, please refer to chapter 8 of this book to ensure that you have applied for the correct order. The types of order available are as follows:

(1) Child arrangements order.

(2) Prohibited steps order.

(3) Specific issue order.

(4) Parental responsibility order.

(5) Variation or discharge of child arrangements order, prohibited steps order or specific issue order.

(6) Special guardianship order.

In the section of the application form requiring you to set out the reasons for your application, you should have in mind the following guidelines:

(i) You should not give a long and detailed account of the history of your relationship. If the dispute is not resolved at the first hearing, the court is very likely to make an order that you prepare a full statement.

(ii) You should give a clear but concise explanation for your application, in bullet point form if possible. An example could be as follows:

- My partner and I were in a relationship for 7 years.

- We separated on 7 January 2014 and I moved out of the house.

- I saw the children whenever Sally would let me, mostly at the weekends on Saturdays or Sundays.

- I have now found a flat and would like the children to stay over with me on alternate weekends and in the school holidays but Sally will not agree to the children staying-over.

- Sally is now saying that I was violent to her during the relationship and that she is scared of me. I was never violent towards her but accept that we rowed and we shouted at each other.

- Sally has said that the children are too young to stay away from her overnight. I do not agree and would like the court to grant me an order to allow this happen.

(iii) As with pre-proceedings letters, always keep your language moderate so that you do not aggravate an already delicate situation. At the first hearing, the court will be seeking to encourage an agreement and will be likely to put pressure on both parties to try to achieve this. You do not want to make agreement impossible by being too aggressive with your language in this section of the application. Be business-like and civil but not emotional.

(iv) Always set out what you are asking the court to order. It can be said very simply, such as 'I would like the children to live with me during the week and see their father every weekend' or 'I would like to share the care of the children with their mother and for them to be in my care on Mondays, Tuesdays and Wednesdays every week'. If you have not set out exactly what you want, the respondent will not be able to say if they agree with the arrangement you are seeking.

You will also have to complete a Form C1A. This form is required by the court where you are alleging that you and/or the children have suffered harm as a result of behaviour by the person who is to be the respondent to your application.

This form is currently in a tabular format. Please complete all the relevant sections of the form. In some cases it is necessary to protect yourself and the children from harm and to do so you have to give a description of the abusive behaviour that you or the children have suffered. It may be that your ex-partner has a mental health problem that impacts on their behaviour or has criminal convictions for offences of violence that you think have an impact on their suitability to see the children. When the circumstances require it, this is the time to set it out in Form C1A.

However, the court very often receives forms that set out a list of allegations that are not serious and would have no impact on whether the children should be seeing the proposed respondent. It is important to remember that when couples separate, people do and say things that they would not otherwise do or say. If there has been violence or verbal abuse that has scared you or the children and you are worried about the impact of this behaviour on the children, and that it may continue, you should always set it out in the form. If you think that the behaviour is what is to be expected when couples separate, you should think carefully before alleging that your ex is a risk to the children, as this will always inflame an already difficult dispute and will make reaching agreement much more difficult.

When you have completed the forms, you will need to take them to the court office and the court staff will check over the content of the form and, if you have completed the form adequately, the court will issue the application. You need to take three copies of the forms with you to the court, as they will all need to be given the case number that is allocated by the court and they will be stamped with the court seal. The court will also prepare a document that provides the details of the date, time and venue of the first court hearing. The court will then 'serve' all the court papers on the proposed respondent (generally the other parent). You should look at the court website to establish if you need to make an appointment to attend the court office to issue your application.

The court will fix a hearing to take place 5 weeks after the proceedings have been issued, unless a request for an urgent hearing has been made on your application form. If you have requested an urgent hearing, as you believe that the child cannot wait until week 5 for the court to consider the case, you should set out your reasons in the application form. On page 1 of the C100, you should include in the section for the order you are seeking 'an order for an early hearing'.

Urgent applications in cases concerning children

There may be circumstances when you believe that your case is so urgent that you cannot wait to give notice to the other party of your application to the court or you believe that you or the child may suffer harm if you give the other party notice of your application to the court.

This situation is governed by paragraphs 4.3 to 4.5 of Practice Direction 20A of the Family Procedure Rules 2010. These rules require that your urgent application is filed with the court on Form C100. You must say in the 'order sought' section that you are applying for an order without giving notice to the proposed respondent. You should provide a detailed explanation within the reasons section of the form setting out why you feel that an order should be made before the proposed respondent has been served with your application.

1

Paragraph 9.3 of Child Arrangements Programme (CAP) provides that urgent applications can be made in one of 3 exceptional circumstances:

(1) If the applicant were to give notice to the respondent and this notice would enable the respondent to defeat the purpose of the injunction, or

(2) The case is so urgent that there has literally been no time to serve notice on the respondent because the injunction is needed now to prevent a wrongful act, or

(3) If the applicant gave notice to the respondent, this would be likely to expose the applicant or relevant child to unnecessary risk of physical or emotional harm.

Responding to an application for an order concerning children

If you receive an application for an order concerning your children, you need to complete 2 forms (that should have been sent to you with the application). You will also receive a document from the court that tells you when the first court hearing is to take place.

The first form for you to complete is the acknowledgment of service in Form C7. You must complete all the boxes on the form and return the form to the court no later than 14 days before the hearing date that the court has listed.

The Form C7 asks if you oppose the application. It does not ask you to give the reasons why you oppose the application. There is a box to tick if you believe the children have suffered or are at risk of suffering harm. If you do, you should complete the second form that you will have been sent. This is the C1A harm form. You should think carefully about what you include in the harm form. Add only what is necessary and impacts on the applicant's relationship with the children.

If you are served with an application for parental responsibility, you will also receive a Form C6 that must be completed and returned. This is the form to complete to respond to the application for parental responsibility. If the application is for a child arrangements order and parental responsibility, you must complete and return C6 and C7.

In urgent cases, a judge or magistrate may have decided that a court hearing needs to take place very quickly and may list a hearing within a day or 2, or sometimes even within a few hours. In this situation, you should attend court on the date directed by the judge.

Applications for divorce of a marriage, dissolution of civil partnership or judicial separation

For the procedure to use when seeking divorce, dissolution or judicial separation, please see chapter 4 of this book.

Applications for a financial remedy

Making an application

Once you have issued your application for a divorce and you wish to make a claim for a financial remedy, you must file you Form A with the court.

The procedure to follow is set out in chapter 9 of this book. In summary you must:

(1) File your Form A with the court.

(2) The court will fix a first directions appointment (FDA) not less than 12 weeks and not more than 16 weeks after the date you file your form A at the court.

(3) Within 4 days of receiving your application, the court will serve the Form A on the respondent with a notice of the date of the FDA. There is a procedure for the applicant to serve the Form A on the respondent but you should avoid this and leave service to the court in the first instance.

(4) You must deliver to the court and deliver to the respondent a copy of your Form E. This must be done 35 days before the FDA.

(5) You must serve a copy of the Form A on any institution that holds a mortgage over your property.

Responding to an application for a financial remedy

You will receive a copy of Form A from the court, together with a notice giving a date for the FDA. You must, no later than 35 days prior to the date of the hearing, deliver to the applicant and the court your financial statement in Form E. Please see chapter 9 of this book for guidance on how to prepare your Form E.

Applications for a non-molestation order or occupation order

Making an application

An application for a non-molestation order or an occupation order can be made in any Family Court. The form to use is FL401. Fill in all sections of the form. The nature of the orders available and the procedure to follow are explained in detail within chapter 7 of this book.

> **Form FL401 and its guidance can be found at:**
>
> http://www.justice.gov.uk/courts/procedure-rules/family/formspage

You will need to take your application to the court with a sworn statement. That means that you will need to write out a statement clearly explaining who you are, who the respondent is, what happened and what order you say you need and why. Your application and the statement will need to be personally served on the respondent. This means that you will need to instruct a process server or some other person to give the papers to the respondent in person. The papers cannot be posted to the respondent unless, once you have tried to serve him personally, the court is satisfied that he is evading service and agrees to make an order for substituted or deemed service.

If you are asking the court to make an order without first serving the respondent with a copy of the application, you will need a specific paragraph in the sworn statement that explains why, with reference to the factors in section 45 of the Family Law Act 1996, you need the court to make an order without giving the respondent the opportunity to give his or her side of the story. Please see chapter 7.

For guidance on statement writing, please see below under the heading 'Preparing a statement for court'.

Responding to an application for a non-molestation or occupation order

If you receive an application for a non-molestation or occupation order, you will also receive a court notice that gives you the date and the time of the court hearing. These applications have to be served on you personally. You should attend the court on the date given as, if you fail to attend, the court is likely to make on order in your absence.

You do not need to prepare a statement in reply to the statement made by the applicant. If the case is not agreed at the first hearing, the judge will direct that you prepare a statement in reply and send it to the court and to the applicant.

You may wish to prepare a position statement for the first hearing so that the judge has some idea of your response to the allegations made and whether you are prepared to submit to and order or offer an undertaking. For guidance on preparing a position statement, see chapters 6 and 8. For guidance concerning the types of orders available and on offering undertakings, see chapter 7.

Case preparation for interim hearings

An interim hearing is a hearing after the issue of the application. The majority of cases that come before the courts are settled at these short hearings. You should always be hoping that your case can be agreed or the issues narrowed at these early hearings. It may be, if the issues are narrowed enough, that the judge can make a decision about what is not agreed at a short hearing without the need for you to give oral evidence from the witness box. It is for these reasons that it is very important to prepare properly for these short hearings. The decisions made at the interim hearings will shape the rest of the proceedings.

Preparing the papers for the court hearing

The Family Court has a practice direction concerning the preparation of the court papers into a bundle for each court hearing. If you are unrepresented but another party in the proceedings is represented by lawyers, the represented party has to take responsibility for preparing the court bundle. If all parties are representing themselves, it is the responsibility of the person that first made an application to the court to prepare the court bundle. It is very important that this is done following the guidance set out in the 'bundles practice direction'.

The rules require that the bundle is contained within an A4 ring binder or lever arch file and does not contain more the 350 pages per file. The bundle must be clearly labelled on its exterior with the court case number and the date and time of the hearing for which it has been prepared.

The bundle must be delivered to the court, by no later than two working days before the court hearing.

The papers within the files must be paginated and there must be an index at the front of the file. The papers within the file must be set out as follows:

- *Section A.* Case summaries and position statements.
- *Section B.* Applications and court orders.
- *Section C.* Statements.
- *Section D.* Care plans (unlikely to be required in proceedings between parents).
- *Section E.* Miscellaneous documents.

Each section should be paginated separately – section A might be paginated as A1 to A45. Section B will not continue on with page 46 but will be paginated as B1 to B56. This allows documents to be added to each section as the case continues and avoids having to repaginate every section whenever a new document is added. Place the page numbers on the bottom right corner of each page.

The rules also require that the other parties to the proceedings are provided with an index to the court bundle no later than 4 days prior to the court hearing. You do not have to copy the bundle and give a hard copy to the other parties. All that you must do is send a copy of the index to them. However, you must deliver a hard copy to the court. Do not email a soft copy to the court office as this will not be printed by the court staff. It is your responsibility to ensure that the court has hard copies of the court bundle.

Do not expect the court to allow you to breach court rules because you are representing yourself. You may harm your case if you do not follow the rules that have to be followed by all litigants, be they represented or unrepresented. The court can make a wasted costs order against you if you do not provide a bundle and court time is lost.

Case summaries

If you are the person preparing the bundle, you must prepare a case summary to be included in section A of the bundle. This needs to be contained on one side of A4 if possible. The case summary should state in a concise way:

(1) Who are the parties to the proceedings?

(2) A summary of the background facts.

(3) What application each party has made to the court.

(4) What has been agreed between the parties?

(5) What is in dispute between the parties?

Use these five points as headings for each section of your case summary, as this will help you focus on what you need to include in your document.

If you are preparing the bundle you can follow the same format for the case summary as that provided for in sections 1 and 2 of a position statement. You will not then need to repeat this information in your own position statement.

A case summary is not the document for you to argue your case. It really is a concise summary of the background so that the judge can get a clear idea of what the case is about. You will need to prepare a separate position statement to argue your case.

For an example of a case summary in a financial remedy case, see chapter 9.

Position statements

All parties to the proceedings must prepare a position statement setting out their case and deliver it to the court no later than

11am on the working day before the court hearing is listed. *This applies to all parties to the proceedings.* For guidance as to what information to include in a position statement, please see chapter 6. For an example of a position statement in a case concerning children, see chapter 8.

You must identify within your position statement the documents in the court bundle that you want the judge to read before the case starts. This is called an essential reading list.

Is a bundle required for every hearing?

It is not necessary to provide a court bundle for all hearings. The rule can be summarised as follows:

(1) If your case is being heard by a High Court judge or if your case is being heard by any judge sitting at the Royal Courts of Justice in London, a bundle must be prepared for all hearings.

(2) In any other court, a bundle must be prepared for all hearings that are listed for more than one hour.

There are special rules for certain hearings in financial remedy cases. Please refer to chapter 9.

Case preparation for fact-finding and final hearings

Scott-Schedules and fact-finding hearings

If a court lists a fact-finding hearing it will often direct the parties to the proceedings to prepare a Scott-schedule. These schedules are also often required for final hearings in

Pre-proceedings Conduct and Case Preparation

applications for injunctions and in any final hearing where there are a number of allegations that the parties are making against each other.

A Scott-schedule is just a table that sets out the allegations made and the responses to those allegations. The table is usually set out in landscape format and looks like this:

	Allegation	Bundle Reference	Response	Bundle Reference	Court Finding
1	The father hit the mother when at the pub on valentines day.	B24 para 15	Denied. The father has never hit the mother in the pub or any where else.	B44 para 2	
2	The father sexually abused Tina when she was 9 years old. The sexual abuse included rape and forced oral sex.	B99 para 7	Denied. The father has never abused his daughter in any way whatsoever.	B107 para 9	
3	On 27th June 20011, the mother was drunk when she came home from shopping. Kevin was crying as he had a very wet nappy as it had not been changed for 7 hours. The mother shock Kevin and threw him into his cot.	B112 para 9 B127 para 44 B149 para 73	The mother has never shaken Kevin The mother has never left Kevin in a dirty nappy for 7 hours	B170 para 3 B172 para 16	
4					

If you are making allegations, then you should prepare the schedule and type in your allegations. You should then send the schedule to the other party by email so they can respond to the allegations and send it back to you. If you send the schedule in Microsoft Word format rather than as a PDF, it can then easily be completed electronically and you should have one completed schedule to send to the court.

It may be that the other party will make allegations against you when replying to your allegations. These allegations should be added at the end of the schedule (so at (4) in the example given above) and the response can then be added.

The Scott-Schedule should be filed within section A of the court bundle. The bundle will need to be updated by the person who initially prepared it. If you prepared the court bundle, you will need to update it with all the evidence that has be served by all parties. You will need to make sure that all the new documents are paginated and inserted into the correct sections of the bundles. You will need to send out copies of the updated index to every party. *This is a considerable administrative burden but it has to be done properly to ensure that: (i) the court has all the documents and (ii) everyone involved in the case has the documents in the same place in the bundle as you do and that the page numbers match.*

At a fact-finding hearing, the court will consider the allegations that each party makes against the other. The court will direct that you file and serve statements (this means file [deliver] to the court and serve [deliver] to the other parties to the proceedings). To prepare for a fact-finding hearing, you will need to read all the statements and be ready to answer the allegations that will be put to you when you give evidence. See below for statement writing guidance and chapter 6 on how to ask questions and give oral evidence.

Final hearings

For the final hearing, the court bundle will need to be updated. The case summary at the beginning of the bundle will need to be updated so that it sets out the issues that remain in dispute in order that the judge can see what he or she has to determine. Each party will need to serve a position statement.

The position statement that you prepare for the final hearing should address the factors that the court has to consider when making a decision in your case, whether you are the applicant or respondent. Some lawyers may prepare 'skeleton arguments' that set out their legal arguments as a separate document or it may be within the position statement. It does not matter which approach you take but give your document clear headings, as this will provide you with a structure to follow.

You should refer to the chapter 6 of this book for more information concerning written and oral advocacy at final hearings.

Financial remedy proceedings

If you are involved in financial remedy proceedings, there are a number of special documents that you need to prepare to properly present your case at court. Please refer to chapter 9 for detailed explanation of how to prepare these documents.

Preparation for hearings under Schedule 1 of the Children Act

If you are making or responding to an application made for financial payments under the Children Act, please refer to chapter 11. For advice concerning pre-proceedings negotiations see above under the heading 'Pre-Proceedings Negotiations and Attempts at Settlement' and for guidance on preparing a court bundle see above under the heading 'Preparing the papers for the court hearing'.

Preparation for final hearings in applications for non-molestation and occupation orders

It may be that an order is made at the first hearing until the court has the opportunity to consider the evidence at a subsequent final hearing or no order is made and the case is then listed for a final hearing. If the hearing is listed for more that one hour, the applicant is required to prepare a court bundle. Please see above for guidance on preparing the court bundle.

You may be directed to prepare a Scott-schedule on the allegations of misconduct relied upon. If so, please see above for an example.

For the final hearing, you will need to prepare a position statement setting out, if you are the applicant, what you are seeking and why you require the protection of the court. You should address the factors set out in the relevant section of the Family Law Act 1996. Please see chapter 7.

If you are responding to an application for an injunction, you will also need to prepare a position statement explaining why you oppose the grant of the order, detailing what you are prepared to offer, if you will agree to give an undertaking. You should address the factors set out in the relevant section of the Family Law Act 1996. Please see chapter 7.

Preparing a statement for court

There is no prescribed format for how a court statement should be presented but if you follow these simple guidelines, you are likely to provide the court with the information it needs in a way that is acceptable to the judge:

Always put the case heading at the top of the first page of the statement. You can usually copy these from other documents served on you. The usual presentation is something like this:

IN THE FAMILY COURT SITTING   CASE NO: BL 14P001123
AT BLACKPOOL
IN THE MATTER OF: TOM SMITH (DOB 12.08.2004)
AND JANE SMITH (DOB 17.07.2010
BETWEEN

                    JOHN SMITH   <u>Applicant</u>
                      And
                    JOAN SMITH   <u>Respondent</u>

FIRST STATEMENT OF JOHN SMITH

Always include a statement at the start of the document recording that you are telling the truth. A usual example would be:

> I, John Smith, of 24 Cherry Tree Lane, Blackpool, provide this statement believing it to be true and understanding that it may be placed before the Court.

Always sign the statement at the end and record, on the statement next to your signature, the date that you signed it. It is important that you read the statement carefully and are sure that the contents are true before you sign it.

It is essential that each paragraph of your statement is numbered and that the pages of the statement are also numbered. It is very difficult for everyone in court if this is not done and it will be difficult for you to refer the judge to the parts of the statement that you want to highlight if it is not properly numbered and paginated.

If this is the first statement, it is helpful to the court to use the first few paragraphs to explain who you are and to describe your family. If it is a case concerning children, then you can describe the background to your relationship, when and why you separated from the other parent and what have been the arrangements for the children since separation.

The statement is an opportunity for you to tell your story to the court and to explain what outcome you want and why. Do not make the statement too long and use 12 point font. Please use 1.5 line spacing. You want to make your statement easy to read so small font typing should be avoided.

Try to present you story in chronological order. If you are describing past events, provide dates whenever you can. If you cannot provide a date but remember it was summer or winter, say so. Giving a context around an event is very helpful.

What you will need to include in your statement will depend on the reason why the statement is required by the court. If the case concerns children, once you have set out all the facts that you want the court to know about, you should address the factors in the welfare checklist (see chapter 8). You can use each factor as a paragraph heading and then provide the court with your views under each heading. If it a case concerning an application for an injunction, you can use the factors that the court must consider under the Family Law Act 1996 as paragraph headings (see chapter 7). If your statement has been ordered in financial remedy proceedings, you will need to address the factors in section 25 of the Matrimonial Causes Act 1973 (see chapter 9).

Try to remain focused on thinking like a family lawyer. Statements prepared by litigants in person can often read like a bit of a rant rather than a considered legal document. You want the judge to think that you are a responsible and reliable witness so do not play into the hands of your opponents by serving statements that are far too lengthy and aggressively worded.

Enforcement

The final phase of the proceedings is known as enforcement. If the court has made an order, be it an order for the payment of spousal maintenance or an order for a child to have overnight visits with a parent, the court expects the order to be obeyed.

If the order is not obeyed, fresh applications have to be made to the court in an attempt to have the order 'enforced' against the party who is in breach of its terms.

Enforcement of courts orders is considered in detail in chapter 12. Enforcement of child arrangements orders is considered in chapter 8. If you are seeking to enforce a child arrangements order, you will need to use Form C79.

> **Form C79 can be found here:**
>
> http://hmctsformfinder.justice.gov.uk/HMCTS/GetForm.do?court_forms_id=2252

Dos and don'ts

DOS

- Remember that you are running your own case and you cannot expect special treatment because you do not have a lawyer

- The court does not conduct proceedings by correspondence. Emails and letters to the court are likely to go unanswered or, if answered, the answer is likely to be that you should make an application to the court. If you have a question, go to the court counter and speak to someone face-to-face. If you want an order changed or made, then you will need to make an application and pay a fee

- ✓ Remember to go for your MIAM. The judge is likely to adjourn your case until you have

- ✓ Always be concise when preparing documents for the court. You can always give greater detail orally when in court

DON'TS

- ✗ Forget to keep a clear diary. When the court orders that you must provide a document by a specified date, you must provide the document by that date. If you do not, the court might make a costs order against you

- ✗ Write anything in haste – remember any documents or correspondence could be seen by the judge. Never send anything 'in the heat of the moment'. Always take time to reflect

Chapter 6

Advocacy – How Best to Make your Case at Court

What you will learn

- How to prepare for the hearing
- How to prepare documents and what the different type of documents are
- How to present your case to the court
- How to question witnesses
- How to deal with the 'day' of the hearing

Introduction

> (i) **What is advocacy?**
>
> Simply stated, it is nothing more than a public statement to the court as to why the court should agree with your terms as opposed to the terms the other side would argue for (or advocate).

Advocacy is also sometimes called the technique of persuasion. So let's see how to go about it.

It is important to point out that in the modern era advocacy very much includes the written word as every judge in the family justice system will rely heavily on position statements, case summaries, chronologies and skeleton arguments in his or her pre-reading of the case (see chapter 5). This is because the system is very busy and it is common for several complicated or difficult cases to be listed for short hearings on the same day with the result that the judge will be hugely assisted by short documents setting out the issues and the arguments. It is only when you get into court before the judge and you have the chance to speak that your skills in oral or spoken advocacy will come to the fore. The trick is to win the argument on paper before you even get into court.

In this context, 'judge' also refers to magistrates, who take an active part in the Family Court.

Before you get to court – what to prepare

What do you want the court to do?

Lawyers speak of 'court orders' which are the formal record of the decision of the court. Every professional lawyer needs to work out from the beginning what it is he wants the court to do. You need to do this too. This means in nearly every case having an idea as to what orders you would like the court to make. This can split into two basic questions:

(1) What is the result I would like at the end of the case; for example, a residence order enabling my children to live with me, or an order for contact that the children can stay overnight?

(2) Litigants (that is the parties to the case) soon realise that if the other side does not agree with the main result you are

seeking it is very unusual (although not unheard of) for the judge to order that to happen at the first hearing of the case. Disputed matters of importance will be decided after:

(i) proper evidence has been gathered, and

(ii) a final hearing has taken place where the court spends more time hearing from both parties and other witnesses and giving a reasoned decision (or 'judgment' as it is known).

So at any hearing other than a final hearing you need to ask what preparatory orders (also known as 'directions') you would like the court to make. Examples of directions include the filing of statements from witnesses, preparation of a Cafcass report and obtaining records from the other party or even third parties such as the police or health services.

> **What is Cafcass?**
>
> This is an organisation known as the Children and Family Court Advisory and Support Service Every year Cafcass helps over 140,000 children and young people who are going through care or adoption proceedings, or whose parents have separated and are unable to agree about future arrangements for their children. Cafcass is the voice of children in the family courts and helps to ensure that children's welfare is put first during proceedings. http://www.cafcass.gov.uk/

Case management documents

Telling the judge on paper what you want and why

When you have worked out what it is you want the court to do and why, type it out in a short document.

It is now obligatory for lawyers representing parties in family cases to prepare short documents (case management documents) summarising the points they wish to make. This makes the judge's life much easier but funnily enough it also makes the lawyers' life much easier in court too as he or she will benefit greatly for having thought about the important points in advance in a considered way and will need to worry less about remembering to make a point if they know it has already been written down and read by the judge.

The main types of case management documents are position statements, case summaries, skeleton arguments and chronologies. Apart from chronologies the other three types of documents basically do the same thing although in slightly different ways. A case summary might be longer and include two or three pages of large type, setting out the history in a summary way. It usually includes a couple of paragraphs on what you want the court to do and why. It is quite a useful document to put in early on as it shows any judge coming new to the case why the proceedings began. A position statement is usually a bit shorter and may be used for hearings after the first directions hearing. It could usefully set out what has happened since the last hearing and what you want the judge to do today.

A skeleton argument usually contains more of a legal argument. So to take a simple example, if after a fact-finding hearing in a contact case the mother wishes to argue for continued supervision of contact in the light of the findings made, she might want to summarise the case-law which gives guidance on the approach the court might take after findings have been made. That could be done in a skeleton argument though, it does not matter at all if she makes the argument in a position statement or case summary.

The documents do need to be kept to a minimum, two or three pages at most and try to pare it down. All the main points can be kept to a page in most cases and punchy points carry more weight. Always remember that the judge is under time pressure and they need to understand the details of your case quickly and succinctly.

So it is best to spare them the misery of wading through pages of single spaced ramblings in which any good points are buried amid repetitious and irrelevant background. Don't do that. Most cases have three or four good points at most. Make them, then stop.

Following are some tips about what should be included in your documentation.

It is helpful to the judge if you set out the heading of the case and case number at the top of the first page. Then give the document a title – *'Position Statement of the respondent father for the hearing on (and give the date)'*. Begin your document with a list of who is involved: so in cases concerning the welfare of a child state:

- the parties' names, addresses, dates of birth;

- the name of the child or children and date(s) of birth;

- where the child or children are living; and

- what the current arrangements are for contact (if any).

Inform the judge about the proceedings:

> 'I am the mother of X who was born on XX.XX.10. This is my application for a residence and a contact order in relation to her. The father is Z. The application was made on XX.XX.14 and the respondent, Z, filed an acknowledgment of service on XX.XX.14.'

It would then be useful to tell the judge what decision you would like him or her to make in the case. You might say; for example:

> 'I am seeking a residence order in relation to X. I seek an order that she sees her father on alternate weekends and during school holidays but that until he is drug free I am opposed to X staying overnight. I am aware that the father seeks a shared residence order and shared care. I oppose this and if the court is unable to resolve the matter today, would suggest that a Cafcass officer be appointed to investigate X's best interests and that we each provide a statement of evidence before the matter is reconsidered by the court. I also ask that the court directs him to submit to independent hair strand analysis to establish whether or not he is taking hard drugs.'

Having said that you might go on to set out how you and your ex-partner have got into this situation and why you oppose his plans.

It would also be useful to refer to an attached chronology of events. A chronology is a list of key events by date order. Usually it comprises a three column table created in a document with several rows. The first column is for dates, the second column for a short description of events and the third can be to reference the event to a page in a statement or the court bundle for ease of access.

So you might say something like this:

> 'Z and I separated in August 2013 by agreement when he left the flat. We agreed that he should see X on Wednesday afternoons after nursery from 3pm to 6pm. Later we agreed that she could stay over with him on Saturday nights from 3pm until 10am on Sundays. On 10 November 2013 a friend of his rang me and said that he was worried as Z had the care of X on Saturday evening and when she was asleep he had friends round and there was heavy drinking and Z took cocaine. I was aware that during our relationship he would occasionally take the drug socially. On the same day I asked Z about the drug taking and he denied it but became angry and aggressive. Since that time I have refused to let X stay overnight and would not be prepared to do so until I know

the truth about Z's drug taking and that he would not take drugs whilst caring for our daughter. Because X is only three and because of Z's work commitments I do not consider that it is in her best interests to live with Z at all and certainly not for half of the week as he suggests.'

So in this case, the mother has within a few lines stated what the case is about, what she wants the court to order in the long and short term and why she has concerns about the father. There are of course no hard and fast rules about this but be clear and succinct and try not to repeat your points.

In a financial case (see chapter 9) the judge will have Form E but will still benefit from a short statement as to what you want and why, a chronology and a table of the assets, liabilities and the incomes of the parties, restricted if possible to one page (Excel is excellent for this).

It is always a good idea to address the legal test directly. Why not say why the order you suggest is more in accordance with your child's best interests than the order that the other side seeks. In similar vein, in financial cases explain why the order you seek is fairer than the one the other side seeks.

Getting ready for the hearing

Try if you can to prepare your documents a few days before the hearing. The judge will be impressed if when he or she opens the file on the day or afternoon before your case, there on the file is your document explaining what it is all about. Find out the email address of the court and if you know which judge is hearing it email it in for his or her attention. Otherwise take two or three copies of it to court with you on the day; but a day or two before is much better.

The other thing you will need to think about is what other documents the judge should have. By far the best way to make sure that he or she has the right documents is to prepare a court bundle as outlined in chapter 5.

> **What is a court bundle?**
>
> A court bundle is essentially papers that are needed by the court for your case. It makes sure that all the information and evidence relevant to your case can be found in one place so that it is easy to refer to during your hearing.

If you are the applicant you are obliged to get a bundle to the judge for any hearing of substance (usually over 2 hours of length and for every hearing in the High Court) and the bundle must be delivered to the court, by no later than 2 working days before the court hearing. Get a receipt for the delivery as it is not exactly unknown for documents handed into the court office to get lost before getting to the judge. Mark the documents with the case number and, if known, the name of the judge. If you are confused about this by all means ask court staff who are known to be helpful with administrative matters concerning filling in court forms, paying court fees and getting papers to the judge.

Try not to get any documents copied by the court office, as the cost is very high. The cost of a 100 page bundle at any high street printer will be a fraction of the cost charged by the court.

On the day

On the day of the hearing try to get to court early, particularly if you are nervous. If you are going to be late and miss the starting time of the hearing be sure to ring the court and let them know.

The court will usually wait for you to arrive but if they do not know that you are on your way it is quite within the right of the court to start on time.

It is quite usual for litigants in person (LIPs) to be accompanied by a friend or family member for moral support. When you arrive and get through security look at the court lists posted in the public areas, find your case name and number and go to the court where the case is listed to identify yourself to the court usher – usually a person in a black gown with a clipboard. This is the time to hand in any documents you have brought for the hearing and have not managed to email in. In fact, even if you have emailed documents into the court the safest bet is to hand in a copy on the morning and tell the usher that you emailed it in too. Take copies to hand to the other side before the hearing.

The period of time before the case is called into court is usually taken up by the lawyers having discussions to see if they can narrow the issues. Some litigants in person are quite happy to discuss the issues and alternative directions with a lawyer on the other side. Others feel a bit intimidated and are worried that they might be 'tricked' into saying something that might be held against them. The rules as to how a barrister or a solicitor should behave towards a litigant in person are clear. They must not knowingly mislead that person, nor bully nor intimidate them. LIPs are much more common these days than was once the case and most lawyers will be experienced in dealing with LIPs in a straightforward and fair manner. Having said that, it is perfectly acceptable for an LIP to say that he/she would prefer to speak to the judge and not explore 'settlement' options until after they had been into court.

If your former partner is also representing him/herself you will have your own view as to whether you are happy to have a face-to-face discussion with them outside court. If it is a case where you are genuinely fearful of being harmed or threatened by your ex-partner in the court building it is perfectly proper to ring the court in advance and ask whether the court can allocate a room for you so that you don't have to share the waiting area with a person of whom you are fearful.

Types of hearing

There are many types of hearing. Your approach to them will vary dependent upon the type of hearing. The main types are as follows:

Cases involving children

First hearing dispute resolution appointment

This is the very first court appointment in private law hearings relating to children. The court will look to mediate a resolution to the dispute without further time or cost. A Cafcass officer will probably speak to the parties and possibly the children if they are old enough. Judges are usually extremely keen to resolve the cases at this stage with some advice on the likely outcome and the rigours of litigation. If the case does not settle the judge will decide whether to appoint a Cafcass officer to investigate further or in less complex cases set the matter down for a final hearing with suitable directions for the filing of evidence.

Interim/directions hearing

This is a hearing which may take place to review the case in the light of the evidence filed. The court will expect the parties to seek to narrow the issues between them. If the case is not resolved at this hearing the court will make further directions for the filing of evidence and fix the date for the final hearing. Some directions hearings are needed when things go wrong such as when evidence ordered from third parties does not come in on time or at all or when one of the parties appears to have disengaged from the proceedings.

Fact-finding hearing

These type of hearings are going out of fashion because they add an extra tier of delay to the proceedings. They are useful when the outcome of the case is likely to depend on the truth of serious allegations made by one party against the other. They are more likely these days in cases of alleged sexual abuse rather than domestic violence but even then some judges will list the matter for an early final hearing as opposed to a two part hearing which may take up to a year to resolve (see chapter 7).

Final hearing

The court usually hears oral evidence from the parties and witnesses and makes an order after argument.

Chapter 8 covers cases involving children in detail.

Financial cases

First directions appointment

A procedural hearing at which the court will review the financial statements and disclosure, decide what further enquiries by questionnaire are justified, make directions for the valuation of assets and fix the case for an FDR some weeks later.

Financial dispute resolution hearing (FDR)

The vast majority of financial cases are resolved as a result of the FDR either on the day or shortly afterwards. The value of these hearings is that the parties can enter into without prejudice negotiations (that is, unknown to the trial judge at the final hearing) in a process driven by the judge who is duty bound if at all possible to give an indication as to the likely outcome of the case. The parties usually set out their proposals in advance and on the day of the FDR usually present the judge with a schedule of assets and income and a case summary setting out the order sought and the justification for it. Typically there is negotiation followed by judicial indication with more negotiation to follow and further trips to see the judge as the issues narrow. Be prepared to be there all day if necessary. If the case does not settle expect further directions for trial to be given including the provision of witness statements and up to date valuations. The FDR judge is not permitted to decide the final hearing of this case.

Final hearing

The court usually hears oral evidence from the parties and witnesses and makes an order after argument.

Chapter 9 covers cases involving financial matters in detail.

Addressing the judge

As explained above it is much more likely in cases dealing with children that hearings which are not final hearings of the case will be decided on what lawyers call 'submissions' meaning spoken arguments and not hearing oral evidence. This is usually because of the lack of time to take evidence and the perception that justice can be achieved at an interim stage without testing witnesses by cross-examination.

How should you approach your submissions? The answer is this: always politely and with clarity and economy.

What should you call the judge? A district judge in the county court will be called 'Sir or Madam', a circuit judge 'Your Honour' and magistrates 'Sir or Madam'. In the High Court the judge is called 'My Lord or My Lady'. Don't worry too much about getting this wrong. Most judges are pretty relaxed about this sort of thing.

> **For additional information about the court formalities go to:**
>
> http://www.judiciary.gov.uk/you-and-the-judiciary/what-do-i-call-judge/.

When you go into court the judge will usually spend a moment or two telling you what he has read and what he thinks the issues are for the hearing. He may also say what the court can and cannot achieve at the hearing and what might have to be left for decision on another day at a final hearing. He will then ask the parties in court to address him.

If you are the applicant you will be asked to go first. It is much easier if you have worked out what you want to say in advance and have written it down to be read by the judge. Then you can use your position statement as a guide to emphasise your points. There may be passages in the written evidence you want the judge to have particular regard to. Don't go overboard but it helps if you have flagged up the references you want to rely on and perhaps give the judge the page number for his note or even read out a short passage from the evidence to emphasise the point. You can probably make all the points you need to make in 5–10 minutes and try not to repeat yourself. Judges tend to be 'on the ball' and nearly all of them get the points first time round. If you know what the other side will say it is perfectly fine to anticipate what they are going to say and to 'get your retaliation in first' before they speak. But never fear, the applicant will have another chance at addressing the court after the respondent has spoken. This is called the 'Reply'.

It is customary to listen to what the other side is saying in silence however tempting it may be to interject and heckle. The judge will be irritated if this happens and will tell the heckler that he/she will have a chance to address the court in a moment. Judges sometimes have to tell lawyers off for this type of thing. It is far better to bite your tongue and address the inaccuracies as soon as you are invited by the court to speak. It is also perfectly proper to ask the court politely for a chance to correct an inaccuracy in the other side's address even if you have used up your chance or chances.

After submissions the judge may give a short ruling and explain his reasons. Try and keep a rough written note of what he says as it may prove useful in the future. He will also say what order he is to make and in all likelihood will either ask the legally represented party to type up the terms of the order and send it in or, alternatively, get the court admin team to type it up, seal (stamp) it and post it to the parties. The drafting of orders is quite technical which is why the judge will look to assistance from any lawyers in the room. Ultimately, however, the order is that of the judge and not the typist.

At an FDR the judge should if at all possible give an indication as to what may be the type or range of orders he would make if he were trying the case. This is the whole point of the FDR: to encourage the parties to negotiate and settle the case in the knowledge of what a judge considers to be the right order. Usually the parties go out for some time and are invited to come back into court when they have settled the case or when they know that they should fix a final hearing for another judge to decide. This often happens at other hearings too when the judge might give a clear but informal indication as to how the case should be resolved.

Dealing with oral evidence and closing submissions

At a contested final hearing the court will often hear the parties and other witnesses.

The order of events is well established:

(1) The applicant 'opens' the case – that is briefly tells the judge what he or she wants, what is agreed and what is disputed and what the evidence is he or she intends to call to establish the case on the disputed elements.

(2) If there is a Cafcass officer often he or she will be heard first. The judge will ask some questions followed by each party.

(3) The applicant then gives evidence and is cross-examined followed by his or her witnesses.

(4) The respondent gives evidence and is cross-examined followed by his or her witnesses.

(5) Closing submissions by each party also called final speeches summarising the evidence and the case.

(6) The judgment delivered by the judge; sometimes in writing but more commonly verbally immediately after the submissions.

This type of hearing can be a nerve-wracking experience for the professional initiated and amateur uninitiated alike. Like may things, however, the key to survival and indeed success is to keep things simple.

The best way to do this is to prepare for the hearing in a thorough and orderly way. Put some effort into it. Here is a list of things to do and consider:

(1) Put the papers in a file. Flag up all the orders, statements and reports. Use coloured tabs to differentiate between documents.

(2) Read all of the papers. Twice. It sounds silly to say read the papers but there may be details which you might have forgotten and overlooked in the months leading up to the final hearing. The best advocates know the papers inside out.

(3) Make a list of the page references of all key documents. Just on one page for your own reference.

(4) Write your final submissions out in outline. Just in outline for the time being because you will need to leave gaps to comment on the oral evidence but in it list all of the main points you want to make and the relevant evidence which is not disputed and the relevant evidence which is disputed.

(e) So in a disputed contact case the basic list might look like this:

F has a tendency towards violence; – see my statement at [bundle ref] and his criminal convictions at [bundle ref] and photos [bundle ref];

F still takes drugs; see hair strand report at [bundle ref];

F left the child with his friend; see his statement at [bundle ref]; and

F did not take child to doctor; see my statement at [bundle ref].

(f) In a financial case the basic principles are the same: work out at the beginning what parts of the case are disputed which you need to prove by the end of the case in order to win. So, for example, if you need to prove that your ex-wife has wasted tens of thousands of pounds on holidays you need to:

(i) make a note of all the page references in her bank statements which demonstrate this; and

(ii) make a note of the fact that you need to put all of this to her when you are cross-examining her.

(g) Do this on an issue by issue basis until you have a complete list of disputed issues and a list of areas you need to challenge and the key page references which back this up.

(h) Call this document 'a case plan' and add to it and cross sections out as the case progresses.

(i) Keep a handwritten note of what is said in court when you are not speaking. It may come in handy later if someone contradicts what they said earlier.

Questioning

There are three recognised parts of witness questioning: examination-in-chief, cross-examination and re-examination.

Examination-in-chief

These are the questions put on behalf of a party to that party to elicit his evidence. They will inevitably be questions designed to put that party or his witness in the best light. There are lots of rules about how a professional advocate should conduct examination in chief which you can look at if you wish but it is right to bear in mind the fact that:

(1) lengthy examination in chief is quite rare where a party's

statement is read into his evidence so he does not need to tell his story from scratch and indeed will not be allowed to in most cases;

(2) if the party is a LIP he will not ask himself questions (!) but the judge may ask a few questions to set the scene;

(3) judges do not expect LIPs to know the rules of evidence and are trained to help and guide LIPs in eliciting evidence in a fair and proportionate way.

Cross-examination

This is slightly different. These are the questions a party puts to the opposing party and his witnesses. They can be hostile in the sense that they may, and in some cases must, challenge the other party's account of events or opinions. Many books have been written about the skill of cross-examination and it is fair to say that advocates of great seniority still differ widely in their approach in terms of style and affect. Do not worry about that. What is essential for you to remember is that there are certain facts that:

(1) you may wish to bring out as confirming your view of events;

(2) you must challenge; and

(3) you may wish to challenge.

It is often useful during cross examination to have a your case plan with a fairly fixed order of topics or even questions set out. Ask short factual questions. If your account of an important event is not seemingly challenged ask the other party to agree in the witness box that this is so. Try to deal with what is agreed as you begin each topic.

There is a clear rule about what you must challenge. If the opposing party gives evidence contradictory to your own about events or relevant matters you must challenge the accuracy/truth of his version when you question him. In the trade it is called 'putting your case' and means that you cannot address the judge at the end of the case and suggest that X is a liar unless you cross-examined him and suggested that to him in your questions. This counts for all relevant disputed events.

Other useful things to question on are a person's previous statements or actions. It may be, for example, that when questioned by the police X said something which he now denies. So put the previous statement to him and ask him if he said it at the time and, if he accepts the police recording, ask him whether he was lying then or now. Or, another example, in a finance case if the husband says that he cannot afford to pay maintenance you may wish to take him through large elements of his expenditure recorded in his bank or credit card statements in the past year and invite him to consider his priorities.

Don't worry if you don't think that you are asking enough questions. Stick to your plan and remember the judge (or magistrates) will always ask questions either during the evidence or at the end of it which he thinks will help him come to a fair and just conclusion.

Re-examination

This is the concluding part of questioning when the party who called the witness is entitled to ask him questions to clarify the answers he has just given in cross-examination. Usually there are no more than one or two questions if any at all.

How to prepare for being questioned

Many lawyers have never themselves been witnesses but will readily agree that for most ordinary people it can be a very stressful experience. However, as a party to the case it is also an opportunity to present a favourable impression with the judge which may have a significant bearing on the outcome.

Again the key to success is preparation. Know the facts inside out. Know your strong areas and weak areas. Anticipate hostile (but polite) questions on the weak areas. Think in advance how you might answer. Having the facts at your fingertips will bolster your confidence in the witness box.

When giving evidence really try hard to answer the question directly. It is amazing how many people are evasive even about the most trivial matters and what a bad impression that can create. This is often due to nerves or the pervasive fear that you are being lured into a trap. Here is the news: The advocate questioning you has exactly the same material as you. There are few hidden traps in family cases. All of the bad stuff is probably there on paper months before the final hearing. So just answer the questions directly in a straightforward manner. And if you did or said something bad which objectively was not justified then say so and move on. Admit where you were wrong. By all means explain how it happened but if it was wrong, then say so. Judges hear so many people evading personal responsibility for things most will view a balanced and straightforward witness as refreshing and impressive.

The judge will not allow you to be questioned in a discourteous, bullying or unfair way. However, if there is a factual dispute expect to have your integrity or at least your memory queried. Politely, of course.

Closing submissions

This is the opportunity to comment on the evidence that the court has just heard and to summarise your arguments as to why the judge should prefer your view. Keep it short. Give the judge three main reasons why you should win. State why your evidence should be believed over the other party when there is a dispute. Maybe the other party gave an inconsistent or unbelievable account in the witness box, or perhaps his account is contradicted by independent evidence and yours is supported by it. Draw the strands of your case together. Tell the judge what you want him to order and why it is the best or fairest outcome of all the other solutions.

Judgment

Take a note of what the judge says and what orders he makes.

Permission to appeal

Nearly all orders require the permission of the judge who took the decision or the appeal court to appeal the decision. Appealing decisions in family cases is difficult as the judges are given wide discretion to resolve difficult cases as best they can. Often there is no absolutely correct answer and the appeal courts give trial judges the latitude to make their best choice between what are sometimes unpalatable alternatives. Having said that if the judge gets the law wrong, or in some ways did not make the decision following due process, or even simply took a clearly wrong decision, the appeal court would be likely to entertain an appeal. This is quite technical stuff and the best course is to seek professional advice on the merits of an appeal before getting your hopes up too much.

Dos and don'ts

DOS

- **DO** spend some time working out what to say. Planning properly will help with your nerves

- ✔ **DO** read all of the case papers twice
- ✔ **DO** prepare brief, punchy documents
- ✔ **DO** email your documents to the court a couple of days before the hearing
- ✔ **DO** get to court early
- ✔ **DO** try and speak to the other side in a constructive way

DON'TS

- ✘ **DON'T** be intimidated by the process, LIPs are very common these days
- ✘ **DON'T** agree with something you don't actually agree with because you feel under pressure. If you don't agree say so and say why
- ✘ **DON'T** feel the need to say everything just in case. Try to work out what is going to help the judge most of all
- ✘ **DON'T** be impolite or aggressive. Be courteous yet firm

Chapter 7

Domestic Violence

What you will learn

- What are non-molestation and occupation orders
- How to make an application for a non-molestation and/or occupation order
- What to do if a non-molestation and/or occupation order is made against you
- What the court takes into account when making orders and the different types of orders that may be made
- Evidence, hearings and enforcement of orders
- What to do, not to do, and where to go for further information and advice

Introduction

This chapter deals with domestic violence and two types of protection from the court ('orders') to help protect you and your children. 'Non-molestation orders' deal with a variety of unwanted behaviours, and 'occupation orders' deal with whether or not people can stay at the family home. Both types of orders are made under Part 4 of the Family Law Act 1996 (FLA 1996).

> For details of the FLA 1996 go to:
>
> http://www.legislation.gov.uk/ukpga/1996/27/contents

The law in relation to occupation orders is set out in sections 33–40 of the FLA 1996 and non-molestation orders at sections 42 and 42A. Sections 43–49 of the FLA 1996 deal with both types of order. The court procedural rules dealing with these types of applications are set out in Part 10 of the Family Procedure Rules 2010, with the associated Practice Direction 10A.

> **What are the Family Procedure Rules 2010?**
>
> The Family Procedure Rules 2010 are rules which provide an essential code of procedure for family proceedings in the High Court, County Court and Family Court.

> **What is a Practice Direction?**
>
> A Practice Direction is issued to provide supplemental or further information to rules of procedure in the courts.

> You can see these Rules if you go to:
>
> http://www.justice.gov.uk/courts/procedure-rules/family/parts/part_10

Non-molestation orders

A non-molestation order is an order preventing a person (the respondent) from 'molesting' an 'associated' person or a 'relevant child'. The term 'molesting' is not defined and covers a wide range of behaviour from violent behaviour to behaviour which is sufficiently troubling or inconvenient so as to require the court's involvement. It covers emotional abuse eg controlling, coercive or threatening conduct. The order is an injunction and prevents the respondent from doing certain things eg using or threatening violence, coming within a certain area near an address, or communicating with the applicant, either altogether or by particular means. Further detail as to the types of order usually made by the court are set out below. It is important to remember, though, that you cannot use a non-molestation order to exclude someone from a home where they are entitled to be: for that, you need an occupation order (see below).

Examples of things that can be prohibited by non-molestation orders

- using/threatening unlawful violence;
- intimidating, pestering, molesting or otherwise harassing behaviour;
- entering, attempting to enter or coming within a certain distance of a property (unless the respondent is entitled to be there);
- sending threatening or abusive letters, text messages;
- communicating with the applicant whether by telephone, text message or other means of communication except through solicitors;
- damaging, attempting to damage, or threatening to damage property; and
- prohibiting the respondent from instructing or encouraging any other person to do anything which he/she is forbidden to do by the terms of the order.

If you seek a non-molestation order against someone, they have to be 'associated' with you. The range of association is wide and is set out in full in section 62(3) of the FLA 1996. The form for an application for a non-molestation or occupation order (Form FL401) is helpful as it sets out (in section 4 of that form) the different relationships and all you need to do is tick the appropriate box.

> **This form is available online by entering 'form FL401' at:**
>
> **http://hmctsformfinder.justice.gov.uk/HMCTS/FormFinder.do**

In summary two people are associated if they:

- are or have been married/civil partners;

- are or have been cohabitants;

- live or have lived in the same household (but not if they were just an employee, tenant, lodger or boarder);

- are relatives;

- have agreed to marry one another or be civil partners (whether or not that agreement has ended);

- have had an 'intimate personal relationship with each other which is or was of significant duration';

- if they are both parents of, or both have parental responsibility for, a child; and

- if they are both parties to the same family proceedings (but not the non-molestation/occupation order proceedings).

Breach of a non-molestation order is a criminal offence. When a non-molestation order is made, a copy should be sent to the local chief of police so they are aware of it. If an officer has reasonable cause to believe that a person has breached a non-molestation order, the officer can arrest that person straight away. Breach of an occupation order is not a criminal offence but a 'power of arrest' can be attached to the order in serious cases, namely where there has been violence or a threat of violence and the court considers that the applicant requires the protection of the power of arrest. Further issues about enforcement of these orders is dealt with under 'enforcement' below.

Occupation orders

An occupation order can do a number of things, including to:

- exclude a person from the family home (to include the surrounding area if necessary) and prevent them from returning;

- allow a person entry to the home and enforce their right to remain there;

- terminate a person's right to occupy the home; and

- regulate the occupation of the home as between people living there, eg use of certain rooms at certain times.

An occupation order is a serious order as it interferes with a person's rights in relation to their home. Unlike with non-molestation orders, courts very rarely make an occupation order on the application of one party alone without the other party being there to put forward his/her position. After a relationship breaks down there is always the difficult task of deciding what to do about the living arrangements, and often this is influenced by what happens about the care of any children involved. However, there might be occasions where an emergency or disagreement arises and you need the court to make an order to sort out the occupation of the home. Before making an application, please consider carefully the factors that the court takes into account in deciding whether to make an order, which is dealt with below.

You will need to apply under the correct section of the FLA 1996 for an occupation order: it depends on your right to occupy the home and your relationship to the other person as to which section applies. This also affects things like how long the order can last for. As mentioned above, the form for an application for a non-molestation or occupation order (Form FL401) is very useful as it sets out (in section 6 of the form) the different categories and you just need to tick the right box. The Notes for Guidance at the end of the form sets out examples eg to help you decide whether you are 'entitled' to occupy the property (the 'dwelling-house'). It is always a good to seek specialist legal advice from a solicitor or a direct access barrister if you can and remember that you may be entitled to legal aid to help you make your application (see further chapter 2).

How to make an application for a non-molestation or occupation order

The application

You can make an application for either order, or both orders, at any Family Court. You will need to complete Form FL401 (mentioned above). At the end of the form – which you can download or collect from the court – there are detailed notes which you should read carefully as they will help you understand and fill out the form.

> To locate your nearest court go to:
>
> https://courttribunalfinder.service.gov.uk/

There is also a leaflet available online or at court called 'FL700' which is a guide to Part 4 of the Family Law Act 1996 in relation to domestic violence. That contains a step-by-step guide to issuing your application and so it is recommended that you read this as well.

> **To find the FL700 leaflet go to:**
>
> http://hmctsformfinder.justice.gov.uk/HMCTS/FormFinder.do

In order to issue your application you will need to:

- Have all the right details to fill in the form (but note that you are allowed to keep your address confidential if you want to – that requires an additional form called C8 which the court can give you or you can find online, see below).

> **To find Form C8 see:**
>
> http://hmctsformfinder.justice.gov.uk/HMCTS/GetForm.do?court_forms_id=2216

> **For an example of a completed Form C8, please go to:**
>
> diydivorce.familylaw.co.uk/

- Take three copies of the completed form to the court to issue (you keep one copy once it is issued, the court keeps one and the other is served on the respondent, usually by a bailiff or process server which the court can arrange at your request – see below). Remember that if you are applying for an occupation order you will need a fourth copy to send to the mortgage company or landlord as appropriate (see below).

- Consider and then set out the terms of the order you are asking for.

- Prepare a statement in support of your application which explains what has happened and why you want the orders you seek. This statement must contain a 'statement of truth' at the end and be signed and dated.

- If you are making an application in relation to a property, it is usually helpful to have information in relation to that property, eg details of the mortgage/tenancy.

At the bottom of the first page of the form there is an option to tick the box telling the court that you want it to hear your application 'without notice' ie without telling the respondent. There will need to be a good reason for this: usually this is done in cases of absolute emergency where it is necessary for a person, the applicant, to go to court and get a protective order before the other person, the respondent, finds out and does something to stop the applicant. Your statement must explain clearly why you have asked the court to make an order without hearing both sides and the judge may well ask you more about this when you are in the hearing. A further hearing will almost certainly be listed after the first 'without notice' hearing (sometimes called an *ex parte* hearing) so that the court can hear from the respondent and decide whether to keep any orders made going forward. See further below for the factors the court will take into account before making an order without notice to the respondent.

The court staff will check the forms you have prepared and then the court staff will 'issue' your application. They will put a 'case number' on the form and then tell you the date and time of your court hearing. If you applied 'without notice' to the respondent, your hearing may well be that same day. If the hearing is 'on notice' ie with both parties there, then the hearing will likely be on another day.

The 'without notice' hearing

If you go before the court alone, without the respondent there, the judge will read your application and statement in support. The hearing takes place in private, so members of the public are not allowed in. If you have a solicitor or barrister, they will speak on your behalf. If you are representing yourself, you are allowed to ask to take in a person as a 'McKenzie Friend'. That person is not allowed to speak on your behalf without the court's permission but can help you with papers and taking notes.

> **What is a McKenzie Friend?**
>
> A non-legally qualified person who helps a litigant in person at court by providing support.

The judge may well have further questions about your application which you must answer honestly: the judge has a duty when hearing from one side alone to scrutinise the evidence carefully to see whether it meets the required standard for an order to be made (see below for the factors the court takes into account). The judge will either grant your application in the terms you seek, or in slightly different/lesser terms if the judge feels that something else is appropriate, or he may adjourn the case for a certain period of time to get both parties back to court so the judge can hear both sides. You may be given the date for the next hearing in court, or you will be told that it will be sent to you.

If the judge makes an order against the respondent then the court will usually 'draw up' the order on the day (ie type it out formally). You should wait to receive your copy of it. If you need to take a copy to someone to get it served, you will need to take that copy too, or you may have asked the court to arrange for personal service of the order and it will then be collected from court by whoever is serving it.

Serving the application (and order)

The application will need to be served on the respondent personally although this does not mean by you, it just means the respondent must be handed it in person, usually by a bailiff or process server (unless the court has said that the respondent should be served in a different way). If you've issued an application and the hearing is on another day, the respondent must be served with the application (including the evidence in support) and the notice of the hearing no less than 2 days before the hearing, unless the court has specified otherwise. If you've issued your application at court, had a hearing and got an order that day, the order must also be served personally on the respondent along with the application, evidence and notice of the next hearing date, which is usually set quite soon.

The court can arrange service if you request this. If you've got solicitors helping you, they can arrange service. You are allowed to arrange for anyone to serve the respondent – it doesn't have to be a bailiff or process server – but whoever does carry out the personal service must complete a 'statement of service' (Form FL415) proving that they have done this. It is usually not a good idea to arrange for service to be done by you directly, or by someone else known to the respondent, as emotions can run high and there might be problems when the respondent is served, so this is best avoided. If it is a bailiff/process server, they will complete the statement of service for you once service has been achieved.

If a bailiff/process server is going to serve the respondent, you will need to provide details of the respondent including what they look like, how tall they are etc. A photograph is usually very helpful, if available. The respondent's address will already be on the application. If service at the respondent's home is unsuccessful you can provide details of another place, for example, their place of work, for service to be achieved.

If you have applied for an occupation order, the application must also be served on the mortgage company or landlord. Check with the court whether you need to do this (by post) or whether the court will do this for you.

If you get an order at court which is a non-molestation order or an occupation order with a power of arrest attached, you must take a copy of the order to your local police station so that the police are aware of the possibility that the respondent can be arrested for doing/not doing certain things, and what those things are. Again, the court will do this for you if you ask it to.

If there are children involved, you might also want to consider whether you need to make an application under the Children Act 1989 at the same time as a non-molestation and/or occupation order, for example you may want to consider whether a 'prohibited steps order' (one of the section 8 orders) is also required to prevent the respondent from removing the children from your care/control, or from their school. See further chapter 8.

What happens if you are served with a non-molestation or occupation order

It is extremely important that if you are served with an order, you must obey it, even if you think the order should not have been made. The best thing you can do is take the papers to a solicitor, a direct access barrister or your local Citizens' Advice Bureau (CAB), to get advice about what you should do in response.

> To find your nearest Citizens' Advice Bureau go to:
>
> http://www.citizensadvice.org.uk/

It will almost certainly be the case that a hearing date has been listed for the court to decide whether the orders should continue in force, be varied, replaced with 'undertakings' [a formal promise to the court which is enforceable as if it were an order] or discharged. You should attend that hearing. It is a good idea for you to get to court at least half an hour before the time the hearing is listed. Do also remember though that it is not guaranteed that your hearing will start at the listed time or last for the time estimate given, so be prepared to take sufficient time off work, or make alternate child care arrangements, so you can stay at court for as long as required. Bring all of the papers to court that you have been served with, so you can refer to them when at court.

At that hearing, often called a 'return date' hearing, the judge will hear from you about your response to the application. It may be that you accept some of the things alleged, but not all of them. You may not accept anything alleged. The judge will consider the types of allegations made and what should happen next. The various options are:

- The orders may remain in force in the terms they were made until a full hearing can take place where you each argue your case ie the applicant has a chance to prove the allegations and the respondent has a chance to challenge them.

- The orders may remain in force but varied slightly. There will then be another hearing as described above to decide on whether, and if so what, final orders should be made.

- The application may be settled by agreement by the respondent offering 'undertakings' or both parties offering 'cross-undertakings' (see below).

- The orders may be discharged but a further hearing listed

- to consider whether they should be made again or in different terms in the future once there is more evidence available.

- The orders may be discharged and the application dismissed but this is very rare, and would only really happen if the application was wholly without merit and some 'knock-out' evidence could be produced showing the applicant had lied to the court the first time and should not have the orders in force.

In the event that no return date hearing has been listed and you contest the order which has been made, there will be provision in the order for you to apply back to court for consideration of the orders. If this happens, go to a solicitor, Citizens' Advice Bureau, or the court counter to ask what you need to do to get a hearing.

It is usual that at the return date hearing, if it is clear that the case will not settle, the court will consider what it will need at a contested hearing and it will make 'directions' setting a timetable for all of the evidence to be completed (see below for examples of 'directions'). The court may say that the evidence should be 'filed and served' by a particular date. This means a copy sent to the court (filed) and sent to the other side (served). It is highly advisable to get a receipt for postage or delivery and to keep a copy for yourself. The timelines are important and, unless you have a very good reason for being late, the court has the right to exclude your evidence from consideration if it is not filed and served on time.

> **What is the return date hearing?**
>
> The hearing when both sides are there after one party has gone to court alone to get an order.

The directions at the return date hearing may also include provision for evidence to be obtained from third parties eg a doctor or hospital, or the police. Whatever the directions are, make sure you understand them before you leave court and you know what, if anything, you need to do and by what date.

Factors the court takes into account

When the court considers whether or not to make a non-molestation order, it will have regard to all the circumstances including the need to secure the health, safety and well-being of the applicant and any relevant children (who will have been named in the application). It is quite a broad test and, as described above, 'molestation' can refer to a very wide range of behaviour. The court's intervention must be required for an order to be made.

When the court considers whether or not to make an occupation order, there is a two stage test. First the 'balance of harm' test and second the court's discretion when taking into account a number of factors.

At the first stage the court looks at the likelihood of significant harm to one party (and any relevant children) and balances this against the likelihood of significant harm to the other party. The court must make the order if the applicant is likely to suffer significant harm as a result of the conduct of the respondent and that harm is greater than any harm that is likely to be suffered by the respondent if the order is made.

The court does have the power to make the order even if the 'balance of harm' test is not satisfied in the applicant's favour. In such cases, the court has to decide whether to use its discretion to make the order ie making the order is optional, not required. The factors that the court takes into account in arriving at its decision are as follows:

- the housing needs and resources of each of the parties and of any relevant child;

- the financial resources of each of the parties;

- the likely effect of any order, or of any decision by the court not to exercise its powers on the health, safety or well-being of the parties and of any relevant child; and

- the conduct of the parties in relation to each other and otherwise.

There are clearly a number of matters that the court has to take into consideration and so the court will need information (evidence) about all of them. For this reason the court very rarely makes occupation orders 'without notice' to the respondent as the court will not be in a position to know reliably what the respondent's resources are nor what the effect the order will have on the respondent, or what the respondent says about any allegations about his or her conduct.

Without notice hearings

A mentioned above, if the case is extremely urgent and you are asking the court to make an order 'without notice' to the other side the judge will consider the following (in addition to the normal 'tests' for the orders):

- all the circumstances of the case;

- any risk of significant harm to the applicant or a relevant child attributable to conduct of the respondent if the order is not made immediately;

- whether it is likely that the applicant will be deterred or prevented from pursuing the application if an order is not made immediately; and

- whether there is reason to believe that the respondent is aware of the proceedings but is deliberately evading service and that the applicant or a relevant child will be seriously affected by the delay involved in arranging for service to take place.

Orders and undertakings

The types of orders that can be made by a court are discussed above for non-molestation orders and occupation orders respectively.

> **What is an undertaking?**
>
> This is a formal promise given by a party instead of, or to supplement, an order. It is enforceable as if it were an order.

An undertaking can last for a defined time or 'until further order' (effectively forever). Breach of an undertaking is not a criminal offence (like breach of a non-molestation order is) but an undertaking is enforceable as if it were an order of the court, so it is a serious matter to offer an undertaking because breaching it is 'contempt of court' ie you can be punished by a fine or committal to prison for up to two years. If you no longer wish to be bound by an undertaking, you would need to apply to the court to be released from it.

Some might say that an undertaking to do/not do certain things is an implied admission but others could just as easily ask why a person would not offer a promise to do/not do something if that person would/would not do it anyway. Remember that FLA 1996 proceedings are private and so what is discussed in court or written in the court papers is not public knowledge. Undertakings can therefore be a good way to settle applications by the respondent making promises which will reassure the applicant regarding certain behaviour about which there are concerns. It avoids the court having to make any findings about whether things did or did not happen. If a court makes a finding then it can be relied on later, eg in proceedings concerning children. It is also sometimes the case that although the applicant has come to court and asked for an order against the respondent, there may well be allegations that the respondent wishes to make against the applicant. Therefore cross-undertakings, ie promises by both parties in the same/similar terms can be a good way to deal with such situations.

It is important to remember, though, that the court will not accept an undertaking in a case where there has been violence, or a threat of violence and where the applicant requires that an order is made so that breach of that order is a criminal offence, or where a power of arrest would have been attached to an occupation order ie in serious situations where it needs to be possible to arrest the respondent for breaching the order rather than bringing the matter back to court.

Remember that a court can make an order only within the confines of the law. However, a party can give an undertaking to do/not do whatever he/she wants but it must be sufficiently clear to be capable of enforcement. Often undertakings are given in the same terms as an order that was made previously, but this can also extend to further things by agreement, such as dealing with issues relating to the children even if Children Act proceedings are not issued. Some of the different types of things that can be promised as an undertaking include:

- agreeing not to bring a joint tenancy to an end unless those parties agree in writing;
- agreeing not to discuss the proceedings with the children or with anyone else in the presence/earshot of the children and not to permit or encourage anyone else to do so; and

- agreeing not to communicate in relation to a joint business save in writing.

Further provisions

In addition to what has been discussed above, the court can make also orders relating to the following (albeit that such orders are quite rare):

- repair and maintenance of the property;

- payment of the rent/mortgage or other outgoings eg utility bills;

- payment of money to the party who has been required to leave a property that they would otherwise be entitled to live in (this is usually considered to 'cancel out' the rent/mortgage unless there is a stark difference in the parties' financial resources);

- granting use of certain furniture or contents in the property; and

- requiring a party to take reasonable care of any furniture/contents and/or to keep certain furniture/contents secure.

If the court is asked to make any of the above orders, it will take into account the financial needs and resources of the parties and the financial obligations which they have, or are likely to have in the foreseeable future, including obligations towards each other and to any relevant child eg child support.

Directions

(i) **What are directions?**

A timetable set up by the court for the future progress of the case with instructions given to each party.

If the court needs to make directions for a further hearing then the sorts of things which may be ordered are as follows:

- the applicant to set out in a schedule the allegations being made, referring to the statement (which would have already been filed with the application);

- the respondent to submit a statement in response to the applicant's statement and also to fill in his/her responses to the schedule of allegations; and

- provision for other evidence eg from a GP or from the police.

Duration

Orders can be made for varying duration. A non-molestation order is usually made for a period of one year, but this could be less or more as required by the situation. You can always go back to court to ask for an extension, but you must do so whilst the order is still 'live' ie, in force. An occupation order's duration depends on which part of the FLA 1996 applies and therefore what is appropriate: these are not usually orders which would last forever and it may be that there is a restriction as to how long the order can last for, or how many extensions there can be.

Often you will see 'until further order' written in an order and the standard interpretation of this is that the order will last until a further order is made bringing the earlier one to an end – or overtaking it with specific reference to the earlier order ie just because another order happens to be made later doesn't bring a non-molestation order or occupation order to an end. Do check with the judge is you are unsure.

Evidence and contested hearings

See chapter 5 for guidance as to how to prepare your case. Set out below are tips specific towards applications for non-molestation or occupation orders.

The statement in support

Summarised below is a list of all the things that should be covered in the applicant's statement in support of the application:

- An introductory paragraph should state your name and address (unless you are keeping this confidential and have completed a Form C8, in which case just say 'of a confidential address' in the statement) and explain briefly what you are asking the court to do.

- Either at the outset or the end remember to set out clearly why the application is made without notice to the respondent, if this is the case.

- Set out in clear, numbered paragraphs, the reasons for your application. Do also number your pages. The statement does not need to be very long and you should concentrate on the most serious and most recent allegations/events and whatever it is that made you apply for the order. It is most helpful if you write this out in chronological order and you should give each event/allegation a date (or approximate date) and include as much detail as you can and not use vague phrases such as 'the respondent was always abusive towards me': you must describe when, how often, and in what way the respondent was abusive.

- For an application for non-molestation orders, make sure your evidence covers issues about the 'health, safety and well-being' of you and any relevant children.

- For an application for an occupation order, make sure you address all the factors that the court takes into account (see above).

- If you are able to obtain any documents or independent evidence in relation to your allegations, you should attach them to your statement, as it will strengthen your case. Refer to these in the statement with page numbers so the judge can cross-refer. These are usually called 'exhibits' to your statement.

- At the end of your statement you must include a 'statement of truth'. This means you must write the sentence: *'I believe that the facts stated in this witness statement are true'*. Then print and sign your name and don't forget to date it.

If the case does not finish or settle (eg, with undertakings) at the return date hearing, the court may need to list the application for a 'contested hearing'. That means a hearing with a longer amount of time to go through all of the evidence and hear oral evidence from the parties. The respondent will have a chance to test the evidence eg by asking questions or presenting documents to challenge it. At that hearing, the court will need to make findings about the allegations to decide what is or is not true and this will help the judge decide whether or not to make the order sought. If this is the case, the judge is likely to want to have a 'schedule of allegations', also known as a 'Scott-schedule'.

Schedule of allegations

A Scott-schedule (see chapter 5 for an example) is, in effect, a table where the allegations are numbered, with one column setting out what the allegation is (with a date) and cross-referring to the place in the applicant's statement where the incident is described (which is why page numbers and paragraph numbers are helpful). The next column is left blank for the respondent to set out his response eg 'accepted' or 'denied' and then to say why very briefly, with reference to the statement the respondent will have prepared. The last column is left blank for the judge to write comments or make a note of his/her findings during the hearing.

Respondent's statement

It is almost certainly the case that if the application proceeds to a contested hearing, the respondent will also be required to file a statement in response to the statement of the applicant. This statement should reply to the allegations in the applicant's statement and cross-refer accordingly. The statement itself should also start with the respondent's name and address and end with a statement of truth, name (printed and signed) and date. If the respondent has any independent evidence to rely on, this should be attached to the statement as exhibits too. Furthermore, if the respondent seeks orders as well eg an occupation order the other way round (requiring the applicant to leave rather than the respondent), then this should also be included in the statement. Some courts may require the respondent to issue his/her own application for this too. Unless already dealt with as part of the response, all of the issues that need to be addressed to deal with that application should be set out (see factors to be taken into account above). It is probably the case that if you have been ordered to do a statement in response, there will also be an order for you to complete your column of the Scott schedule as described above.

> **What is a statement of truth?**
>
> This should be added at the end of the document and would say *'I believe that the facts stated in this witness statement are true'*.

The hearing

A contested hearing will start with the judge hearing a short introduction to the case if this is not already clear from the papers, usually by the applicant but he may hear briefly from the respondent too if necessary. Then the judge hears oral evidence as follows:

- The applicant goes in the witness box and either swears on a religious book or gives the non-religious affirmation, then states his/her name, address (unless confidential) and confirms to the court that his/her statement is true and that this should be treated as the applicant's main evidence. If there is a need to add some updating information, this can be done (but should not be lengthy – it is not an opportunity to repeat what is already in the statement).

- The respondent is then allowed to ask the applicant questions about his/her statement and challenge what is said in there and/or to challenge any evidence provided in support.

- The judge may intervene at any point to stop inappropriate questions, to help re-phrase questions or to add questions at the end.

- The opposite then happens: the respondent goes in the witness box and events occur as above but the other way around so that the applicant is able to challenge what the respondent has said.

- If either party has any witnesses in support of their case, they usually go before the relevant party but can go afterwards, depending on availability. The conduct of the hearing is up to the judge. Do warn any witnesses that they may be required to wait.

- Remember that the oral evidence part is about challenging what has been said or produced in evidence rather than arguing about why the court should or should not do something – those arguments are 'submissions'.

- The parties then make 'submissions' and draw together the reasons why the court should or should not make the order sought. This is a chance to comment on the evidence and tell the judge why you say your version of events is 'more likely than not' to be the truth (that is the test for the judge to apply, also known as the 'balance of probabilities').

- The judge then may want some time to consider what he/she has heard and will then give a 'judgment' describing the order that will be made and why.

> **What are submissions?**
>
> These are arguments which analyse and comment on the written and/or oral evidence.

The sorts of things you might want to think about when preparing/challenging evidence include:

- Is there external, independent evidence in support or which will refute a point made? Documentary and unbiased evidence is usually likely to be most reliable. Is there a failure to produce evidence that might otherwise be expected?

- Are there internal inconsistencies within the documents produced or between the documents and what was said in court? Timings and locations can often change between versions which may highlight a weakness or a lie.

- Is what is alleged inherently unlikely? Consider what detail is provided or left out? Can the person describe other things eg, where the children were or where certain furniture was? Are reactions proportionate to the situations?

- Is the person seemingly making things up as he/she goes along and adding things that weren't there before: why is this the case, why was that detail left out earlier?

- Are there any reasons to doubt a person's credibility? Do remember though that just because a person has lied about one thing does not mean they will lie about others, but it is likely to affect the way a judge considers how reliable a witness or party is if they can be shown to have lied at some point in their evidence.

See further chapter 6 for assistance with presenting your case.

Appeal

If you consider that the judge was wrong to arrive at his/her order, you are entitled to appeal the order. You are required to have the court's permission to appeal and this can either be obtained from the judge who gave the judgment and made the order or from the appeal court. You can ask the judge on the day for permission to appeal or you can include in your appeal application a request for permission to appeal. You have 21 days from the date of the judge's decision to appeal it. Permission to appeal will only be given where the court considers that the appeal would have a real prospect of success or there is some other compelling reason why the appeal should be heard.

Successfully appealing a decision of a judge who has exercised his/her discretion and who has based the decision on hearing evidence from parties is difficult: the appeal court does not hear the evidence again and will take seriously the impressions formed by the judge at the original hearing (the 'first instance' hearing). It is advisable to seek legal advice promptly if you consider you may want to appeal a decision because if you appeal and lose, you are at risk of having to pay the other side's appeal costs.

The rules in relation to appeals are set out in FPR 2010, Part 30 and the associated Practice Direction 30A (see start of chapter for a link to these Rules).

Enforcement

There are two things not to be confused in relation to enforcement, namely the 'penal notice' and the 'power of arrest'.

The penal notice is a notice written on the order, addressed to the appropriate party (usually the respondent) making clear that if he/she does not obey certain parts of the order, he/she will be in contempt of court and may be sent to prison or fined. A penal notice should always be included in a non-molestation or occupation order as both orders are 'injunctions' and require a person to do/not do something and so that person must be warned of the consequence of disobeying that order. Any order with a penal notice should have been served personally on the respondent unless the court directs otherwise.

> **What is contempt of court?**
>
> Contempt of court is an offence for being disobedient to a court of law. Examples of contempt of court are failing to comply with an order or request of the court, withholding evidence or being disruptive during court proceedings. If you are found to be in contempt of court you may be fine or sent to prison.

A power of arrest can be included on an order if the court wishes to give a police officer the power to arrest a person named in the order (usually the respondent) if he/she has reasonable cause to believe that that person has breached the order. Without the power of arrest, the other party (usually the applicant) would have to come back to court first to ask the court for a warrant for arrest. As described at the start of this chapter, breaching a non-molestation order is a criminal offence and it is an arrestable offence. Therefore a power of arrest is not applicable to a non-molestation order.

In relation to occupation orders, section 47 of the FLA 1996 provides that a power of arrest can be attached to an occupation order in serious cases, namely where there has been violence or a threat of violence and the court considers that you require the protection of the power of arrest.

If a person breaches an undertaking, remember that this is enforceable as if it were an order. An undertaking is sometimes written out on a form which already has the warning notice on it, but if not on that form, then wherever it is written it must have a warning notice on it, similar to the penal notice mentioned above. You cannot attach a power of arrest to an undertaking: if the harm/threatened harm is sufficiently serious to require a power of arrest, the court should not be accepting an undertaking in the first place.

In summary, the following options are available when it comes to enforcement:

> Non-molestation orders only:
>
> - Arrest of a person for breach of a non-molestation order and criminal prosecution in the criminal courts: this can result in a fine or imprisonment for up to five years

> Both occupation orders and non-molestation orders (if this is not punished via the criminal system as described above eg, if for some reason there is no prosecution or the prosecution is unsuccessful):
>
> - Proceedings for contempt of court within the family court system, which can result in a fine or imprisonment for up to two years.

Further information is set out in chapter 12.

Further information and guidance

If you are in fear for your safety or your children's safety, **you can always call 999**. Your doctor, midwife or health visitor may be able to help you, or refer you to someone who can. The local Citizens' Advice Bureau can tell you about local organisations and solicitors who can advise and support you. Alternatively you can contact any of the following organisations to get help and advice about domestic abuse:

- **English National Domestic Violence Helpline**, 0808 2000 247 (24 hour)
  www.nationaldomesticviolencehelpline.org.uk

- **Women's Aid**
  www.womensaid.org.uk

- **Men's Advice Line**, 0808 801 0327
  www.mensadviceline.org.uk

- **National Centre for Domestic Violence**, 0844 8044 999
  www.ncdv.org.uk

- **Broken Rainbow** (for lesbian, gay, bisexual and transgender people), 0300 999 5428
  www.broken-rainbow.org.uk

Dos and don'ts

DOS

- **DO** seek legal advice if at all possible (CAB, solicitor, direct access barrister) or ring a helpline (see information above)

- **DO** read all of the forms and guidance notes thoroughly

- **DO** consider carefully what exactly you are asking for and also whether any other orders might be required eg, relating to any children

- **DO** make sure allegations are as specific and detailed as possible, focus on the most recent and most serious

- **DO** think about what evidence you have or you need to get to support your position

- **DO** think about the factors the court takes into account

- **DO** keep a note of what happens, including of any events after your application especially if any of the orders are breached

- **DO** consider whether you can settle the case by agreement eg, by offering 'undertakings'

DON'TS

- **DON'T** disobey orders made against you, even if you disagree with them

- **DON'T** think that domestic abuse only involves physical violence. You may have experienced emotional or verbal abuse which has made you afraid for yourself or your children and this is treated as domestic abuse

Chapter 8

Children

What you will learn

- What you need to do before asking the court to make an order about a child
- The new child arrangements programme
- The practical steps to take to start the process
- How to gather evidence
- The practical steps to take to complete the process

Introduction

The procedure for all family cases is contained in the Family Procedure Rules 2010 and in Practice Directions which appear alongside the Rules. Both are available online.

> (i) **What are the Family Procedure Rules 2010?**
>
> The Family Procedure Rules 2010 are Rules which provide an essential code of procedure for family proceedings in the High Court, County Court and Family Court.

The Rules are divided into Parts, each dealing with a separate topic. Each Part has at least one Practice Direction to go with it.

> **(i) What is a Practice Direction?**
>
> A Practice Direction is issued to provide supplemental or further information to rules of procedure in the courts.

> **To see the Family Procedure Rules 2010 go to:**
>
> www.justice.gov.uk/courts/procedure-rules/family/rules_pd_menu

Part 12 of the Rules deals with most applications relating to children. It does not deal with parental order proceedings or applications in adoption, placement and related proceedings. It has sixteen Practice Directions to go with it: PD12A–PD12P.

Parental order proceedings (applications under the Human Fertilisation and Embryology Act 2008) are dealt with under Part 18 of the Rules. Applications in adoption, placement and related proceedings are dealt with under Part 14 of the Rules.

Resolving children disputes

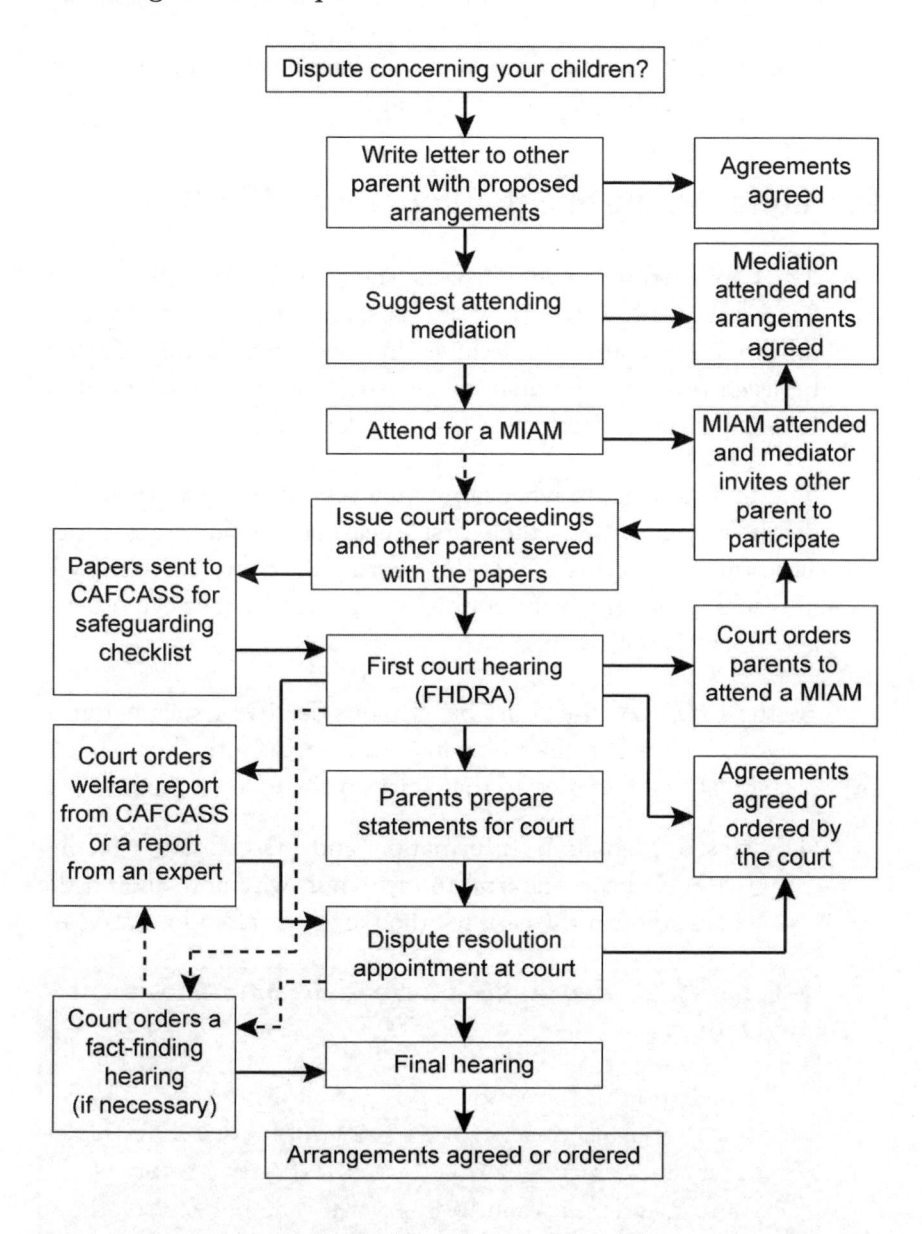

- Dispute concerning your children?
  - Write letter to other parent with proposed arrangements
    - Agreements agreed
    - Suggest attending mediation
      - Mediation attended and arrangements agreed
      - Attend for a MIAM
        - MIAM attended and mediator invites other parent to participate
        - Issue court proceedings and other parent served with the papers
          - Papers sent to CAFCASS for safeguarding checklist
          - First court hearing (FHDRA)
            - Court orders parents to attend a MIAM
            - Court orders welfare report from CAFCASS or a report from an expert
            - Parents prepare statements for court
            - Dispute resolution appointment at court
              - Agreements agreed or ordered by the court
            - Court orders a fact-finding hearing (if necessary)
            - Final hearing
              - Arrangements agreed or ordered

How to start proceedings

The procedure to use to make an application to the court concerning a child is set out in chapter 5.

The Child Arrangements Programme (CAP)

The Child Arrangements Programme (CAP) came into force on 22 April 2014. CAP provides a set of rules that must be followed for court proceedings in cases concerning children between private individuals (it does not apply to cases brought by local authority children's services departments).

The first hearing, in what family lawyers refer to as private law disputes, is called the first hearing dispute resolution appointment (FHDRA). At this hearing the court will assist you in reaching an agreement yourselves or it may impose an order if agreement is not reached.

At the FHDRA, the court has to consider five issues before it moves to consider the substance of the dispute. You should prepare answers to give to the court on the following points:

(1) Has a Mediation Information and Assessment Meeting (MIAM) been undertaken or, if not, why not? Should the court adjourn the case for the parties to attend a MIAM?

> *(i)* **What is a Mediation Information and Assessment Meeting?**
>
> A Mediation Information and Assessment Meeting (or MIAM) is a meeting between you (with or without your partner) and a mediator which you must attend before you can make an application to the court. The purpose of the MIAM is to see if you can resolve your difficulties through mediation rather than going to court.

(2) Should the parties to the proceedings attend a separated parent information programme or is any other form of dispute resolution appropriate?

(3) Is the allocation decision correct?

(4) Does an expert need to be instructed?

(5) Is a section 7 welfare report required?

It is not until the court has consider the five factors set out at (1) to (5) above, that it will then consider whether an order is appropriate at this early stage of the proceedings, and if so, what order should be made.

CAP is a court procedure that has been designed specifically for use by litigants in person. You should download it, read it and take a copy of it with you to court.

> **You can find a copy of CAP at:**
>
> http://www.justice.gov.uk/downloads/family-justice-reform/pd-12b-cap.pdf

At the FHDRA, the court will have received a letter from Cafcass that sets out the results of an initial investigation into the circumstances of the family and whether there are any safeguarding issues.

> **What is Cafcass?**
>
> This is an organisation known as the Children and Family Court Advisory and Support Service. Every year Cafcass helps over 140,000 children and young people who are going through care or adoption proceedings, or whose parents have separated and are unable to agree about future arrangements for their children. Cafcass is the voice of

> children in the family courts and helps to ensure that children's welfare is put first during proceedings. http://www.cafcass.gov.uk/

If you have a history of involvement with the police or social services, you should be prepared to answer questions about this at the FHDRA. If there have been any calls to the police during the course of your relationship due to arguments or allegations of domestic abuse, this is likely to be set out in the Cafcass letter so you should be ready to answer any questions that the judge might raise.

The court will read the C100 application form and the C7 response form, together with any C1A forms that have been filed. You should not send a statement to the court before the FHDRA appointment and should not take one to court with you. Paragraph 13.1 of CPA provides that no evidence shall be filed until after the FHDRA. The court will give directions (orders concerning the gathering of evidence) at the FHDRA.

Should I prepare a position statement for the FHDRA?

If your ex is represented, their barrister or solicitor may prepare a position statement for the hearing. This is a summary of the case and a summary of what the client is seeking from the court at that hearing. The FHDRA will be listed for less than one hour so there is no requirement for a position statement to be filed, unless specifically ordered by the court. However, there is nothing in CAP that prevents litigants in person from sending a position statement to the court. Indeed, you might feel that you are at a disadvantage if the judge has read a document prepared by the other party's lawyer but has not read a document prepared by you. The court will have read the reasons given by the applicant for bringing the proceedings but the Form C7 does not seek an explanation for why you may oppose what is sought.

Preparing a position statement is your opportunity to set out in summary form why you oppose the court making the order sought or why you agree, or what you do agree and what you do not.

If you decide to prepare a position statement, you should follow these guidelines:

(1) A position statement must be brief. More than two sides of A4 is likely to be unnecessary and long documents are less helpful for the judge who is likely to have a very long list of cases and limited time for pre-reading. The trick with a position statement is to be concise so the judge can quickly read your document, know what your case is about and know what you are asking the judge to do at the hearing.

(2) In the first paragraph, set out who the parties to the proceedings are, their ages and addresses. Give the full names of the children, their ages, where they live and where they go to school.

(3) Do not use your position statement as a substitute for a full evidential statement. Many judges believe that it is counter-productive to order the parties to file statements at an early stage of the proceedings, as this requires them to take positions and express, often negative, views about each other. This can make a bad situation worse, make settlement more difficult and thereby delay decision making for the children. The court will give directions for the parties to file statements but only when the court has decided that this is necessary. This means that your position statement has to give the court a brief summary of the background but must not be a detailed account of the history. It is often useful to give a chronology in your position statement. This will help you to keep the information you provide brief. The following is a formula that you can adopt for your position statement:

POSITION STATEMENT ON BEHALF OF JOHN SMITH FOR HEARING
LISTED AT BLACKPOOL FAMILY COURT ON 15TH AUGUST 2014

1. The Parties to the Proceedings

The applicant is the John Smith. Mr Smith was born on 3 April 1969 and is 44 years old. He lives at 24 Cherry Tree Lane, Blackpool.

The respondent is Joan Smith. Mrs Smith was born on 2 March 1970 and is 43 years old. Mrs Smith lives at 97 Matrimonial Road, Blackpool.

The children are Tom Smith, born on 12 August 2004, aged 9, and Jane Smith, born on 17 July 2010, aged 4. The children live with their mother at 97 Matrimonial Road, Blackpool and attend school at Blackpool Academy.

2. The Background to the Case

31.12.2002	John and Joan meet and start relationship
01.07.2003	John and Joan move in together
10.04.2004	Parties marry
12.08.2004	Tom born
13.08.2005	Parties move to 97 Matrimonial Road
11.12.2008	John gets new job in Manchester and traveling for work regularly
13.03.2009	John and Joan have a trial separation. There had been many arguments since John started his new job
April 2009	Parties attend 6 sessions with *Relate* and reconcile
17.07.2010	Jane born

24.12.2010	There is a big argument at Christmas as Joan not happy with the lack of support she says she gets at home from John. John has to leave home at 6am and gets home at 7.30pm each weekday
August 2013	Joan tells John that she feels they have grown apart and she wants a divorce. John leaves the home and rents a flat close to the railway station. John sees Tom and Jane on weekends, usually a Saturday for the whole day
January 2014	John meets Pauline and they start a relationship
02.05.2014	Tom and Jane meet Pauline when they have contact with John
03.05.2014	Joan tells John that he should have asked her before introducing the children to Pauline. Joan says that the children felt uncomfortable meeting Pauline and Joan says that she will no longer allow any contact as she will not force the children to go if they don't want to
14.05.2014	John receives a letter from a solicitor instructed by Joan that tells him to stop sending emails to Joan asking to see the children as Joan has made her position clear and will contact John should the children ask to see him. The letter says that any further emails will be treated as harassment and an injunction might be sought
15.05.2014	John sends an email to the solicitors asking if Joan will attend mediation
28.05.2014	John issues an application for a child arrangement order, as he has had no response from Joan's solicitors despite a number of emails chasing them for a reply
13.06.2014	John receives Joan's Form C7 stating that Joan opposes the application for an order permitting him to see the children. The letter sent with the form states that the children have said that they do not want to see him

3. The Father's Application at the FHDRA

The father seeks an order requiring Joan Smith to make the children available to see him. It is not accepted that the children do not want to see their father. If the court is concerned about the children seeing Pauline, the father will agree not to bring the children into contact with Pauline to enable visits to recommence but this cannot be a long-term position as the father and Pauline are in a committed relationship.

John Smith
13 August 2014

(4) More detailed guidance on the preparation of position statements is found at chapter 7. What you need to include in a position statement depends upon what type of hearing and what type of case you are involved with.

If the case is not settled at the FHDRA, the court may list a further interim hearing. The court will give directions for the gathering of evidence. For example, the judge might order as follows:

(1) An officer of Cafcass shall, by 26 November 2014, file and serve a section 7 report on the father's application for contact.

(2) The mother shall, by 27 August 2014, file and serve a statement setting out the reasons why she opposes the father's application for contact.

(3) The father shall, by 10 September 2014, file and serve a statement in reply.

(i4) No further evidence shall be filed by either party unless permission is granted by the court.

The next hearing is likely to be listed after the court has received a section 7 (welfare) report or an expert assessment, if one is ordered. A welfare report may be ordered to investigate the wishes and feelings of the children concerning the issue before the court. The author of the report will also speak to the children's school and make other enquiries so that the court is given a detailed picture of the children's lives from which it can, having heard from both parents, make decisions.

The court may list the next hearing as a review hearing, to see how successful contact has been, or as a dispute resolution appointment (DRA), a fact-finding hearing or a final hearing.

Review hearings

If the court lists a review hearing, it is likely to be listed for less than one hour so the bundles practice direction is unlikely to apply. The purpose of a review hearing is generally to see how the arrangements made for the children at the FHDRA have been going and whether it is possible to make a final order and bring the court proceedings to an end.

It will be for you to decide if you want to prepare a position statement for a review hearing. If you do, you should set out what directions were made by the court at the last hearing and whether they have been complied with. If you have not done what you were supposed to do, you should give a reason why and be prepared to answer questions about this at court.

In your position statement you should set out your view on how the arrangements made for the children have been working and how you would like to court to proceed. If there have been problems with the arrangements for the children, you should say what they have been and what you think can be done to improve things.

At the review hearing, the court will read and hear what each party has said and decide if a final order can be made or if a further court hearing is required. The court will always be wanting the parties to reach an agreement. CAP discourages judges from listing review hearings as review hearings became too common and proceedings were being extended unnecessarily, so you may find that the judge in your case will not want to list a review hearing but will make a final order and ask Cafcass to monitor the operation of the order made.

Dispute resolution appointments

If the court lists a DRA, you should read paragraph 16 of CAP. To prepare for the hearing, you should consider the factors listed at paragraph 16.3.5 of CAP and address them in the position statement you prepare for the court and be prepared to answer questions about them at court. You should always prepare a position statement for a DRA so that the court has advance notice of the case that you will be arguing.

At the DRA, the court will be considering the following issues:

(1) What are the key issues in the case and how can they be resolved? Can they be resolved or narrowed at the DRA?

(2) Can the court make a final order at the DRA?

(3) What evidence is required to resolve any issue that cannot be resolved at the DRA?

(4) What directions are required, particularly:

   (a) The filing of further evidence.

   (b) The filing of a statement of issues/issues requiring determination.

   (c) The filing of a witness template and skeleton arguments.

   (d) Ensuring compliance with the bundles practice direction.

   (e) Listing a final hearing.

The court will take a robust approach at the DRA. The intention is that cases that have not been resolved at the FHDRA should be capable of resolution at the DRA by the judge hearing argument from the parties and, if necessary, some limited evidence from the witness box. The court will then make decisions on the issues that remain between the parties.

You should expect the judge to be forthright in his or her approach at this hearing and challenge you as to why you cannot reach an agreement about arrangements for the children. The court will not let the parties use the court proceedings to make allegations against each other unless the truth of those allegations would have an impact on whether the children should have a relationship with one of the parents or would impact on how arrangements should be made to ensure that the children, and the parents, are safe when the children spend time with them. Generally speaking, the court can hear arguments or limited evidence if deciding how much time the children spend with each parent and where and how handovers of the children are to take place. If the dispute is simply about the amount of time with each parent and the practical arrangements to be made for this, you should expect the court to determine these issues at a DRA and make a final order.

To prepare for a DRA, you should set out in your position statement what you want and give reasons why you think this is in the best interests of the children. Always remember that the children are the focus for the court – they are the paramount consideration – so always address your arguments to what is good for them rather than what is good for you. It is helpful for the judge if you use bullet points, for example.

> The children should see their father on alternate weekends from after school on Friday until 6pm on Sunday because:
>
> - The visiting contact each Saturday has gone very well. The children have enjoyed the time with their father and have often been reluctant to leave at the end of the visit.
>
> - The children have said that they would like to spend more time with their father and have asked to stay over at the house.
>
> - The children have now met Pauline and they have a good relationship.
>
> - The father has 2 spare bedrooms to accommodate the children if they come to visit.

- It would be good for the children to see their father on alternate weekends for the whole week so they would then have a full weekend with their mother that would enable them to enjoy their mother's company and see friends local to her home at weekends. The current weekly visiting contact does not provide any full weekends for them at their mother's home.

- The children would have a better opportunity to see members of their paternal extended family if they had staying weekends with their father.

Alternatively, your position statement might say:

The children should live with their mother and see their father at a contact centre for 2 hours on alternate Saturdays because:

- John is a man who quickly losses his temper and bullied the mother throughout the relationship, although there was no physical violence.

- The mother had hoped that the father would be able to behave appropriately during the time he saw the children under the terms agreed at the FHDRA.

- The children have told the mother that the father has been constantly quizzing them about what the mother is doing and if she has a new partner.

- The children have told the mother that the father is constantly comparing the mother with the father's new partner and saying how much better Pauline is as a partner than the mother. The children have told the mother that the father has said that Pauline is much better looking, a better cook and that the mother is stupid.

- When the mother went to collect the children from MacDonald's on 19 June, the father and the children were not there. The mother waited for 30 minutes and sent texts to the father. He did not reply and when he arrived he was abusive to the mother saying that she was neurotic. There was an argument that was witnessed by the children with the father being abusive and insulting to the mother.

- The children were scared by what they saw and no longer wish to have contact with their father.

- The mother accepts that the children should have a relationship with their father but believes that it should take place in a safe venue where the mother and the children will be protected from the father's temper.

Fact-finding and final hearings

The court may be invited by the lawyers, advised by Cafcass or make an order of its own motion that a fact-finding hearing takes place. This is a hearing where the court is not making a final determination of the best interests of the child but will hear evidence on factual matters that are disputed so as to inform the welfare decision that it will make at a later hearing. These finding-of-fact hearings are often used when serious allegations have been made against one parent. It may be that an allegation has been made that the father has sexually abused one of the children or the mother has caused an injury to a child. The court may list a hearing to deal with these allegations and then consider whether to hold another hearing to make a decision about what order to make regarding the arrangements for the child. The reason why these separate hearings are often listed is that if the allegation is found not to be proved, then the court may not need to make an order concerning the child at all and time is saved by dealing with the factual issues as soon as possible.

Fact-finding hearings are also listed when allegations have been made that one parent has been the perpetrator of domestic abuse against the other. If these allegations are denied, it is necessary for the court to consider the evidence and decide what allegations that it finds to be proved so that it can assess what risk there might be to the children or the parent who was the victim of the abuse. That assessment of risk will then inform the court's thinking as to what child arrangement order to make.

If the court lists a final hearing, it will hear all the evidence and make a decision. You will be ordered to file a statement with the court before the final hearing, if this has not already been ordered. For guidance in preparing a statement, see chapter 4.

Expert evidence

The court must specifically consider whether there is a need for any expert evidence. The parties are required to comply with Part 25 of the Family Procedure Rules and the associated Practice Direction, PD25A.

Part 25 states that expert evidence will be restricted to that which is necessary to resolve the proceedings. The court's permission is required for expert evidence to be put in evidence. The costs of any expert required will be considered by the court.

The court has a duty to consider whether the costs of an expert and any delay caused by an appointment is proportionate 'to the nature, importance and complexity of the issues'.

Any application by a party for expert evidence must be made by formal written application. This should include the expert's CV, timescales to report and the costs. A draft letter of instruction to the expert should also be provided. PD25A sets out matters to be included in such letter. Any party wishing to instruct an expert should also submit a draft order for directions dealing with the instruction.

Enforcement

If the court makes an order which is not complied with by one party, an application may be made to the court by the party seeking compliance.

If the court is satisfied so that it is sure that a person has failed to comply with the child arrangements order, it may make an order (an 'enforcement order') imposing on the person an unpaid work requirement.

There is also a provision for applying for compensation for financial loss when a child arrangements order has been made and not complied with, and a person has suffered financial loss as a result of the breach.

A child arrangements order may be enforced by seeking an order requiring the other parent to 'deliver up' the child to the parent in whose favour the child arrangements order has been made. The court has the power to punish a person for breach of its order either by way of a fine, not exceeding £5,000, or to commit the parent to prison until the breach has been remedied or for a period not exceeding two months. In order to seek such enforcement, you must ensure the party alleged to be in breach has been 'served' with a copy of the child arrangements order.

Costs

The court has power to make a costs order against another party, that is to say an order requiring that other party to pay the other party's legal costs.

The general principle is that the court may, at any time, make such order as to costs as it thinks just. The general rule in civil cases that the unsuccessful party is ordered to pay the costs of the successful party does not apply to family proceedings. In children cases orders for costs against another party are rare unless there is behaviour that has caused another party to incur costs and which is deemed by the court to be unreasonable. The court is allowed to take into account conduct in relation to the litigation before and during proceedings.

The general view is that an award of costs against another party in children proceedings may lead to a situation where a parent may feel punished and may reduce co-operation from them and ultimately impinge on the welfare of the child concerned. This view does not prevail in the case of the enforcement of a child arrangements order nor to appeals or fact-finding hearings. The judge is required to approach such cases with a clean sheet.

Appeals

If a party is not happy with the decision made, there is sometimes an opportunity to seek an appeal against it.

The grounds for appealing family orders are governed by strict legal parameters. The discretion of any court, hearing an application is wide and usually an appeal will not be merited unless the decision appealed is 'plainly wrong.'

There is much case law surrounding appeals and whether there are grounds to appeal an order will usually be best explained by an experienced family lawyer based on his/her experience and legal knowledge.

Generally appeals are rare and if public funding is sought to conduct it, the Legal Aid Agency must be satisfied that the appeal has merit. Appeals from district judges or magistrates are allocated to circuit judges by the Designated Family Judge (DFJ). Appeals from circuit judges and second appeals will continue to be heard by the Court of Appeal.

Appeals must be lodged or started within strict time limits and sometimes permission is needed to start an appeal. Permission is not needed to appeal against a decision of the magistrates. Any permission needed should be sought from the judge who gave the decision. If the appeal is from a decision of a circuit judge or High Court judge, a fee will be payable: it is currently £465.

The notice of appeal must be filed within the period directed by the lower court (which should be no more than 35 days) and where the lower court makes no direction, then within 21 days of the date of the order, and it must be 'served' on the respondent/s no later than seven days after its filing at court.

Such hearings are dealt with as a review hearing unless the court considers it is in the interests of justice to hold a re-hearing.

Further research

The following publications may be helpful:

- Lord Justice McFarlane and Madeleine Reardon, 'Children and Adoption Law' (Jordan Publishing)

- His Honour Judge Mitchell, 'Child Law: Essential Materials' (Jordan Publishing)

- Deborah Cullen and Mary Lane, 'Child Care law in England and Wales' (British Association of Adoption and Fostering)

Tips and traps

The court is wholly concerned with what is best for the child, not the adults. Try to look at things from the perspective of the child and what he/she would want, ie to see the other parent regularly or maintain some sort of contact with them.

Parents have human rights but usually children's rights 'trump' these in a Family Court.

Courts hold much store by indirect arrangements, that is to say, writing to a child: a card or letter is viewed as very beneficial for a child.

Court deadlines – dates and times for the filing of evidence – are there for a reason and need to be adhered to, unless there is a very good reason why a certain direction has not been complied with, for example ill-health substantiated by a doctor's note.

Proceedings are not a competition with the opposing party and the proceedings are not about winning and losing.

Maintaining courteous and pleasant relations with all relatives around a child is vital to their well-being: courts like to see this.

Generally, it is best not to involve children in adult issues and disputes, and the less they are aware of disagreements the better. Talking to them about who/when they want to see a parent, is generally discouraged. Clearly, there will come a time/age when this will change, but still err on the side of caution and avoid involving children in adult disputes. Also avoid informing them of court proceedings if possible.

Having parental responsibility: sections 2 and 3 of the Children Act 1989

What does it mean?

- 'Parental responsibility' means all the rights, duties, powers, responsibilities and authority which by law a parent of a child has in relation to the child and his property.

- The courts have said that parental responsibly confers on the committed father the status of parenthood for which nature has already ordained he must bear responsibility.

- If a father does not have parental responsibility there are some situations in which he may be at a disadvantage. If a father without parental responsibility finds himself applying for another order (eg a child arrangements order) it is often sensible to apply for parental responsibility as well.

Who has automatic parental responsibility for a child?

- The birth mother of a child will always have parental responsibility for a child from the moment the baby is born.

- Where a child's father and mother were married to each other at the time of his birth, they each have parental responsibility for the child.

- Where a child's father and mother were not married to each other at the time of his birth the mother shall have parental responsibility for the child.

- Otherwise, it needs to be acquired: see below.

How does it work if more than one person has it?

- Where more than one person has parental responsibility for a child, each of them may act alone and without the other (or others) in meeting that responsibility.

- There is a clear expectation that parents work co-operatively together.

- Whilst small, day-to-day matters do not need consultation between the parents, big decisions, such as which school the child should attend, should be subject to consultation.

- Where there is conflict between parents the issue of who has parental responsibility and how it is exercised can be a source of conflict and concern.

- Where trust is running low there may be concern that it will be abused.

- A father without parental responsibility may fear the mother will use her parental responsibility and his lack of it to sideline or exclude him from important decisions in their child's life.

- A mother who is caring for a child on a day-to-day basis may fear that if the father requires parental responsibility he will abuse it and seek to dictate arrangements or to meddle in the minutiae of her care for their child.

Acquiring parental responsibility: section 4 of the Children Act 1989

Do fathers named on the birth certificate have parental responsibility?

- A father of a child whose birth was registered after 1 December 2003 will have parental responsibility for the child if his name is on their birth certificate.

- Acquisition of parental responsibility occurs when his name is placed on the birth certificate when the baby's birth is registered (or re-registered).

- To have his name registered on the birth certificate an

unmarried father will need to have the mother's agreement and will need to attend with the mother when the birth is registered (or re-registered).

- Once the unmarried father has parental responsibility because his name is on the birth certificate registration he can only lose it by order of the court. Only very rarely will the court remove parental responsibility from a birth father.

- An unmarried father whose name is not on the birth certificate may apply to the court on his own (or with the mother's support) to have the birth re-registered so that the certificate shows him as the father.

What if the wrong person is named on the birth certificate?

- Sometimes a man is named on a child's birth certificate as the child's father when in fact he is not.

- Sometimes this is by mistake but sometimes it is the result of misplaced wishful thinking.

- It is never appropriate for a birth certificate to have recorded upon it the incorrect identity of a child's father.

- If this is the case the birth certificate should be rectified. The General Records Office (GRO) can provide advice as to how this can be done.

- It is very likely that a DNA test either proving the identity of the biological father, and that therefore the registered name is incorrect, or a DNA test proving that the registered father is not the biological father, will be required.

- Before obtaining a DNA test it is advisable to check with

the GRO as only the testing of accredited laboratories is acceptable and you may waste your money if you do not use an accredited lab.

- It is also possible to obtain a court declaration but this is more costly and complicated and so enquiries of the GRO are a sensible first port of call.

Does a father who subsequently marries the mother acquire parental responsibility?

- If the parents of a child get married the father will acquire parental responsibility for that child, and any future children he may have with his new wife.

- The father will not acquire parental responsibility for any stepchildren born to the mother (who are not biologically his) simply because he marries their mother.

- There is a requirement that the parents of a child who is legitimated by their subsequent marriage must re-register the child's birth within 3 months of the date of the marriage by virtue of which he was legitimated.

Can parents otherwise agree that the father should have parental responsibility?

- The father and the child's mother can make a 'parental responsibility agreement' providing for him to have parental responsibility for the child.

- This is the cheapest option but requires agreement.

- Both parents need to attend the Family Court to sign the document and their signatures need to be witnessed.

- To do this you need to enquire at your local Family Court

- If you are a mother considering whether to agree to parental responsibility it is worth noting that if an application for parental responsibility was to be made to court it is very likely that the application would be granted. The court approaches the issue on the basis that it is in a child's interests to have both his parents identified and responsible for him.

If an unmarried father is not on the birth certificate and the mother does not agree to his having parental responsibility, can the court order it?

- The court can order that a father shall have parental responsibility for the child.

- The father would need to issue an application at court for this. This is Form C100. A fee will be payable to issue the application.

- Where the court makes a child arrangements order in favour of an unmarried father naming him as a person with whom the child is to live, it must also, if he would not otherwise have parental responsibility for the child, make a parental responsibility order. So even if the child arrangements order came to an end, the parental responsibility order would still remain.

- If a court makes an order providing for a child to live with any other person (eg a grandparent or a step-parent), that other person acquires parental responsibility. If that order came to an end, that person's parental responsibility would end at the same time.

What should the court consider when deciding whether to grant parental responsibility to a father?

- The court considers the degree of commitment the father has shown towards the child, the degree of attachment between him and the child and the reasons why he is applying for the order.

- But these three requirements, though a starting point, are not intended to be exhaustive and the court must take into account all the relevant circumstances.

- It is generally considered that it is in the interests of a child to know who their father is. Parental responsibility is a basic recognition of the identity of the child's parents. With that recognition comes both rights and responsibilities.

- Only in exceptional circumstances will a court refuse to grant an application for parental responsibility.

How does acquiring parental responsibility relate to seeking to spend time with a child?

- The law is clear that the granting of parental responsibility is a separate consideration from arrangements for a child to spend time with a father.

- However one would not expect a father who spends time with his child to be refused parental responsibility.

- It is also perfectly reasonable for a father who has limited or restricted time with his child (there may be a number of reasons for this) to have parental responsibility for his child.

- It would be a mistake to see the issues as the same.

Can a mother apply to court to impose parental responsibility upon the father?

- No – but if the mother thought the father was shirking his responsibilities, she could apply for financial support under Schedule 1 of the Children Act 1989 or a section 8 order, depending on what she is seeking to achieve.

- Parental responsibility and maintenance are separate issues. A father with or without parental responsibility is still liable to provide financial provision (maintenance) for his child.

Can a step-parent apply for parental responsibility?

- The step-parent may obtain parental responsibility if both (birth) parents agree to them having it. This will then be a parental responsibility agreement.

- If there is not agreement between the two birth parents, the step-parent may make an application to the court.

- The step-parent's parental responsibility can only be terminated by application to the court by any person who has parental responsibility or by the child himself (provided he has sufficient understanding of the consequences of the application).

Child arrangements and other orders in respect of children: section 8 of the Children Act 1989

The court has power to determine who the child lives with and to sort out the arrangements for the child to spend time with their other parent.

These arrangements used to be called 'custody' and 'access'. Some non-lawyers continue to use these terms which became known in October 1991 as 'residence' and 'contact'. In April 2014, there were further changes to the law and the terms 'residence' and 'contact' have been scrapped. There are now 'child arrangements orders'.

Section 8 of the Children Act 1989 sets out the main orders regularly sought to settle arrangements for children or sort out disputes between parents about specific issues.

These orders can only be made once a baby has been born. The court cannot make these orders in respect of an unborn child.

A 'child arrangements order' means an order regulating arrangements relating to any of the following:

(1) with whom a child is to live, spend time or otherwise have contact;

(2) when a child is to live, spend time or otherwise have contact with any person.

A 'prohibited steps order' means an order that no step which could be taken by a parent in meeting his parental responsibility for a child, and which is of a kind specified in the order, shall be taken by any person without the consent of the court.

A 'specific issue order' means an order giving directions for the purpose of determining a specific question which has arisen, or which may arise, in connection with any aspect of parental responsibility for a child.

The thinking behind these orders is to give the court flexibility and a wide choice of orders so that any question which arises concerning the welfare of a child or arrangements to be made for him can be sorted out.

Prohibited steps orders

These are orders that prohibit a parent from doing something they would otherwise be entitled to do as part of exercising parental responsibility for their child.

Common examples of prohibited steps orders are orders prohibiting:

- One parent from attending at the child's school (or from attending without a prior appointment).

- One parent taking a child abroad.

- One parent applying for a passport or travel document.

Specific issue orders

These are orders that resolve an issue between parents in respect of an issue concerning their child.

Common examples of specific issue orders are orders deciding:

- The school which the child will attend.

- Whether a child should have a vaccination or other procedure.

- Whether a child may be taken abroad on holiday or to move to live abroad or to relocate within England and Wales.

- Whether a child may obtain a passport or other identity document.

Decisions about children: section 1 of the Children Act 1989

When the court decides any question with respect to the upbringing of a child (such as where the child should live or whom the child should see), it must take account of the following principles:

- The child's welfare is paramount.

- The general principle that any delay in determining the question is likely to prejudice the welfare of the child. In other words, the court should aim to resolve matters as soon as possible, balanced with the need to make informed decisions based on proper evidence and enquiries. Delay should be avoided unless it is necessary or has purpose to it.

- The welfare checklist.

- Where a court is considering whether or not to make one or more orders under this Act with respect to a child, it shall not make the order or any of the orders unless it considers that doing so would be better for the child than making no order at all.

The welfare checklist consists of ALL the circumstances, but with particular regard to the following factors:

- The ascertainable wishes and feelings of the child concerned (considered in the light of his age and understanding).

- His physical, emotional and educational needs.

- The likely effect on him of any change in his circumstances.

- His age, sex, background and any characteristics of his which the court considers relevant.

- Any harm which he has suffered or is at risk of suffering.

- How capable each of his parents, and any other person in relation to whom the court considers the question to be relevant, is of meeting his needs.

- The range of powers available to the court in the proceedings in question.

The court's approach to the child's wishes and feelings tends to be as follows.

- Clearly a very young child will not have sufficient maturity or understanding to express their view.

- Younger children also may struggle with the wish to please both parents.

- All children may suffer harm if pressure is put on them to take sides.

- The wishes and feelings of a mature child do not carry any presumption of precedence over any other factors.

- It may be appropriate for an older child to speak with the judge. This is more likely to be the case where decisions are being made as to their living arrangements or schooling.

- Cafcass may be asked to prepare a report. This may be a full report investigating all aspects of their care and welfare. In some cases it is appropriate to request a 'wishes and feelings report' which would assist the court in understanding the child's wishes and feelings about the issue to be determined.

The court's approach to physical, emotional and educational needs tends to be that most children have the usual needs of other children of their age. Some children have special needs that need to be factored in to the decisions to be made for them.

Examples of relevant change would include:

- A move of house.

- Spending more or less time with a parent or siblings or half-siblings.

- Change of school.

- Disruption of friendships.

- A child's relationships with their extended family (grandparents, cousins etc) may be relevant for consideration.

Age, sex, background and relevant characteristics are a catch all, giving the court a wide area of focus to tailor the decision to the child concerned. Particular factors might include:

- Cultural background which may be rich and varied; arrangements may benefit the child to enable him to enjoy all aspects of his heritage.

- A child may have a relative other than a parent who is important to them or has played particularly important role in their life. It may be important to recognise this when deciding arrangements for that child.

The issue of harm extends to risk of future harm as well as harm already suffered. The following considerations apply.

- The concept of harm is broad and not restricted to physical assault.

- Where there is parental conflict a child may suffer emotional harm as a result of being caught up between his parents.

Under the head of capability of parents, these are some of the considerations.

- Most parents are capable of providing good enough care to their children. They can feed them, clothe them and get them to school.

- A parent may have a difficulty with their physical or mental health or with alcohol or drug misuse that is relevant to the arrangements to be made for a child. Trivial complaints are not helpful but if there is genuine concern the court may well request an expert report (from a doctor, for example) or scientific testing (usually of hair) if the issue is substance misuse.

- Any expert report or hair strand testing will need to be funded. The court will not meet the costs of this. If a party has the benefit of legal aid the court may be able to order that the cost of any assessment or testing is funded by Legal Aid.

- In the context of divorce and separation one parent's attitude to the other and their ability to promote a positive attitude of the other parent is important. It is very difficult for children to have to deal with a sense that they love both their parents but their parents hate each other.

- A parent's capacity to keep their differences with their ex-partner to one side and to have a functioning and co-operative relationship as parents is crucial to the wellbeing of the children.

As for the court's powers, by the time the court comes to decide whether to make an order it should be clear what orders are being sought.

- The court has very wide powers to make an order which best provides for the interest of each of the children concerned.

- The court must consider first whether an order is required at all.

- It will consider the least level of interference that is necessary in the case. The court has to be clear that the order being made is necessary and proportionate. That is to say it is not 'a sledge hammer to crack a walnut'.

The 'no order principle' means that the court will not make an order simply for the sake of it. There has to be an advantage to the child in an order being made. The court must ask itself 'is it better for the child to make an order or not?'

If the dispute has got as far as going to court, even if agreement is then reached, it is often best that the arrangements are recorded in an order so that the agreement is kept to and there is no need to go back to court.

Sometimes it is helpful to set out the parties' intentions as a preamble to an order. That is a paragraph recording what has been agreed but not made as part of a formal order. However if this is done and the agreement is breached the court's powers of enforcement are weaker than if an order has been made.

Dos and don'ts

DOS

- **DO** remember that the court's main focus is on the welfare of the child

- **DO** think about the emotional impact of long court proceedings on your children – and on you

✔ **DO** follow the court's directions – on time

DON'TS

✘ **DON'T** conduct trial by email or text: allegations and counter-allegations usually make things worse

✘ **DON'T** spend too much time worrying about minute detail: how many extra hours in a year may seem important now but will it in twenty years' time?

✘ **DON'T** raise your voice when talking about the case – whether to your former partner, to the court or to somebody else

Chapter 9

Finances

What you will learn

- How to bring a financial claim
- The different kinds of financial orders available
- The various stages of the court process and how to prepare for them
- How the court will manage the case along the way
- How the court will reach its final decision on the case

What are financial remedy proceedings?

This description covers the range of orders that can be made when a couple separate and one of them makes an application to the court for financial provision. The court has the power to make financial orders in proceedings between those that are married, those in a same sex civil partnership and those that live together. However, the law relating to people who merely live together is different to the law relating to married/civil partners, and is considered in chapter 10. This chapter deals with those who are married or in a civil partnership.

The procedure for these types of applications are set out in Family Procedure Rules 2010, which can be referred to online. If you see an abbreviation 'FPR', it is a reference to these rules.

> (i) **What are the Family Procedure Rules 2010?**
>
> The Family Procedure Rules 2010 are Rules which provide an essential code of procedure for family proceedings in the High Court, County Court and Family Court.

> **To see the Family Procedure Rules 2010 go to:**
>
> www.justice.gov.uk/courts/procedure-rules/family/rules_pd_menu

What type of orders can a court make?

The court can make a broad range of financial orders. It can make capital orders that, for example, change the ownership of the family home (often described as the *'former matrimonial home'*), or which transfer the ownership of investment properties. It can make an order for a lump sum to be paid, and/or an order for the capital value of a pension to be split (or 'shared' as it is described in the legislation), leaving each party with pension funds of their own. Orders can be made requiring the sale of property, such as the former matrimonial home. These types of order are made only once.

> (i) **What is the former matrimonial home?**
>
> This is the home where you last lived as a family.

The court can also make income orders, which are known formally as orders for *'periodical payments'*, and are known informally as orders for maintenance. Maintenance orders can be made in favour of a spouse, and/or, if there is agreement between the parents, in favour of children of the family. However any order for child maintenance made by the court, on the basis of an agreement between the parties, will automatically be cancelled out a year after the order is made *if* one or other parent asks the Child Maintenance Service (formerly the Child Support Agency) to make a calculation.

> **What is the Child Maintenance Service?**
>
> This is a government service which deals with the organisation, calculation of and arrangements for payment of child maintenance when parents cannot agree how much child maintenance should be paid.

The court cannot impose a child periodical payments order and if there is no agreement between the parents it will be necessary to refer to the Child Maintenance Service (CMS).

The court does have the power to order maintenance for children of the family where one of the parties is not the biological parent but the child has been treated by that person as a child of the family. One factor in that situation will be the ability of the natural parent to provide or contribute to the child's maintenance. If the court does make a periodical payments order in respect of a child this will be frequently be expressed to continue until they attain the age of 18. An order can extend beyond that age in circumstances where the child will be receiving further education or training (university being the obvious example, but so would an apprenticeship) or in what is described as 'special circumstances' (which includes physical or other handicap).

Maintenance orders for former spouses end automatically if they marry again (or if they enter a civil partnership) or if one of them dies. There is no automatic end to a periodical payments order if the spouse starts to live with another person, although the court can always vary the level of maintenance downwards in those circumstances. Much may depend on the means of the new cohabitee.

The level and the duration of periodical payments can be varied by the court from time to time in the light of a change of circumstances. Typically this might involve an increase or decrease in one party's income; it might also arise from one party wanting to bring an end to the maintenance payment. The court can do this by capitalising the maintenance order by ordering the payer to make a one-off lump sum payment which replaces the on-going maintenance.

Before leaving this topic, mention should be made of the court's powers to unravel transactions which are intended to reduce or frustrate the financial provision that should be made. Sometimes a party trying to reduce the provision to be made to the other will transfer property or money to a third person and suggest that it is no longer available to them. The court has the power to set aside such transactions, if it is satisfied that it has been done with a view to reducing financial exposure to the other party, and it will not hesitate to use those powers where necessary. These powers are in section 37 of the Matrimonial Causes Act 1973 (the Act of Parliament which contains the law which the courts will follow in matrimonial financial disputes). An important part of those provisions is the presumption that any transaction made less than 3 years before the issuing of an application to set aside is presumed to be done with the intention of defeating the claim for financial relief.

Principles governing the way in which the court decides what order to make

The judge who deals with your case will have to consider a number of factors that are set out in the relevant statute, which is the Matrimonial Causes Act 1973. The various factors are set out in section 25 of the Act, and they are considered in more detail below. You should become familiar with them yourself, and have them always in your mind when preparing your case.

The function of the judge is to consider the various factors set out in section 25, to give first consideration to the welfare of any children under the age of 18, and to arrive at a fair result. This gives the judge a very broad discretion, and makes predicting the likely order quite difficult, for we all have different views as to what is fair. A party who works very hard might think it unfair to have their bonus shared out with their estranged spouse, but that spouse might equally argue that they are doing what they can by caring for the children and that they should not now be prejudiced by the way that they arranged their roles during the marriage.

One thing is absolutely clear in this area of law is that the courts have repeatedly emphasised that there should be no distinction between the homemaker and the breadwinner. It might be suggested by the breadwinner that they should get more of the assets because they generated them. This argument will receive pretty short shrift from the court because it is discriminatory.

The judge-made case-law ('precedent') says that in searching for fairness, the judges should also be guided by three principles, which are: needs, sharing, and compensation.

Compensation is rarely relevant. It has been restricted by a number of cases which have emerged since its birth. It might still be relevant only in a case of two equally high-earning career spouses, both of whom are/were on track for even higher earnings, but one of whom has given up that career to look after children.

Most cases will be determined on the basis of need. This obviously means housing needs and income needs. It is not often that there is more than enough to meet these twin needs. How to prepare your case on the basis of a needs argument is addressed later in this chapter.

As to the meeting of on-going need, by way of a maintenance order, the court is obliged by the statute to consider whether it is possible to effect an end to the financial obligations between the parties – a 'clean break'. A spousal maintenance claim might be bought off by payment of a capital sum, if there is the money to do it. Or the court might order spousal maintenance only for a limited period of time, if it is satisfied that the receiving spouse can become self-sufficient within that period. Clean breaks of this sort are less common when there are young dependent children.

> **What is a clean break?**
>
> This is where an order is made which deals with all claims between the parties once and for all.

As for the principle of *'sharing'*, this means essentially that the parties should share (usually equally, though subject to need) whatever they have generated during the marriage, or what has been described as *the fruits of the marital partnership*. If needs cannot be met by way of an equal division, then the division may have to be unequal. A shorthand way of describing assets built up during the marriage is – unsurprisingly – *'matrimonial assets'*! Then we have non-matrimonial assets.

> **What are 'non-matrimonial assets'?**
>
> Typically, these will be money brought into the marriage by one party; the obvious examples are inheritance or gifts or lottery wins from one side of the marriage, arising either before or during the marriage. They might also include assets acquired after the separation but before the case has

> come before the court. The key distinction for you to consider is whether the asset was generated within the marriage by each of you doing your bit, or whether the asset comes from a source completely outside of the marriage partnership.

You might quite naturally conclude from this that if the asset is non-matrimonial it should be retained by the party who created it or received it. Unfortunately, things are not so simple as that because an argument based upon need might mean that some of the non-matrimonial property should also be invaded to meet that need. This is part and parcel of the wide discretion that the court retains; of course with this comes an uncertainty in predicting the outcome.

Section 25 factors

> (*i*) **What are the section 25 factors?**
>
> These are the factors which the court will take into account in deciding what order to make.

You will need to become familiar with these if you are representing yourself because these are the points that the court is obliged to consider in exercising its discretion. Section 25 reads as follows:

> (1) It shall be the duty of the court in deciding whether to exercise its powers under section 23, 24, 24A or 24B above and, if so, in what manner, to have regard to all the circumstances of the case, first consideration being given to the welfare while a minor of any child of the family who has not attained the age of eighteen.
>
> (2) As regards the exercise of the powers of the court under section 23(1)(a), (b) or (c), 24, 24A or 24B above in

Either spouse can issue an application for a financial order against the other, or both can issue applications if they wish to. It does not matter which of you was the petitioner in the divorce itself and which was the respondent.

You yourself might need to serve a copy of the Form A on third parties, as required of you by the Family Procedure Rules, for example on the mortgage lender on the matrimonial home, or on the trustees of any pension scheme that you are seeking a share of. This is dealt with in more detail below.

At the same time the court will notify both of you, by order, of the date for the first hearing in your case – the 'first appointment'. That date will be between 12 and 16 weeks after the filing of your Form A. That may seem like a long time away, but you will have a lot to do in that time.

The order will contain a timetable for certain documents to be produced by both of you (see below) and you might find it helpful to prepare a diary note for when you are meant to do specific things.

The financial information form – Form E

The first document that the court will order each of you to complete, and to produce to each other and to the court, is the Form E, which is a pro forma that, when completed, gives full details of your financial position.

> **What is Form E?**
>
> The standard form in which each party must make full, clear and up to date disclosure of their financial means.

> The Form E can be found and downloaded from:
>
> http://www.justice.gov.uk/courts/procedure-rules/family/rules_pd_menu

The Form E needs to be filed with the court and mutually exchanged with the other party not less than 35 days before the date of the first appointment.

> For an example of a completed Form E, please go to:
>
> diydivorce.familylaw.co.uk/

The first thing to be said about completion of Form E is that it should be done truthfully and accurately. The form itself contains a written reminder that each party is under a <u>duty</u> to the court to *'give full, frank and clear disclosure of all your financial and other relevant circumstances'*. A failure to give accurate information in Form E may undermine the validity of any final order resolving the proceedings, and so lead to further litigation, and/or to criminal prosecution for fraud/perjury. It might also lead to the court coming to the view that the person who has been untruthful has something to hide, and so the court may conclude that there are some hidden resources. The final point to mention might be this – the better the Form E the less likely it is that the other party will have genuine questions to raise about it.

You should ensure that you complete the form neatly, so that it is capable of being easily read and readily understood. Judges can quickly lose patience with a form which has been completed scruffily and/or illegibly.

The form itself is quite user-friendly with explanatory notes built in to the body of the form explaining how to complete it. Additional pages can be added if there is insufficient space on the form itself, though one should always aim to be concise where possible. Although conduct is a section 25 factor, it will only be relevant in *exceptional circumstances*, as the form itself says. Many people use that box on Form E to unburden themselves of years of marital grievance, but it is unlikely to be relevant and it will probably serve only to irritate the judge.

Certain documents must be attached to Form E, as set out in a list on the form itself, for example 12 months' worth of bank statements, two years' worth of accounts for any business you operate, a cash equivalent transfer value document from the managers/trustees of any pension scheme you have, that sort of thing. These documents are required so as to support the figures that you have already set out in the body of the Form E. The form should be dated and signed by you as being true.

If you are having trouble completing your Form E, see a solicitor or a direct access barrister and take some advice. You ought to be able to agree a fixed fee so that you know exactly how much you are spending to get the Form E prepared and sent to the court.

Gathering your own information about your spouse's financial means

Disclosure of information should be achieved through the usual court process of Form E and questionnaire (see below). It is not appropriate for you secretly to rifle through documents or through a computer belonging to your spouse in order to gather information which you believe may become useful to you at some later stage in the proceedings. Unless such information has been freely shared during the marriage in an entirely open way, this behaviour may amount to a breach of confidence, and could conceivably result in a civil action against you for damages or, worse, a criminal prosecution. Moreover the spouse whose confidence has been infringed could apply for the return of all such documents and all copies, and you might be ordered to pay the legal costs of that application.

That said, it is never a straightforward question to answer whether married people have kept financial information confidential from each other during the course of a marriage, and judges will be keen to guard against a party to proceedings being permitted to present a false financial picture to the court.

Other documents that you must produce prior to the first appointment

Apart from Form E, there are four other documents that each of you must produce prior to first appointment.

> **What is the first appointment?**
>
> The hearing at which the court makes directions to ensure that the parties have full disclosure of the financial means of the other party for the purposes of the next hearing, the FDR hearing.

You must file them with the court and serve them on each other, not later than 14 days prior to the first appointment. They are:

(1) A concise statement of the issues between the parties.

(2) A chronology.

(3) A questionnaire setting out any further information and documents requested from the other party.

(4) A notice (Form G) stating whether you will be in a position at the first appointment to invite the court to use that hearing also as the FDR hearing (see below).

The first three of those documents cannot be downloaded as pro formas. You have to draft them yourself. Instruction on how to do so is set out below. The fourth document, the Form G, is a pro forma which can be downloaded.

Other documents that you might choose to produce prior to the first appointment

The rules provide (FPR PD9A, para 4.1) that you should try to agree with the other side the contents of a schedule of the assets/debts. This is almost always the most important document in a financial remedies case. Even if it is not possible to agree such a schedule, you should still try to produce one. If you able to do so using a computer computer package such as Excel, so much the better. If possible, the schedule should be limited to one sheet of A4. Forms E are lengthy documents. It will be of enormous assistance to a busy judge to have the Forms E summarised by you in a small schedule of assets, and it may be the first document that the court relies upon, so it gives you a measure of control over the proceedings. An example of a simple Excel schedule of assets is set out at the end of this chapter. You will note that the schedule identifies the net value of the assets; in other words the sum of money that would be left in your hands after the asset were sold and all liabilities relating to the asset including any secured borrowing, costs of sale and tax are paid.

The same rules provide that you should try to agree with the other side the contents of a case summary, which sets out, as concisely as possible, a summary of the main features of the case, for example:

(1) Who are the parties to the proceedings.

(2) A summary of the background facts.

(3) What applications each party has made to the court.

(4) What has been agreed between the parties.

(5) What is in dispute between the parties.

Use these five points as headings for each section of your case summary as this will help you focus on what you need to include in your document. A case summary is not the document for you to argue your case. It really is a concise summary of the background so that the judge can get a clear idea of what the case is about.

A format to follow for your case summary can be as follows (you can copy this and substitute your own information and facts):

CASE SUMMARY ON BEHALF OF JOHN SMITH FOR FIRST DIRECTIONS APPOINTMENT LISTED AT THE CENTRAL FAMILY COURT ON 15 AUGUST 2014

1. The Parties to the Proceedings

The Applicant is the John Smith. Mr Smith was born on 3 April 1969 and is 44 years old. He lives at 24 Cherry Tree Lane, Camden.

The Respondent is Joan Smith. Mrs Smith was born on 2 March 1970 and is 43 years old. Mrs Smith lives at 97 Matrimonial Road, Barking.

The children are Tom Smith, born on 12 August 2004, aged 9, and Jane Smith, born on 17 July 2010, aged 4.

The children live with their mother at 97 Matrimonial Road, Barking and attend school at Barking Academy.

The parties met on 31.12.2002 and moved in together on 01.07.2003.

The parties married on 10.04.2004.

The parties separated In August 2013. John left the former matrimonial home [FMH] and rented his current accommodation. Joan remains in the FMH.

On 13.03.2013, Joan issued divorce proceedings.

On 25.05.2013, the court pronounced decree nisi on the basis of John's unreasonable behaviour. John did not oppose the granting of the decree.

John works as a tractor sales manager based from an office in Peterborough.

Joan works as a classroom assistant at the children's school.

The parties have not attended mediation as John refused to attend a MIAM.

2. The Background to the Proceedings

The court is respectfully referred to the chronology attached hereto.

3. The Applications before the court

Joan issued her Form A on 20.05.2014. The parties have communicated with each other as required by the pre-action protocol.

Joan seeks spousal and child maintenance, a property adjustment order concerning the house and the savings, and a pension sharing order.

John seeks a property adjustment order.

4. What has been Agreed between the Parties

(a) Joan has made an application to the Child Maintenance

Service and John has submitted the information requested and is waiting to hear what the child maintenance assessment requires him to pay.

(b) John agrees that he will need to pay Joan some spousal maintenance but he does not agree that Joan cannot improve her income by getting a better or a second job.

(c) John agrees that the children will live with Joan during the week but he wants them to be able to stay with him at the weekend.

5. What is in Dispute between the Parties

(a) John does not agree Joan's schedule of expenses.

(b) John does not agree that Joan should have all the family savings. John wants the savings to be shared.

(c) John does not agree that Joan should stay in the house. John believes it should be sold and the loan taken out to pay for the conservatory should be paid from the proceeds of sale.

(d) John does not agree that Joan should have any of his pension.

(e) The value of the home.

(f) Joan's earning capacity.

John Smith
14th August 2014

The first appointment

The essential purpose of the first appointment is to identify the issues in the case and to fill in any important information gaps that exist following the exchange of Forms E. The court at the first appointment is interested only in securing information which needs to be filed before settlement discussions can begin in earnest. For this reason the first appointment is generally *not* a hearing at which the court will try and broker an overall agreement, although if there are no information gaps then it is possible to use the first appointment as a financial dispute resolution appointment ('FDR') as we shall see later in this chapter.

For a first appointment to be successful the parties need to comply with the rules (FPR 2010, rule 9.14) which requires both to send to each other at least 14 days before the hearing the documents set out below. These documents will be read by the judge before the hearing (or at least should be) and sometimes this is all the judge will read (though usually they will try and read the two Forms E as well). The point of the documents is to help the judge work out what the main issues in the case are and what further information is needed to get it into shape so that settlement can be achieved. The documents that you must send to the other side are the following;

(1) <u>A Statement of Issues</u>. This can be pretty short and should be as neutral as possible. It will be read by the judge before the hearing begins and so should try to identify what the real points of dispute are so that the judge can focus on those issues. Examples of 'issues' might be as follows;

　　(a) 'Whether our house should be sold immediately and the proceeds shared out (as [X] suggests or whether it should be transferred to [wife/husband]'.

　　(b) 'We do not agree what the value of our home is'.

　　(c) 'Whether the wife has an earning capacity and, if so, how much she could reasonably be expected to earn'.

　　(d) 'Whether there should be any spousal maintenance paid to the wife and, if so, how much for how long'.

(e) 'Whether there should be any pension sharing orders'.

(2) If you have not explored settlement and do not know what the precise stumbling blocks to settlement are then you will have to do your best to predict the issues eg based on comments in the other side's Form E, or in correspondence. However do not refer to 'without prejudice' correspondence in your Statement of Issues because the judge should *not* see the without prejudice letter at this stage.

(3) A Chronology – ie a list of the *important* dates in the case, eg the parties' dates of birth, the date of first living together, of marriage, of separation and so on. If there have been any proceedings relating to the children then the dates of applications and hearings should be included here. Some Chronologies run to a few pages but most are made up of between 5–10 dates.

(4) A Questionnaire ie a document which contains questions for the other party to answer, and/or requests for the production of copy documents, so that you have a full and clear picture of that party's financial means:

(a) In order to understand the way Questionnaires work it is important to understand the rather unusual rules that apply to information in Financial Remedy proceedings. Be warned – it gets pretty fiddly.

- Firstly there is a strong distinction drawn between 'information' and 'documentary evidence'. Examples of 'information' might include the fact that you are going to be made redundant, or promoted at work, or are about to get a new state benefit paid to you or that you are cohabiting. Examples of 'documentary evidence' would include a letter from your employer informing you of the redundancy, or the offer of a new job, or a letter setting out the state benefits etc.

- Secondly it is a key aspect of the law that all parties are under a duty of 'full and frank disclosure', so you *must* share all relevant *information* with the other side even if it is unhelpful to you. If you don't do this then you will criticised and can be punished with costs orders or, in extreme cases, the court may even assume that you are deliberately hiding financial resources and will base its awards on this assumption. This is known as 'drawing adverse inferences' against a non-disclosing party. Your Form E should therefore contain all your relevant *information*, whether it is helpful to you or not.

- However it is for the court to decide what *documentary evidence* you should be obliged to provide to the other side. You must of course provide all of the documents required by Form E but, other than that, strictly speaking it is for the court to decide what documents you should provide. Some courts will require some persuading that it is necessary to go any further than the documents required by Form E itself. As we will see this rule begins to get blurred the closer you get to a final hearing even though the Rules specify otherwise, see FPR 2010, rule 9.16.

(b) You should send a Questionnaire to the other side if you think that the other side has either 'information' or 'documentary evidence' that you need to have in order to try to achieve a settlement. Your Questionnaire must be a series of questions, with each question given a separate number. You can ask as many questions as you like but the other side will only be required to answer questions that the court agree are relevant to the issues in the case and which are proportionate and will strike out any questions which do not meet that test. A typical Questionnaire will ask for 'information' and 'documentary evidence', eg:

- 'Please state how many jobs you have applied for in the last six months and state the salaries on offer for each job?'

- 'Please provide a copy of each job application you have made in the last six months'.

(5) Remember to send to the court copies of the Statement of Issues, Chronology and Questionnaire that you send to the other side, and remember to keep copies for yourself as well.

(6) Form G. The court will send you a blank Form G. You should complete this form to state whether or not you want to use the first appointment as an FDR. You will probably only suggest that you are able to use the first appointment as an FDR if you feel you already have sufficient information and don't require further information. If you have felt it necessary to raise a Questionnaire, and you have not received replies to it well before the first appointment, it is unlikely to be appropriate to use the first appointment as an FDR.

Service on mortgage companies/trustees etc

If you are the applicant and you seek orders against a property with a mortgage or against a trust then make sure you have served your application Form A on the mortgage company, or the trustees in question in accordance with the rules (FPR 2010, rule 9.13). The purpose of this is to permit the mortgage company or trust to intervene in the proceedings if they see fit. It is very rare that mortgage companies do intervene, but trustees of a trust do occasionally intervene.

The first appointment hearing

At the first appointment the court will look to fill information gaps so that the court will have all the information it needs at the FDR. This 'gap-filling' will generally be achieved by one of two methods, ie:

(1) Ordering evidence from experts – often called 'expert evidence', or

(2) Ordering disclosure from the other parties in response to the questionnaire.

Expert evidence

Not every case requires expert evidence but many do.

> *(i)* **What is expert evidence?**
>
> This is an opinion from an expert, contained in a report eg valuation of a residential property.

The most common expert evidence is evidence from an estate agent as to the value of the marital home and any other property. Each party will have given an estimated value in the Form E and will have provided copies of any valuations but it is very common for the Form E values to be quite a long way apart. If expert evidence is required the court will usually order that one expert (the *single joint expert*) shall be instructed by the parties jointly. That process will require one joint letter of instruction to be written to the agent. Neither of you should be making contact with the agent without informing the other party. The most common expert evidence is from estate agents, as to property values. Other examples of expert evidence might include:

(1) A report from a GP as to one party's health and its relevance as to earning capacity.

(2) A report from a chartered surveyor if a property is very valuable, or in some way is unusual, or is a commercial property.

(3) A report from a specialist valuer if there is a particular asset that is valuable but the value is in dispute, eg the value of a painting, a piece of furniture, or a classic car etc.

(4) It is quite common for one party to have their own business or to be a shareholder in a business. There can often be issues as to whether that business or shareholding is valuable. This book is not the place for a detailed explanation of the law regarding company interests, as it is fiercely complex, but where a company looks to be substantial the court might direct that an independent accountant (sometimes called a forensic accountant) prepares a report to provide an opinion as to:

(a) the value of the shareholding/business;

(b) the 'liquidity' of the shareholding/business ie what money (if any) can it afford to provide to the owner without jeopardising its ability to trade, and

(c) the income generating potential of a shareholding/ business, eg because it may be said that the spouse who is the business owner is alleged to be taking a lower income than the business can really afford.

(5) Be aware however that forensic accountant reports can often be very expensive to obtain and so a court will need a lot of persuading before it orders one. A full report may cost £5,000—£10,000 to obtain. It is possible to get cheaper reports eg 'desk-top' reports from companies such as Pinders but you get what you pay for and 'desk-top' reports can be quite superficial.

(6) It is quite common for a court to order a report from an accountant to provide an opinion on the tax consequences of the transfer and sale of assets.

A court will expect each party to come to court with the names and CV for any proposed expert they want to instruct, together with their estimate of their likely fees and timescales for any report they want to instruct and will expect this to have been served on the other party well in advance of the hearing. Indeed the Rules now require you to prepare a draft letter instructing the expert in advance of the hearing and for this to be sent to the other party in advance of the hearing.

Questionnaires

The other 'gap-filling' procedure is to order each party to answer the other's Questionnaire *as amended by the court*. At the hearing the court may go through each Questionnaire, question by question, striking out irrelevant ones, so make sure your questions address significant issues. It is not possible to give a list of relevant matters and much will depend on the scale of assets and income in a case. Generally however courts dislike questions about each party's day-to-day spending such as '*Why* do you say in Form E that you need to spend £50 a month on haircuts' or 'Please provide your petrol receipts for the last 6 months'.

Ordering the FDR appointment

The final thing that the court will do at first appointment is list an FDR appointment, probably two or three months after the first appointment.

> **What is the FDR appointment?**
>
> This is the financial dispute resolution hearing, at which the judge will help the parties to try to resolve the case by agreement.

Some courts will list it then and there so bring your diaries with you so that you can make sure it is not listed on a day that is inconvenient. Other courts will leave it to the court office to decide the date so you might want to come to court with a list of any weekdays that you cannot attend court on in the weeks and months following the first appointment.

Preparing for the first appointment

So, in preparing for the first appointment you should:

(1) Prepare your Questionnaire, Chronology and Schedule of Issues and send these to the court and the other side at least 14 days before the hearing.

(2) At the same time send in your completed Form G stating whether you feel the hearing can be an FDR. You will only do this if you feel you do not need more information before deciding on what is a fair settlement.

(3) Serve any mortgage companies or trustees with a copy of your application and keep a record for the court to see.

Remember you must attend the first appointment unless the court has given you prior permission not to. If you do not attend without prior permission you will probably be penalised with a costs order made against you.

A first appointment will usually be allocated 30 minutes of court time. Yours will probably be one of a number of first appointments listed at the same time. The court will usually call cases on in the order in which the parties indicate that they are ready to proceed.

Steps following the first appointment

Once the first appointment is finished and it is clear that the case will proceed to an FDR then you should:

(1) Diarise the *dates* for:

   (a) Questionnaire replies – both yours and the other party's;

   (b) Securing the valuations;

   (c) Other expert's reports.

(2) Make sure you comply with your obligations under the first appointment order and, most important of all, if the other side fails to comply with their obligations you must chase them, in writing. If their failure has been a wholesale one, eg failure to provide any Replies, then a simple one-line email chasing for those Replies is probably enough. If they have answered some Questions but ignored others then you should spell out in your email or

letter which Questions are still to be answered. Having chased once, then chase again and again, every week or so, until they comply.

(3) If they still fail to comply you can write to the court asking for a penal notice to be attached to the order. If they ignore this then it might be open to you to have the other party punished for their non-compliance. However the real purpose of the chasing letters is to give you the material to persuade the court at any further hearing that you should have your legal costs paid by the other side if that hearing is rendered worthless by reason of the non-disclosure, or that a costs order is needed to reflect their lack of compliance with the Rules. However, perhaps more important, chasing letters that are ignored can sometimes give you the basis for an argument at any final hearing that the other side is a deliberate non-discloser, ie that the court should draw adverse inferences against that non-disclosure and assume that they are hiding assets or other resources.

Using the first appointment as an FDR appointment

If you do not need to take any of the steps outlined above and you consider that you are ready to use the first appointment as an FDR appointment ie you consider that you are ready to reach overall agreement then use the first appointment as an FDR. Doing so can result in a substantial saving in time and costs. However to be effective you must:

(1) Send in your completed Form G not less than 14 days before the hearing indicating that you are ready to use the first appointment hearing as an FDR. It is important that *both* parties send in completed Forms G, so chase the other side to do so. However if they state that they aren't ready to use the first appointment hearing as an FDR most courts will respect this.

(2) Write separately to the court asking for more time to be allocated to the hearing, eg one hour as FDR's take longer than first appointments. In the bigger courts this can ensure that your hearing is allocated more time and can ensure that you have an effective FDR.

(3) Take all of the other steps needed to prepare for an FDR (see below).

It is rare that you will not need *some* further information before the case is ready for an FDR. If there is a reasonable degree of cooperation between you and the other party it is quite common to provide voluntary *'replies to questionnaire'* and also to cooperate in securing valuations. If this is done well in advance of the hearing it can then be possible to use the first appointment as an FDR.

The financial dispute resolution appointment ('FDR')

The FDR is a key hearing as most cases will settle at this hearing. It is described by the Rules as a hearing that *'must be treated as a meeting held for the purposes of discussion and negotiation'* – see FPR 2010, rule 9.17(1).

How does an FDR work?

The theory behind an FDR is as follows;

(1) At the FDR:

　(a) The court should have read the parties' respective Forms E and will have a broad understanding of the parties' assets, liabilities, incomes, outgoings as well as details of their ages, the children, the length of the marriage etc, and

(b) The court should be presented with each party's proposed outcome for the case, ie their preferred overall settlement.

(2) Armed with this information and, after having heard each party explain the fairness of their proposed solution at the hearing itself, the court will then give a verbal assessment of what it considers is the 'fair outcome'. This is often referred to as the judge's 'indication' and its purpose is to assist the parties in negotiating a compromise without the expense, stress and delay of having to have a final hearing (as to which see below). Having heard what the judge considers is fair you should then go out of court and negotiate. You should have in mind in advance what you really need and what you are, at a push, prepared to give way on. Some litigants in person may find it stressful to negotiate directly with their ex-spouse, or even with the lawyer representing their ex-spouse, in which case the court may be persuaded to allow discussions to take place in the courtroom itself with the judge present.

A word of warning however. The quality of judicial 'indications' varies greatly from court to court. Some judges are very reluctant to offer an opinion at all, which can be very frustrating and is not in accordance with the thinking behind the Rule. Other judge's will only give a 'bracket' of possible fair outcomes, eg 'spousal maintenance of somewhere between £250 and £500 per month, or 'a sale of the house and payment to the husband of between 20% and 40% of the proceeds' and so on. Clearly the parties must then negotiate the precise sums. Other judges will offer very specific indications. Given that they only have a 'snapshot' of the case this can risk them making an error but generally the more precise an 'indication' is the better the chances of reaching agreement.

FDR – key points

The key points to remember about the FDR hearing are as follows:

(1) The FDR hearing is entirely 'without prejudice'.

> (i) **What does 'without prejudice' in the FDR hearing mean?**
>
> 'Without prejudice' means any evidence cannot be referred to at a final hearing. It is privileged, meaning secret. This mechanism is designed to encourage parties to speak freely in their efforts to reach agreement, without fear that they are making concessions that they cannot withdraw for the purposes of a final hearing if overall agreement cannot be reached.

This means that any proposals for settlement made at the FDR cannot be referred to at any future hearing unless overall agreement is reached. Indeed nothing said at an FDR may be referred to at a subsequent hearing. For this reason, and to encourage the parties to speak openly at the hearing about their proposed outcomes, the judge will disqualify him/herself at the end of the hearing and will not be permitted to hear any further hearings in the case. This does not prevent the judge from making a directions order on that day at the end of a failed FDR, but that will usually be the last step the judge should take. For this reason the judge will remove all 'without prejudice' documents from the court file at the end of the hearing so that a future judge hearing the final hearing does not come across them accidentally.

(2) There are only three possible types of orders that a judge can make at an FDR:

(a) *A final order reflecting overall agreement in the case*

- this happens when the FDR is successful in reaching overall agreement;

(b) *A directions order including listing for a final hearing* – this happens when it is clear that the FDR will not result in overall agreement. The need for a final hearing is likely to take many months of further delay;

(c) *An order adjourning the FDR to another hearing date* – this happens when the court feels that overall agreement is a possibility but that one party needs further time to reflect or some additional information is required before overall agreement is possible.

(3) Neither party can be forced to reach a settlement. The court cannot impose its preferred outcome however clear that solution might be. Either you or the other party will negotiate an agreement or you won't – you cannot be made to. The judge will apply pressure but cannot impose an overall order. That said, it would be very unwise for you to disregard what a judge has said about your case, even if it is not what you had hoped to hear.

(4) If agreement is reached between you and the other party then the court should try to approve it in principle, often before the final order is drawn up. Once an overall agreement is 'approved' then it is as strong as an order, even if the drawing up of the actual order has not taken place.

(5) If agreement is not reached and an adjourned FDR is not appropriate then the court will make a directions order, as to which see below.

Preparing for an FDR appointment – before the hearing

In order to have the best chance of reaching agreement at an FDR appointment you must prepare for it appropriately. This includes complying with the rules but also taking a few practical steps.

Preparation – the rules

The Rules require the following steps to be taken;

(1) The directions order made at the first appointment must be complied with, and

(2) Not less than seven days before the FDR hearing date the party who is the applicant must file with the court copies of all offers of overall settlement that have been made by either party.

(3) Personal attendance. As with the first appointment you must attend the hearing personally or else risk a costs order being made against you.

Preparation – other steps

Making proposals

Exchange offers well before the hearing

For some self-representing litigants the process of formulating an overall proposal is daunting and occasionally they will leave it to the FDR judge to 'decide' what's fair. Generally however it is a good idea to form your own view of a fair settlement and to make an offer of overall settlement to the other party well before the FDR appointment. If you delay this and make your offer at the hearing itself then it can often prove too much for the other side to absorb at the hearing itself and the hearing can be wasted. If you make the proposal in advance they will have a chance to adjust to it before the hearing itself.

Offers – 'without prejudice' or 'open offer'?

Generally all such offers made before the FDR appointment are headed 'without prejudice' which will ensure that only the judge at the FDR hearing will see it and not any judge at a final hearing. The opposite of a 'without prejudice' offer is an 'open offer' (headed 'Open Offer'). This is an offer that the judge at the final hearing *can* be shown. There is nothing to prevent you making 'open offers' from the very outset of proceedings, including in the Form E, but generally the practice is that proposals made before FDR are 'without prejudice' whereas those made after FDR are either without prejudice or open depending on tactics.

Structuring proposals

The key to a good proposal is ensuring that it is easy to understand what precisely is being proposed. Generally proposal letters will have a short preliminary section which explains the 'thinking' underpinning the proposal but good offer letters will then go on to provide a concise 'shopping list' of key component parts of the proposal, such as for example:

(1) Sale of the property.

(2) Division of the proceeds equally after payment of the joint account overdraft.

(3) No pension sharing.

> **ⓘ What is pension sharing?**
>
> Pension sharing is a division of the capital value of a pension, so that each party emerges from the case with pension funds of their own.

(4) Child maintenance to be regulated by the Child Maintenance Service.

(5) Spousal maintenance of £300 pcm for five years ending on [date].

(6) No order as to costs.

When proposing the sale of an asset and a sharing of the proceeds of sale it is generally regarded as wiser and safer to suggest that the proceeds are shared in *'percentage'* terms rather than in 'fixed sums', particularly when there is uncertainty as to the sale price the asset will achieve. Thus it is better to suggest *'… a sale of the property and the net proceeds shared 60:40 in my favour'* rather than *'… a sale of the property and you shall have the first £50,000 and I will have the balance'* because in the latter scenario an unexpected rise or fall in the value of the property can rapidly make unfair what would otherwise have been a perfectly fair proposal.

Filing offers at court

Make copies of all offers that are made before the FDR appointment and ensure that copies are sent to the court. This is the applicant's responsibility under the Rules but the main thing is that this task is completed so, even if you are the respondent, you should consider doing it in any event.

Try to agree a schedule of assets/liabilities/incomes with the other side prior to the FDR

Some courts will make a direction at the first appointment that you should try to agree such a schedule but, even when no direction is made, it is a good idea to try and agree such a schedule. As far as possible, such a schedule ought to contain up-to-date figures, rather than the figures in Form E which, by now, may be somewhat historic. Send your schedule to the other side a couple of weeks before the hearing and ask the other side to identify anything they do not agree with. In this way you will both know in advance which assets/liabilities/income levels are controversial.

Summarise your case in writing

Before an FDR lawyers will generally prepare a document which summarises:

(1)   the assets, liabilities and incomes of the parties;

(2)   the background eg ages of parties and children, date of and length of marriage, important events etc;

(3)   the parties' respective settlement positions, and

(4)   why their own client's proposal is fair and the why the other party's proposal is unfair.

Very often these documents will run to half a dozen pages, possibly even longer. The court will have limited time for reading so the longer the document the greater the risk of it not being read by the judge before the hearing. They are generally *not* exchanged before the day of the hearing itself.

The court will not expect a Litigant in Person to prepare such a document but it will welcome such a document and they can be very effective in reinforcing your case. So it is a generally a good idea to put down on one side of A4 a few of the key points as to:

(1)   Why your proposal is fair, and

(2) Why the other side's proposal is unfair.

(3) Summarising the assets/debts etc as they are before settlement and how those same assets would be shared if your proposal was approved by the court.

The FDR hearing

Get there early. You should generally attend the hearing at least one hour before the time it is listed to begin, with a view to trying to negotiate a settlement with the other side. There's not much point in being there on your own and so make sure the other side attend at the same time before the hearing.

Listen to the judge. Experience tells us that FDRs are usually successful where the parties follow the court's 'indication' as to a fair settlement. If you try to persuade the other party that the judge was wrong you probably won't get far.

Be prepared to argue your corner. The judge will usually expect both parties to be able to explain why they consider their proposal fair. Even if the judge's initial 'indication' is unfavourable to you it may be possible to persuade the judge that his/her initial view is unfair to you. Judges are always conscious that they are offering 'indications' based on limited opportunities to pre-read and reflect and so, sometimes, they can be persuaded to change their minds. So don't be afraid to argue.

Be willing to compromise. Without some meaningful 'give and take' you are unlikely to get an overall agreement. However it is sometimes possible to depart from the judge's indication where both of you have an interest in such a departure. So, for example, the wife may wish to keep the home for herself whilst the husband may want a sale and a share of the proceeds, but at the same time the husband wishes to get an income clean break and not pay maintenance to the wife while the wife seeks spousal maintenance. The judge's 'indication' at the FDR may be that (i) the house is sold and the proceeds shared but (ii) the husband has to pay spousal maintenance. In this scenario it may be possible to negotiate a transfer of the house to the wife on the basis of a clean break as to spousal maintenance provided that the wife's reasonable income needs can be met. Generally however cases will reach overall agreement at an FDR when that agreement reflects the judge's 'indication' as to a fair outcome.

If you reach agreement – drawing up a final order

If you are able to reach agreement it will be necessary to draw up a final order. This can be a lengthy task and can also be extremely technical and is generally beyond most litigants in person. Courts vary as to their practices.

(1) Some judges will draw up the order then and there, but this is likely to happen only in the simpler cases and if there is time.

(2) Some courts may require you to take your agreement to a solicitor *instructed by both parties* to convert the agreement into an order. This will involve a cost, usually shared equally and will also require that a document is prepared summarising the key points of the agreement, often referred to as Heads of Agreement, which should be (i) signed by both parties and (ii) approved by the court and (iii) copies given to each party and the original held on the court file with the judge's approval endorsed on it.

(3) Other courts may list a further hearing to draft the order or to finalise any disputes about the detail of the order.

If you fail to reach agreement – directions order

If you do not reach agreement then, because the court cannot impose an agreement, the judge will either adjourn the FDR to a new date if the judge thinks that an agreement might be reached at another hearing. However more commonly the court will make a directions order.

> **What is a directions order?**
>
> A directions order is a procedural order which the court makes to get the case ready for the next hearing.

The directions order will typically:

(1) List the case for a final hearing – which may be estimated to take anywhere between one hour or several days, depending upon the complexity of the case and which will often be listed for hearing in several months' time.

(2) Direct disclosure of any further information or expert valuations required before the final hearing. Usually the single joint expert will be asked to update their previous valuations and each party will be asked to update the information in their Forms E. If you feel that the other party is withholding information or documents, come to the FDR with a further Questionnaire seeking that information. If the case settles then you won't need it but, if the case does not settle, you will be armed with a document to put before the court.

(3) Specify which witnesses are to give evidence at the final hearing. Some courts will direct the parties also to prepare witness statements containing their own evidence (known as section 25 narrative statements) summarising what they would want to say about the section 25 criteria (see below).

> **What is an section 25 narrative statement?**
>
> This is evidence in writing, addressing the section 25 factors, designed to save you giving that evidence orally in court, and giving advance notice to the other side of what your case is.

The list of possible section 25 issues is endless but common issues include:

(i) The cost of meeting their respective housing needs – courts will often require the parties to provide estate agents' property particulars,

(ii) The extent of the parties' future earning capacities,

(iii) Their health,

(iv) The financial needs of their children,

(v) The extent and timing of contribution of pre-marital assets or inheritances received during the marriage.

The final hearing

If your case does go to a final hearing then you are unlucky as most will have resolved themselves by the time of the FDR appointment, or at some time between the FDR appointment and the final hearing. However the final hearing is the occasion at which the court will impose a settlement on parties who are, for whatever reason, unable to reach an agreement themselves.

Before the final hearing – general updating

The directions order made at the end of the FDR will sometimes require each party to update their financial information and may set a date by which this is done. If no such direction was made there is nevertheless a clear understanding that you must provide the other party with updated figures for your bank accounts, policy surrender values, share values, debt levels etc and are entitled to expect the same in return. The Rules suggest that you should only provide updated documents that have been ordered by the court but the culture is to provide updating material prior to the final hearing whether or not this has been ordered.

As well as general updating you must of course comply with any other specific directions made by the FDR judge.

Before the final hearing – exchanging 'open proposals'

At the final hearing you *must* have an 'open proposal' that you will be suggesting to the final hearing judge because without such a proposal the hearing will lack all structure. An 'open proposal' is exactly what it suggests, ie your suggested overall settlement for the case that is not marked 'without prejudice' and therefore can be seen by the judge hearing the final hearing. Moreover the Rules require that you tell the other side your 'open proposal' in advance of the final hearing and, in particular:

(1) The applicant must send to the respondent his/her open proposals not less than 14 days before the final hearing, and

(2) The respondent must send his/her open proposals to the applicant not less than seven days before the final hearing and this applies whether or not the applicant has sent his/her open proposals in accordance with the rules.

The rival open proposals will set the benchmark for the judge deciding the final hearing. The judge is permitted to ignore the open proposals if he/she thinks it fair but that is very unusual and the final hearing is usually about deciding which party's open proposals are the fairest and what adjustments, if any, need to be made to them to make the overall settlement fair.

It is not permitted for the trial judge to see any *without prejudice* proposals, such as those which were shown to the court at the FDR hearing.

Preparing 'the court bundle'

> **What is a court bundle?**
>
> A court bundle is essentially papers that are needed by the court for your case. It makes sure that all the information and evidence relevant to your case can be found in one place so that it is easy to refer to during your hearing.

The Rules require the applicant to file with the court a 'hearing bundle'. This must be prepared in such a way that it complies with Practice Direction 27A of the FPR 2010, so do look that up. It is a laborious process but the smooth running of the hearing depends on it. If you are the applicant and the respondent has legal advisers acting for him/her then the Practice Direction requires the respondent's legal team to prepare the bundle for the hearing.

There is a set format for the bundle and the relevant Practice Direction states that it must be prepared as follows (and if possible ensure the contents are agreed with the other party):

'Contents of the bundle

4.1 The bundle shall contain copies of all documents relevant to the hearing, in chronological order from the front of the bundle, paginated and indexed, and divided into separate sections (each section being separately paginated) as follows:

(a) preliminary documents (see para 4.2) and any other case management documents required by any other practice direction;

(b) applications and orders;

(c) statements and affidavits (which must be dated in the top right corner of the front page) (note this includes Forms E and the documents exhibited to them);

(d) care plans (where appropriate – not relevant to financial proceedings);

(e) experts' reports and other reports and

(f) other documents, divided into further sections as may be appropriate.

4.2 At the commencement of the bundle there shall be inserted the following documents (the preliminary documents):

(i) an up to date summary of the background to the hearing confined to those matters which are relevant to the hearing and the management of the case and limited, if practicable, to one A4 page;

(ii) a statement of the issue or issues to be determined ... at the final hearing;

(iii) a position statement by each party including a summary of the order or directions sought by that party ... at the final hearing;

(iv) an up to date chronology, if it is a final hearing or if the summary under (i) is insufficient;

(v) skeleton arguments, if appropriate, with copies of all authorities relied on (this really only applies to lawyers); and

(vi) a list of essential reading for that hearing.

4.3 Each of the preliminary documents shall state on the front page immediately below the heading the date when it was prepared and the date of the hearing for which it was prepared.

4.4 The summary of the background, statement of issues, chronology, position statement and any skeleton arguments shall be cross-referenced to the relevant pages of the bundle.

4.5 The summary of the background, statement of issues, chronology and reading list shall in the case of a final hearing, and shall so far as practicable in the case of any other hearing, each consist of a single document in a form agreed by all parties. Where the parties disagree as to the content the fact of their disagreement and their differing contentions shall be set out at the appropriate places in the document.'

As you will see the process of preparing a bundle can be complex and demanding. In reality most courts will not expect a litigant in person to prepare an immaculate bundle but bear in mind the following:

(1) If you are the applicant and there are no legally represented parties then you must take on this task. If you do not attempt it you may be criticised.

(2) You must put separate page numbers on each page of the bundle, to help the court in dealing with evidence and submissions.

(3) You must prepare four copies of the bundle ie one for you, one for the other side, one for the judge and another one for the witness box. If you are in doubt ask the judge at the FDR how many to produce. The other party should pay for the copying charges for their bundle. It is usually best to get the copying done by a professional copying company.

Finally the copies of the bundle should be delivered to the court at least two full working days (ie this does *not* include weekends) before the final hearing is due to start.

The final hearing itself

At the final hearing each party will be expected to attend and give evidence to the court. This is easy enough if you are represented as your legal team will assist you with this. However when you are representing yourself the position is less easy.

The structure of the final hearing is ultimately a matter for the judge who is hearing the case but there is a well-established pattern which is as follows:

(1) The applicant has the first word and is able to explain the background to the case and explain his/her proposal.

(2) The applicant then gives his/her evidence. This happens in three stages and will almost always involve the witness taking the oath to '… tell the truth, the whole truth etc'. Once sworn in, the three stage process is as follows:

   (1) **Evidence in Chief** – the applicant provides their own evidence as to the issues the court needs to decide, eg housing needs, income needs, earning capacity etc.

   (2) **Cross-Examination** – the applicant is then cross-examined by the respondent. This is a process by which the respondent asks questions of the applicant with a view to undermining their case, eg:

   - How many job applications have you made?
   - Why do you need a five bedroom house?
   - Have you explored your ability to raise a mortgage?

- Why have you not provided a letter from your employer about your redundancy payment even though you were ordered to do so?

If you are acting in person then cross-examination raises the possibility of you asking questions of your ex-spouse directly. The courts will be very concerned to ensure that this process does not develop in to argument and bullying and so the judge may well step in to manage the process.

(3) **Re-Examination** – when cross-examination is over the applicant has an opportunity to add any further evidence but only in relation to the issues that arose during cross-examination.

Once the applicant has completed his/her evidence then any witness called by the applicant will give evidence and the same three-stage process applies.

This at least is the theory. In practice courts find that litigants in person tend to ask very few (if any) questions in cross-examination and so judges are experienced in extracting the necessary evidence from the parties themselves.

Once the applicant and any witnesses have completed their evidence it is the respondent's turn (together with any witnesses called by the respondent) and, again, the same three-stage process applies.

Once all of the evidence is completed the parties have a final opportunity to 'sum up' their case in 'closing submissions'. Quite often the court does not really need to hear yet further comments and it will then go on to give its judgment.

The hearing will usually be recorded on tape (or digitally), and this is in case either party wishes to appeal or in case there is a dispute about what was said at the hearing. Getting a copy of the recording will involve you applying to the court and paying a fee to an independent transcriber.

Judgment – drawing up the order

The court will deliver a judgment and then give its decision. These are two separate stages although the one follows the other. The judgment is the court's summary of all the relevant factual and legal matters that apply to your case. This involves the judge explaining the court's 'thinking' about the case, the history and all of the legal matters that need to be addressed. It might take 30 minutes or so and, if possible, it is sensible to try and take a note of the judge's judgment. The judge will then go on to announce his/her decision and explain what orders are to be made, eg as to the sale of the home or payment of a lump sum or of maintenance etc.

The process of drawing up the order has already been considered. If there is time the judge will draw up the order there and then. If there is a legally represented party the judge might expect that party to draw up the order and email it in to the judge. Sometimes the judge might expect unrepresented parties to approach a solicitor to draw up the order for them, although this is unusual.

After the order has been made

Once the order is drafted the case is usually over. There are however some things to consider.

Costs orders

Before the case concludes it is open to either party to ask the judge to make an order for 'costs' ie that the other party pays them a sum of money to compensate for costs spent. In some cases a Litigant in Person can claim an hourly rate of £18 per hour legal costs for their own time. Generally costs orders are very rare and are only made where one party has not complied with the rules or has been unreasonable in their conduct of the case or in not accepting a sensible open offer made by the other party.

Permission to appeal

If you are unhappy with the outcome you should ask the judge for permission to appeal. It is very rare that this is granted by the judge but one should ask anyway. If permission is refused, you may make a second application for permission, to the appeal judge (see below). The 'grounds' upon which you can successfully appeal are limited and discussed below.

Implementing the final order/'liberty to apply'

Once the order is made it goes without saying that you must then implement it. This may involve selling properties or closing bank accounts, paying lump sums of money etc. Most final orders will include a provision that each party *has liberty to apply to the court as to timing and implementation*. This means that if there are problems with implementation either party can take the matter back to court for the court to make orders resolving those problems.

Appeal

The system does not encourage appeals. For legally represented parties the legal costs of going to appeal can be a major deterrent but, for obvious reasons, this is less true for litigants in person.

Nevertheless the prospects of succeeding with an appeal are usually slim because in order to do so you must demonstrate to the appeal judge (usually this will be a circuit judge – ie the next up the judicial hierarchy from the district judge who decided your case) – that the district judge made a decision that was 'wholly wrong'. Because there is no formula in financial remedy cases and because each decision is tailored to the specific facts of each divorce there is always a wide range of possible orders that can be made at a final hearing. If your decision falls within that range of possible orders then you will not succeed on appeal. Only if the decision was one that no reasonable court could have made will the appeal be successful.

Permission to appeal – time limits

You cannot appeal without 'permission to appeal' and you can only get 'permission to appeal' if you can show that you have a realistic chance of succeeding on appeal. You must apply for 'Permission to Appeal' within 21 days of the decision that you are complaining of. You must bear in mind that the 'decision' is the order that the district judge explains and, if there is a delay between the judge explaining the order and the actual order being typed up and sent to you, then the 21 days can be said to begin on the day of the hearing and not the later date when the typed order is sent to you.

To launch an appeal you must set out your 'grounds of appeal' in a document called an 'appellant's notice' and file this at court within the 21 day time limit. You should also send it to the other party. Your grounds of appeal must explain precisely how and in what way the district judge was 'wrong'.

The court will then list the appeal for a hearing unless a judge reading your appellant's notice considers that your appeal is obviously hopeless and doomed to fail in which case the judge can simply dismiss the appeal 'on paper'.

If you attend at a hearing and your application for permission to appeal is rejected that is generally an end to the appeal. You cannot launch an 'appeal' against the court's order refusing you permission to appeal.

Appealing 'out of time'

Sometimes something happens long after the 21 day time limit has expired that causes you to want to appeal. In some very limited circumstances you can launch an appeal out of time but generally the event that has happened must be:

(1) such as to completely undermine the basis of the final order, and

(2) must be unforeseen, and

(3) must have happened within a relatively short time of the final hearing itself.

Examples of such appeals are rare but can include cases where the other party dies or falls very ill, or where the other party wins a very large lottery payment or such like. Parties often complain that assets change in value after the final hearing but generally a drop or rise in property prices will rarely be sufficient to be the basis for a successful appeal 'out of time'.

The appeal – a review and not a rehearing

For the appeal hearing you should obtain a transcript of the district judge's judgment and put this before the court. You should also prepare a bundle for the appeal hearing. This may be the same as the final hearing bundle but often it will be much smaller as only limited documents will be needed.

The important thing to appreciate is that an appeal will not generally involve the court hearing evidence from the parties again. Instead the court conducts an overall review of the case to see if the order made was 'wrong'. Appeals therefore are generally conducted without new evidence being considered. Arguing the case on an appeal can get pretty technical and so you might want to consider securing some legal advice, especially if a lot of money is riding on the outcome.

New evidence

Importantly it is not generally possible to introduce new evidence that was not considered at the final hearing, especially where the 'new evidence' (sometimes called 'fresh evidence') could have been available at the final hearing. If you do want to introduce 'new evidence' make this clear in your appellant's notice. And specifically ask for permission to do so.

Respondent's notice

If you are the respondent and, having seen that the appellant is appealing, you decide that you yourself would also wish to appeal (known as a 'cross-appeal') then you can do so by filing a respondent's notice setting out the 'grounds' upon which you cross-appeal. Your respondent's notice must be filed at court and sent to the appellant within 14 days of your being served with an appellant's notice. Usually you will also require permission to appeal and so you must request this in your respondent's notice.

Stay

Just because a final order is subject to an appeal does *not* automatically prevent it being put into effect. If you want to put the final order on 'hold' until the appeal has been decided then you must ask for a 'stay' of the final order in your appellant's (or respondent's) notice. The court will usually order a hearing to decide on the question of a 'stay' and will only usually 'stay' those parts of the final order that might be changed if the appeal is allowed and the final order altered.

Variation

Some final orders can be varied in the future and some can't. Generally speaking:

(1) Periodical payments orders *can* be varied as can lump sum orders where the lump sum is payable by instalments.

(2) However simple lump sum orders (ie not payable by instalments), property transfer orders and pension sharing orders are *not* variable in the future.

If a periodical payments order was unaffordable or otherwise unfair at the time it was made at the final hearing then you should launch an appeal against the order and not simply try to vary it. If however a periodical payments order was affordable when it was made but since then has become unaffordable eg because your income has reduced, then you should apply to vary the original order rather than seek to appeal it.

It is possible to vary a lump sum order if it is an order for lump sums by instalments but it is not easy to do so.

Although it is not strictly speaking necessary, an application to vary an existing order will only generally be made where there has been a significant change in a party's circumstances. Sometimes this can be that the other party (usually the party receiving maintenance) has inherited a lot of money or otherwise become much richer but more often than not the reason is that the party paying the maintenance has experienced a drop in income so that the maintenance is no longer affordable, eg because of unemployment, illness, etc. Be aware that if you are made redundant or otherwise receive a pay-off upon leaving your employment the court may well expect you to use some of the redundancy/dismissal lump sum payment to meet your maintenance obligations, at least for a while.

Variation applications are made by issuing a new Form A and will require the whole procedure of Forms E, first appointment, FDR and final hearing to be pursued again so be sure that this is really what you want. The fees involved will be considerable and very often there is only limited 'cost/benefit' in pursuing such an application. However if you cannot afford to pay maintenance that has been ordered then, unless the other party agrees to you paying a reduced amount or agrees to no payments at all, you have little alternative but to make an application because otherwise you will be breach of the order and it can be enforced against you.

The general rule is that only the last 12 months' of 'arrears' of maintenance (ie sums that were meant to be paid under the maintenance order but haven't been paid) will be enforced and any arrears that built up more than 12 months before an application to enforce will be 'remitted' ie cancelled so that they cannot be enforced.

Interim hearings – maintenance pending suit, costs allowances and injunctions

You will now have seen in broad terms how a financial remedy case runs from issue of Form A to conclusion of a final hearing. However there are a number of specific applications that can be made before final hearing. The general purpose of these applications is to deal with matters that arise in the case in the interim prior to the final determination of the claim. The most common of these interim applications are maintenance pending suit applications under section 22 of the Matrimonial Causes Act 1973, costs allowances under section 22ZA of the Matrimonial Causes Act 1973 and injunctions under section 37 of the Matrimonial Causes Act 1973.

If no or insufficient maintenance is being paid it is clearly necessary for a party to be able to apply to the court for assistance prior to the final determination of a claim. Whilst it is not possible to obtain an interim capital order (save by way of a costs allowance – see below), it is possible to apply for an order whereby you receive maintenance from your spouse, pending the overall resolution of the application for financial remedies. This is called an application for maintenance pending suit.

> **What is an application for maintenance pending suit?**
>
> This means maintenance to enable you to meet your needs on a short-term basis until your case is resolved.

To apply for maintenance pending suit, you must follow the procedure set out in FPR Part 18. It is a good idea to submit a short statement to the court, not more than say 4 sides of A4, which should concentrate on two issues; first, the reasonable income needs of you and your family unit; and second, the ability of your spouse to assist you in meeting those needs by paying maintenance. The statement should be dated and signed by you as being true.

As to reasonable needs, you should set out in your statement a short-term monthly budget. You might already have completed a long-term monthly budget in Form E. On an application for maintenance pending suit, you should pare that budget down, so that it cannot be said to be extravagant and contains only essentials.

> **What is a budget?**
>
> A budget is a record of your monthly/annual living costs.

That said, if the standard of living you enjoyed during the marriage was a good one, the court will have regard to that standard when setting the appropriate level of interim maintenance. You might want to give two or three examples of that standard in your statement, but keep it short. An application for maintenance pending suit will almost certainly be dealt with by the judge on the basis only of the documents which have been put in, so it is important to you make you document readable and compelling. You should certainly type it if possible.

As to the ability of your spouse to pay, this is equally important. Whatever your need, no court will order your spouse to pay an amount that they plainly cannot afford. It is important therefore that you address that point in your statement. If you allege that the presentation of your spouse, as to their income, in their Form E, is misleading, you should state (as shortly as you can) how/why you say so.

You should expect to receive a similar sort of statement from your spouse. The hearing will take place over an hour or two, and will almost certainly be dealt with on paper alone.

A costs allowance is the provision of a sum that is meant to cover part of the applicant's costs of legal representation. The justification for the ability to make such an order is relatively clear. Why should a party with sufficient assets and the ability to fund their own legal expenses leave their former partner with no or limited ability to afford legal representation? To be eligible for a costs allowance the applicant has to show that they cannot secure legal representation by any other means (for instance, they cannot get a loan to fund their lawyers, they have no capital assets that can be used to fund lawyers, and there is no public funding available).

If a costs allowance is ordered it has to be referable to legal costs and the party who is paying is entitled to see evidence that this is how it is being spent. The guidance from the courts is that a costs allowance should not, in the first instance, extend beyond the FDR hearing.

Some spouses are tempted to move or dissipate their assets prior to trial with the intention of trying to materially reduce their ultimate liability to the other spouse. If you feel that there is evidence to suggest this is going to happen you need to act fast. A court can make an order to stop a party from transferring their assets or dissipating them. The best advice that you can be given is to seek legal advice as a matter of urgency. The applications to prevent dissipation are difficult to make and if you get it wrong you will normally have to pay the other side's legal costs.

Dos and don'ts

DOS

- DO make a full, clear and up to date presentation of your own financial means throughout the proceedings
- DO pitch your claim and/or your offer at a reasonable level
- DO focus on the main issue(s) in the case
- DO comply with the directions which the court makes along the way

makes no difference in the eyes of the law whether you lived with your partner for one year or 25 years; you will still not be given the same financial rights on the breakdown of the relationship as someone who is married. This can and frequently does cause enormous hardship on the breakdown of cohabitation.

> (i) **What is cohabitation?**
>
> Two people in a stable relationship who live together in the same household who usually pool resources.

There is nothing lawyers or indeed judges can do about this anomaly. It is a matter for Parliament to change the law. If you were living together and unmarried, family lawyers will refer to you as a cohabitant and on the breakdown of your relationship, should a dispute arise, it will be described as a cohabitation dispute.

If there are any children of the relationship it will be necessary to deal with their living and care arrangements as a matter of priority. The law in this country is focussed on the welfare of the child and it makes no difference whether parents are married or unmarried when issues arise in respect of children. So chapter 8 of this book will be just as relevant to married and unmarried parents. Similarly the status of the relationship of the parent makes no difference to entitlement to child maintenance.

> (i) **What is child maintenance?**
>
> This is the provision of financial help with a child's everyday living costs.

The options of family based arrangements, or if that is not possible the use of the Child Maintenance Service apply to both married and unmarried parents.

> Helpful information and support on child maintenance can be found:
>
> at www.cmoptions.org

> **What are family based arrangements?**
>
> These are child maintenance arrangements which parents have agreed between themselves.

> **What is the Child Maintenance Service?**
>
> This is the government body that collects child maintenance.

Chapter 9 deals with how the financial resources of spouses are reallocated on divorce. In very broad terms financial resources such as income, savings, property and pensions are reallocated between spouses in accordance with what is considered to be fair. No such jurisdiction exists following the separation of cohabiting couples. On the breakdown of cohabitation, if there is a child of the relationship, there is the possibility of making an application for financial provision under Schedule 1 of the Children Act. This topic is dealt with in more detail in chapter 11. However any order made under Schedule 1 is an order made for the benefit of the child and not for the direct benefit of one of the parties to the relationship. So on the breakdown of cohabitation, whether or not there was a child of the relationship, there is no statutory jurisdiction to reallocate financial resources for the benefit of one of the parties to the relationship.

A hypothetical set of facts will illustrate the consequences of the absence of a jurisdiction to reallocate resources in favour of one of the parties to the relationship on the breakdown of cohabitation. A man and a woman cohabit for 30 years. They do not marry. The male was throughout the relationship the main breadwinner. The female worked during the early part of the relationship. The couple had three children together. The female stopped work in order to bring up the children. At the end of the relationship the children had all left home and were independent. The female had not worked for over 25 years and there was now no prospect of her obtaining employment. At the end of the relationship the male was earning a large salary, had significant savings and a large pension. The couple lived in a home that the male bought in his own name. If the couple had been married, the female would probably be entitled to an order for half of the capital and pension assets and an order for periodical payments in her favour for the remainder of the male's working life. On the breakdown of cohabitation the court does not have power to make any of these orders in her favour.

At the end of the marriage the court has what is known as 'discretionary jurisdiction' (under the Matrimonial Causes Act) to reallocate resources based on what is 'fair'. There is no equivalent jurisdiction in a cohabitation case. If the female in the example above is able to establish an interest in any of the male's capital resources then on the breakdown of the relationship she would be entitled to receive what was hers in any event. Establishing a proprietary interest is an absolute concept; it is not based on discretion. Either you have an interest or you do not. In order to establish ownership of an asset on the breakdown of cohabitation, the parties are thrown back on concepts of property law. Claims to an interest in property are determined by application under the Trusts of Land and Appointment of Trustees Act 1996. For obvious reasons this is known as a 'TOLATA claim'.

The Trusts of Land and Appointment of Trustees Act 1996 (TOLATA) can be viewed on-line at:

www.legislation.gov.uk

On a breakdown of cohabitation, the most common and financially significant property dispute is that which relates to ownership of the former home of the parties.

The flowchart on the next page summarises the issues that unmarried partners should consider on the breakdown of their relationship.

DIY Divorce and Separation

```
┌─────────────────────┐
│ Do you have children│──────┐
│ with your former    │      │
│ partner?            │      │
└──────────┬──────────┘      │
           │                 ▼
           │         ┌──────────────┐
           │         │     YES      │
           │         └──────┬───────┘
           ▼                │
        ┌─────┐             │
        │ NO  │             ▼
        └──┬──┘
           │
           ▼
┌─────────────────────┐
│ Do you have a       │──────┐
│ property with your  │      │
│ former partner      │      │
│ which you have an   │      ▼
│ interest in (whether│   ┌──────┐
│ legal or equitable?)│   │ YES  │
└──────────┬──────────┘   └──────┘
           │
           ▼
        ┌─────┐
        │ NO  │
        └──┬──┘
           │
           ▼
┌─────────────────────┐
│ This section does   │
│ not apply to your   │
│ case                │
└─────────────────────┘
```

YES

- Applications for child maintenance are normally made to the Child Maintenance Service ('CMS') - see Chapter 11 for the website address and to check your case falls within the remit of the CMS.
- Applications for a property, a lump sum of money and for child maintenance (in certain circumstances) are discussed further in Chapter 11
- Applications concerning the welfare of your children (e.g. where they are going to live, how often they are going to see the other parent) are discussed further in Chapter 8

YES

- Applications for a share in a property (whether or not you have children with your former property) are dealt with in Chapter 10
- If you also have children with your former partner you will need to consider whether it is better for you to make an application under the process described in Chapter 10 or in Chapter 11

Introduction to TOLATA claims

Being a litigant in person in traditional family proceedings, such as an application under the Children Act or a financial remedies claim brought under the Matrimonial Causes Act, is difficult enough. However, the difficulty is manageable since the key concepts are relatively easy to understand if you are a non-lawyer. Raising arguments as to what is in the best interests of a child or whether a reallocation of assets or income is fair are concepts that are not overtly complex at a basic level. Litigants in person are also assisted in traditional family proceedings in that the general rule is that one party will not be required to pay the other side's costs of the litigation. The perhaps misleading simplicity in the basic concepts of family law and the absence of a costs sanction make family law an ideal arena for the litigant in person. However TOLATA claims are highly technical and turn on hard to understand concepts of trust and property law. Many lawyers and indeed judges find this area of law difficult. This is also an area of law where costs do follow the event; in other words the general rule is that the loser pays the winners legal costs. It should not therefore come as a surprise to discover that being a litigant in person in a TOLATA claim comes with very real warnings.

If you don't want to engage a lawyer try to mediate a settlement (see chapter 2). Even if you do instruct a lawyer to provide you with advice on the merits of your case you should still consider mediation as a realistic and cost effective form of dispute resolution. If you are unable to instruct lawyers throughout the process, consider taking strategic legal advice from a solicitor or a direct access barrister. Strategic advice is best taken prior to starting your claim and after the filing of witness statements. A direct access barrister can also assist you with drafting the necessary court documents called 'statements of case', which used to be known as pleadings. In TOLATA claims, drafting statements of case can be both complex and technical. Come what may, it is essential to obtain some input from a lawyer on the merits of your case. It is always better to be forewarned of any difficulties in your case – because there is a very real risk that if you have mistakenly evaluated your prospects of success and you lose the litigation, you are likely to be paying your former partner's legal fees.

> **What is a beneficial interest?**
>
> This is a right to the proceeds of sale of a property.

The main applications that are brought are for declarations that one party has a beneficial interest in a property and for the extent of the interest to be determined. In other words the court will state whether you have an interest in the property and if you do, your percentage share of the equity. Note that the application is one to declare the existence of an interest; not to alter the ownership of an interest in the property. Once the nature and extent of an interest in property is declared the court is frequently asked to deal with an order for an account and an order for sale. The applications are brought under sections 14 and 15 of TOLATA.

> **What is an order for an account?**
>
> This is a process where contributions to mortgage and building works are potentially credited to and debited from the owner's share of the proceeds of sale.

Basic principles

Take a deep breath and make yourself a very strong coffee. The law that you are required to be familiar with on a TOLATA application is both extensive and complex. Teaching this area to law students would take months! What follows can be no more than the briefest of introductions to some basic principles.

Hopefully this section will make your life slightly easier if you choose to undertake the further research identified at the end of the chapter or it will help you to better understand any legal advice that you choose to obtain.

The ownership of land is conceptually divided into two; namely legal and beneficial ownership. The owner of the legal title is the person whose name is registered at the Land Registry. The holder of the legal title is entitled to exercise powers of management in respect of the property. The owner of the legal title holds the property for the benefit of the beneficial owner. The owner of the beneficial interest in the property is the person or persons who are entitled to receive the net proceeds of sale or rent from the property. The beneficial owner may or may not be the same person as the legal owner. You may well have heard reference made to the equity in a property. In broad terms the equity in the property is the beneficial interest.

A joint tenancy is an equal but undivided share in property. A tenancy in common is a divided share in property. Imagine an orange with 10 segments owned equally by 2 people. Whilst the peel remains on the orange the owners own the orange as joint tenants since their share is undivided. When the peel is removed from the orange and the segments divided equally, ownership is as tenants in common.

The legal title to property held by more than one person must always be held as a joint tenancy. The beneficial interest may be held as either joint tenants or tenants in common. A beneficial interest held on a joint tenancy can be severed into a tenancy in common in equal shares. Acts of severance include serving notice to sever and issuing proceedings for an order for sale. A beneficial tenancy in common may be held in equal or unequal shares.

Where the parties have declared their respective interests in property the declaration of trust is usually determinative. In the absence of a declaration, disputes as to the extent of beneficial ownership can be categorised into either sole name or joint name cases. You should also obtain a copy of the file prepared by the solicitors who act on the purchase of the property. The file usually contains useful evidence about ownership intention. A sole name case is a case where the legal title to property is vested in one person. It is therefore for the person whose name is not on the legal title to establish that they have a beneficial interest in the property. In a joint name case the legal title to the property is vested in two or more people as joint tenants. The starting point for these cases is that the beneficial interest is held on a joint tenancy. In joint ownership cases it is upon the joint owner who claims to have other than a joint and equal beneficial interest to establish their claim. In other words, if a joint owner believes that the beneficial interest is not held equally, they have to establish that fact.

'Joint names' cases

The law in respect of joint name cases has undergone clarification and simplification following the two key cases of *Stack v Dowden* [2007] 1 UKHL 17 and *Jones v Kernott* [2011] UKSC 53. If a property is held in joint names at law, the outcome will be equal ownership of the equity unless a party is able to show that the joint intention was otherwise. This task is not lightly to be embarked upon and a full examination of the facts at trial is likely to involve disproportionate costs. In joint names cases it is unlikely to lead to a result other than equal ownership of the equity unless the facts are very unusual. The following points were made in *Stack v Dowden*:

- Merely contributing unequally cannot be enough to justify unequal ownership. Each case will turn on its own facts. Many more factors than financial contributions may be relevant to diving the parties true intentions. These include: any advice or discussions at the time of the transfer which cast light upon their intentions then; the reasons why the home was acquired in their joint names; the reasons why (if it be the case) the survivor was authorised to give a receipt for the capital moneys; the purpose for which the home was acquired; the nature of the parties' relationship; whether they had children for whom they both had responsibility to provide a home; how the purchase was financed, both initially and subsequently; how the parties arranged their finances, whether separately or together or a bit of both; how they discharged the outgoings on the property and their other household expenses.

- When a couple are joint owners of the home and jointly liable for the mortgage, the inferences to be drawn from who pays for what may be very different from the inferences to be drawn when only one is owner of the home. The arithmetical calculation of how much was paid by each is also likely to be less important. It will be easier to draw the inference that they intended that each should contribute as much to the household as they reasonably could and that they would share the eventual benefit or burden equally.

- The parties' individual characters and personalities may also be a factor in deciding where their true intentions lay. In the cohabitation context, mercenary considerations may be more to the fore than they would be in marriage, but it should not be assumed that they always take pride of place over natural love and affection.

- At the end of the day, having taken all this into account, cases in which the joint legal owners are to be taken to have intended that their beneficial interests should be different from their legal interests will be very unusual.

In a joint names case the joint legal owner starts from the position that he or she already has a beneficial interest and the issue for the court to determine is the quantification of that interest. In order to quantify the interest the primary search is to ascertain the actual shared intention of the owners whether expressed or inferred from conduct. Where it is impossible to divine a common intention as to the proportions in which the equity should be shared the court may impute an intention based on what the parties intentions as reasonable and just people would have been had they thought about it at the time.

'Sole name' cases

There are two stages to a sole name case. At the first stage the party whose name is not registered on the title to the property has to establish an interest in the property. Unfortunately like much of this area, the law on establishing an interest in property when your name is not on the title is difficult to understand. The second stage once an interest is established is that of quantification. The quantification of an interest in a sole name case follows exactly the same route as the quantification of the extent of an interest in a joint name case. We have dealt with this in the paragraph above.

At the first stage of a sole name case, the initial search is for an express declaration of trust setting out whether there was an agreement that the party who was not the owner of the legal title was to have a beneficial interest in the property. An express declaration of trust will generally be conclusive unless it is overturned by fraud or mistake or subsequently varied. The most common document in which to find a relevant declaration of trust is the TR1 document that is lodged at the Land Registry when the title to the property is registered on a transfer.

In the absence of an express declaration of trust the court is looking in the domestic context to infer a common intention that was detrimentally relied upon that the party whose name is not on the legal title was to have a beneficial interest in the property. You will need to consider whether there is sufficient evidence to establish an oral agreement to this effect. Establishing an oral agreement is however notoriously difficult due to the passage of time and conflicting recollections. A common intention may also be inferred from the conduct of the parties. The best evidence upon which to rely in order to infer such a common intention is a direct contribution to the purchase price or the payment of mortgage instalments. One line of cases suggests that there is a doubt that anything less than this will do; however another and more recent line of authorities suggests that the law has moved on and should be moved on further from such a restrictive approach by the law taking a wider view of what is capable of counting as a contribution towards the purchase of a property. It may therefore be the case that sufficient payment of household expenses relieving the legal owner of expenditure enabling him to pay the mortgage, may count as a contribution to the purchase price of a property enabling the court to infer the existence of a common intention that the claimant was to have a beneficial interest in the property.

Obtaining a declaration from the court as to the existence and quantum of a beneficial interest in property is all well and good; but on a separation following cohabitation the practical remedy following such a declaration is an order for sale and an account. After all it is only on a sale that the interest in a property is turned into money. It is a surprisingly common mistake not to apply for an order for sale and an account at the same time as the application for a declaration as to whether and the extent to which a party has an interest in property.

An application for an order for sale is made under section 14 of TOLATA. The court exercises a discretionary power when deciding whether to order a sale. The statute identifies a number of matters to which the court is to have regard when exercising its discretion. These matters include the intentions of the settlor (if any), the purposes for which the property held subject to the trust is held, the welfare of any minor who occupies or might reasonably be expected to occupy the property as his home; the interests of any secured creditors and the wishes of the beneficiaries entitled to occupy the property. The court will also consider the position of the parties when determining an application for an order for sale. Every application for an order for sale is therefore fact specific. A good example of a judge exercising his discretion on an application for an order for sale can be read in *The Mortgage Corporation v Shaire* [2000] EWHC 452 (Ch).

Having established and quantified an interest in property and after having obtained an order for sale, the next issue to consider is an account. There are no hard and fast rules about accounts. An account results in debits and credits being made against a parties' share of the net proceeds of sale. The account does not alter the size of the beneficial interests. The general rule is that the accounting period runs from separation until sale. There are a number of commonly encountered issues that arise on the taking of an account. On the breakdown of cohabitation one party may remain in the property to the exclusion of the other paying the mortgage. That party is usually treated as being liable for an occupational rent which is usually treated as equivalent to the value of the mortgage interest that has been repaid. Any repayments of mortgage capital may additionally be taken into account. For example if the beneficial interest in a property is owned equally and one party remains in occupation post separation paying the capital instalments on the mortgage, then he or she ought to be credited with half of the monthly payments that are made. Similarly if the party remaining in occupation does work on the property that materially increases the value of the property on sale there is clearly an argument to be made that this factor should be brought into the account.

Procedural overview

The procedural rules that apply to TOLATA claims are the Civil Procedure Rules (abbreviated by lawyers to 'CPR'). You will clearly need to read the CPR if you are representing yourself. These rules may be found on line at www.justice.gov.uk. In addition to the rules, there are practice directions appended to many of the rules. The practice directions (abbreviated for example to 28 PD) should be read alongside the rules. The practice directions provide assistance in understanding how the rules operate. The authoritative procedural textbook relied upon by judges and lawyers alike is a book called Civil Procedure. The book is colloquially known as The White Book. I would recommend that if you embark upon litigation it would be beneficial to read the commentary to the relevant rules in a law library. I know that finding a law library is not easy, but buying the book is expensive (two volumes cost over £700!). Yes you can represent yourself just by reading the rules themselves; but you will help to level the playing field between lawyers and yourself if you have had access to the White Book. Make sure you read the latest edition of the White Book. It is published annually with updates. Be aware that reading an old version of the book may be dangerous since the law may have changed. A cheaper and perhaps more practical alternative is to buy a student textbook on Civil Procedure. The student textbook that most lawyers are brought up on is O'Hare & Browne: Civil Litigation – which is currently in its sixteenth edition. The cost of the book is £95; which is still expensive for a non-legal book; but the investment will be worthwhile. At the very least in addition to reading the CPR on line you will need to read O'Hare.

Providing commentary on the relevant CPR is beyond the remit of this book. However a birds' eye summary would assist with providing focus and direction in the event that you choose to represent yourself in your dispute.

The initial step in any dispute should be to write a detailed letter before claim that complies with the Pre-Action Conduct Practice Direction Annex A. The Pre-Action Conduct Practice Direction can be found on the www.justice.gov.uk website. The letter before claim should set out your full name and address, the basis on which the claim is made, a clear summary of the facts on which the claim is based, what you want from the defendant and an explanation of how any financial loss has been calculated. The letter should also list the essential documents on which you rely, the type (if any) of alternative dispute resolution that you consider most suitable and the date by which you consider it reasonable for a full response to be made to your letter.

> **What is alternative dispute resolution?**
>
> Also known as ADR, this is a process that tries to enable parties with differences to come to an agreement instead of engaging in litigation and going to court.

A letter in response should be received from the other party to the dispute. Thereafter the parties should actively consider mediation as a method of dispute resolution. If mediation is attempted and fails the next stage would be to issue proceedings. Following proceedings being issued the parties need to define their claim and defence in documents generically described as statements of case. Following the conclusion of this stage the case will come before court for the first hearing: which is called a case management conference. At that hearing the court will make such directions as are proportionately and reasonably required to take the case forward. A typical timetable in a TOLATA claim will deal with disclosure, inspection, exchange of witness statements, the dates for trial and the valuation of the property that is the subject of the TOLATA proceedings. Disclosure is the process by which a party identifies in a list the relevant documents in the proceedings. It may come as a surprise to learn that relevant documents that have to be disclosed include documents that harm as well as support your case. Inspection is the process whereby copies of the documents are obtained. Further details about disclosure and inspection can be found in CPR Part 31. Evidence is given by witness statement and the time for mutual exchange and filing of statements will be set out. The relevant CPR dealing with evidence is CPR Part 32. In default of agreement a single joint expert valuer will usually be instructed to place a valuation on the property. If the case runs smoothly the dispute will then be dealt with at trial in front of a judge who will decide the outcome and deliver a judgment.

Starting proceedings

Proceedings are usually started in the county court at a hearing centre nearest to the property that handles civil claims. The rules on starting proceedings are to be found in CPR Part 7 and CPR Part 8. If the property is in one of the major metropolitan centres start your proceedings in the Chancery List. There are Chancery Lists in the Central London, Birmingham, Bristol, Cardiff, Leeds, Liverpool, Manchester and Newcastle County Courts. If you start proceedings in these courts, you will need to read The Chancery Guide, which can be found on the justice.gov.uk website. If the property is not within the major metropolitan centres the proceedings are best issue in the local county court. I would recommend where possible to issue in one of the Chancery Lists. The Chancery judges are more familiar with property law concepts than more generalist judges in the local county courts.

A difficulty frequently encountered is whether to issue a claim under Part 7 or Part 8. In short, if there is to be a substantial dispute of fact, the proceedings are best started under Part 7. It is sometimes difficult to say in advance whether a dispute will involve a substantial dispute of fact. If proceedings are started under Part 8, the court is able to give directions at the case management conference for the filing of statements of case to identify the issues in dispute. Part 7 and Part 8 claim forms can be downloaded at www.justice.gov.uk/courts/procedure-rules/civil/forms.

Of course you may not chose to issue proceedings; you may have proceedings issued against you. Ignoring the claim against you is never a good idea. You will need to respond to the claim form and to acknowledge service. A failure to do so may lead to judgment in default being entered against you. The rules on responding to claim forms and filing acknowledgements of service are contained in CPR Parts 9 and 10.

Statements of case

If a Part 7 claim is issued, particulars of claim are required to be drafted by the claimant. The defendant is required to respond to the particulars of claim in a document called a defence. The claimant's formal response to the defence is contained within a document known as a reply. The particulars of claim, defence and the reply are collectively called statements of case. The practice and procedure surrounding the drafting of statements of case is contained in CPR Part 16.

Drafting statements of case is technical. You need to frame your arguments concisely and with sufficient particularity. Drafting these documents is very much an art form in itself and there are also technical rules that need to be abided by. If you wish to draft your own statements of case, visit a law library and read Atkins Court Forms and the examples of draft statements of case in TOLATA claims. However the best advice I can give is to instruct a lawyer to draft your statements of case.

Of course sometimes whether inadvertently or by design, a statement of case may be difficult to understand. It is essential to understand exactly the way in which the other side may be putting their case so that you can prepare your case accordingly. Part 18 of the CPR provides a mechanism by which requests can be made for clarification of any matter and the provision of additional information. In the first instance a request is made for a voluntary response to the questionnaire. Usually a period of 21 days is given for the reply to be received. In the absence of a reply or a satisfactory reply an order may be made by the court requiring the Part 18 request to be answered. It is sensible to raise the requests well in advance of the case management conference so that a direction can be obtained, if necessary, for replies to be given to the request.

> **What is a claimant and a defendant?**
>
> If you start proceedings you are a claimant and if you oppose the proceedings you are a defendant.

When bringing a claim, you are required to identify the person or persons against whom the claim is being brought. In TOLATA proceedings the identity of the proposed defendant is usually straightforward; it is any person or company who owns or claims a legal or beneficial interest in the property against which a claim is being made.

Case management

CPR Part 26 deals with case management. When a defendant files a defence each party must file an allocation questionnaire. As a litigant in person you will be served a copy of the allocation questionnaire by the court along with a notice informing you when the questionnaire is required to be returned. Note that you are required to return an estimate of costs in accordance with para 6.4(1) of the Costs Practice Direction along with the allocation questionnaire. The purpose of the allocation questionnaire is to enable the court to allocate the case to one of three tracks; namely the small claims track, the fast track and the multi-track. Different procedural rules will apply depending on the track that a case is allocated to. TOLATA claims are invariably allocated to the multi-track and CPR Part 29 and PD29 are essential reading.

Case management directions may be made either by consent and approved by a court or made by the court at a case management conference. The directions will deal with amongst other things the need for a reply to a defence, any amendments to a statement of case, any outstanding Part 18 requests, the timing for disclosure, inspection and witness statements, the need for and the manner in which expert evidence is to be provided, the length of and date of trial. As a litigant in person, the other side if legally represented will prepare a case summary. If both parties are unrepresented the claimant ought to file a case summary in accordance with PD 29, para 5.7(1).

Trial

Representing yourself at trial especially with a barrister representing the other side will be a daunting experience. But, like going to the dentist, the anticipation is likely to be worse than the actual experience. The relevant parts of chapters 5 and 6 of this book should provide you with assistance and when reading those chapters you should note that in family proceedings a trial is euphemistically called a final hearing. There is no such pretence in a TOLATA claim. CPR Part 32 will also provide you with some useful background.

It is essential to prepare thoroughly for trial. You will need to work over a prolonged period of time. Don't leave all the preparatory work until very shortly before the trial date. Work long and hard on your skeleton argument. Try to read the document dispassionately in order to determine whether it is clear and makes all the points that you wish to make. Perhaps ask a lawyer or a trusted friend to read the document to critique it. Prepare your opening, cross-examination and closing speeches meticulously in advance. If you need some guidance on what you should be doing during the trial ... ask the judge! You may get a helpful response. Buy yourself some small sticky Post-It Notes to mark pages that you want to turn to. Note down what is being said in court by the judge, your opponent and any witnesses since you may need to refer to what was said in closing submissions.

Costs

It is essential to come to terms at the earliest opportunity with the fact that TOLATA claims are unlike family cases in that there is usually a clear winner and loser in the litigation and the loser will generally pay the winner's legal costs. You will likely be served with costs estimates that will give you some indication of the costs that you may have to meet if you lose the litigation. These costs estimates will focus your mind. The Costs Rules are contained in CPRs Parts 44 to 48. Read these rules carefully. Of course you may in fact win the litigation. You will need to pay particular regard to CPR Part 48.6 which deals with what costs may be claimed as a litigant in person. It is likely that you will at some stage during the process take some legal advice. Disbursements in respect of legal advice are recoverable in full if reasonable. You must remember to keep a record with receipt of all disbursements. You will also be able to recover up to two thirds of the amount that would have been allowed if you had been represented by a lawyer. You will need therefore to obtain evidence of the legal costs that would have been charged for the work that you carried out. How do you get this evidence? By obtaining an estimate for the cost that lawyers would charge for the work that you performed. In the absence of this evidence you will be left to recover a paltry sum by way of fixed costs.

You will also need to read CPR Part 36 *very carefully*. In short, Part 36 enables you to make offers in settlement that are not brought to the attention of the court until the conclusion of proceedings. Costs consequences follow if you are a claimant who fails to obtain a judgment more advantageous than a defendant's offer or if you are a claimant who obtains judgment against a defendant that is at least as advantageous to the claimant as the proposals contained in the claimant's Part 36 offer. The costs consequences include making the party who failed to beat the Part 36 offer pay costs of the litigation plus interest on the legal costs incurred at a rate not exceeding 10% above base. The rationale behind Part 36 is to encourage and facilitate the making of without prejudice offers to settle. The costs consequences of failing to beat a Part 36 offer are potentially very serious. It follows that careful consideration should be given to making Part 36 offers and reviewing whether to fight on after receiving such an offer. It may be that you decide that the making or reviewing of Part 36 offers is an appropriate time to obtain legal advice.

Appeals

At the end of the trial a judgment is handed down and an order of the court is made. Either party may potentially appeal the outcome of the case. In a TOLATA case the ground of appeal most frequently relied upon is an error in law made by the trial judge. If the judge applied the wrong legal tests to the case before him there is a good prospect of an appeal succeeding. It is possible to appeal against findings of fact made by the trial judge. However appeals against findings of fact are difficult.

The practice and procedure governing appeals is dealt with under CPR 52. Take legal advice to determine the basis on which you can appeal.

Further research

There are a number of sources that will assist you. We have identified in the text a small number of cases that really help explain some of the issues that you will be dealing with. We have also set out some books and websites that help with matters of practice and procedure. Insofar as the law is concerned textbooks that will help include Megarry and Wade's *The Law of Real Property* and Snell's *Equity*. These books are practitioners' texts and accordingly assume quite a bit of knowledge on behalf of the reader. They come with a warning that they will be difficult to understand. Try Hanbury & Martin *Modern Equity* (19th edition) and read the section dealing with *Kernott v Jones*. Case-law may be obtained free online at www.bailii.org.

Do's and don'ts

DOS

- Obtain a copy of the Land Registry title to the property. Go to www.landregistry.gov.uk

- If you are able to, obtain an up-to-date redemption statement for any mortgage secured against the property

- Using the average of three estate agent's market appraisals is a cost effective way to obtain a broad valuation of most residential property

- If you jointly own the property sever any beneficial joint tenancy so that your share in the property does not fall outside of your estate in the event of your death

✔ Keep records of payments made in respect of the property post separation to assist with any potential account

✔ Try mediation

✔ Do everything that you can to try to obtain funding for legal advice and representation. TOLATA claims are not easy to bring and defend if you are not a lawyer

✔ If you are not a legal owner of the property subject to the dispute you will need to ensure that the property is not sold or mortgaged without your interest being protected. Speak to a lawyer about entering the appropriate notice against the property at the Land Registry

DON'TS

✗ Don't take your case to trial without obtaining legal advice on the merits of your claim. There may be severe costs consequences if you lose!

Chapter 11

Obtaining Money for your Children from the Court

What you will learn

- When you can make an application through the courts rather than through the Child Maintenance Service

- How to make an application and what the court process will be like

- Examples of what things the courts will be looking for and how to run your case successfully

- How to make an application for the costs of running your case, how to recover your costs at the end and how to defend these type of applications

Introduction

The court has the power in certain circumstances to make orders for financial provision for children. You may hear this area of law referred to as Schedule 1 of the Children Act 1989. This is not an easy area of family law so be warned! Most of the time

Schedule 1 of the Children Act 1989 doesn't involve child maintenance. For that you need to make contact with the Child Maintenance Service.

> **What is the Child Maintenance Service?**
>
> This is a government service which deals with the organisation, calculation of and arrangements for payment of child maintenance when parents cannot agree how much child maintenance should be paid.

There is lots of useful information online to help you get started.

> For information about the Child Maintenance Service, including the choices available or for help setting up a new child maintenance arrangements go to:
>
> www.gov.uk/child-support-agency

Who qualifies?

Here are some examples of what can and what cannot be dealt with under Schedule 1 of the Children Act 1989.

> **WHAT CAN BE DEALT WITH**
>
> - Child maintenance only:
>   - If the parent without the day to day care of the child earns more than £104,000 net per annum
>   - For school fees
>   - For a disabled child

- — Where the child or the parent without day to day care lives abroad

- — If the child is over 18: for university fees/vocational training or if there are 'special circumstances'- see definition below

- — If the child is over 16 but under 18 and not in education

- Applications for the payment of a lump sum to cover capital expenses

- Settlement of property to provide a home for the child (and the primary carer of the child)

WHAT CANNNOT BE DEALT WITH

- Child maintenance if none of the exceptions above apply

- Provision of a pension

- Provide a home for a child if/when the child is over the age of 18 at the time of application unless the child is in tertiary education

- Make a lump sum payment to compensate for a perceived lack of child maintenance being received from the Child Maintenance Service

Although the above sets out the most common types of applications which fall under Schedule 1 of the Children Act 1989, it is not an exhaustive list and there may be other situations when the court does have the power to deal with your case. If in doubt you may want to speak to a solicitor or barrister.

What else do you need to know before making an application under Schedule 1?

Usually for unmarried parents: Although technically Schedule 1 of the Children Act 1989 can be used whether you are married or not, this area of law is usually used by unmarried parents (whether you are cohabiting or not). If you are married it is easier and more advantageous to make a different legal application to sort out the finances for both you and your children. There is a section in this book which can help.

Who can make an application? Any parent, legal guardian or special guardian can make an application or anyone who has a residence order made by court in their favour which is active at the time the application is made. So, if you are a grandparent you would not be able to make an application unless the child or children in question are living with you under a residence order. If you are a parent however you can always make an application, even if you are the parent who the children live with or have contact with less of the time. A major loophole is that gay and lesbian parents, even if they live together as a family with the child, cannot make a claim against anyone who is not the **biological** parent of the child.

The child in question must be under 18 years old. However, if the child is in tertiary education (ie post A-level or equivalent) or is undergoing training for a trade, profession or qualification (whether or not they are employed at the time) then regular maintenance payments may be extended to cover this. The court also **may** permit payment for a gap year either before or after tertiary education. This is also the case if 'special circumstances' apply. 'Special circumstances' is obviously a very wide term. Most usually it is applied to a child who has a physical or other disability when the expenses associated with living with that disability will be considered by the court in the widest possible terms. There is law which says that 'special circumstances' will not include either the extreme wealth of the father or the possibility that the child will not inherit on his death.

Financial and welfare benefit: Applications made under this section are not just made for the financial benefit of a child but can also be made for the child's welfare benefit. So for example if the child lives outside of the UK an application could include a fund to travel to see them for contact.

If your case does fall into one of the 'can apply' categories and you fulfil the other criteria to make an application, then read on!

How to make an application

The application process

If you need to make an application to court under Schedule 1 of the Children Act 1989 see the flowchart below for a step-by-step guide:

Application for child over 18
- By the child themselves;
- Undergoing tertiary education or training for a trade, profession or qualification OR where there are special circumstances;
- Where there is not a live periodical payments (i.e. regular payments of money for their benefit) order in place immediately before they are 16
- Where their parents are not living together

Application for child under 18
By a parent, guardian, special guardian or holder of a residence order

Make sure the other side have a copy of the application
- The Court will do this within 4 days after the application is issued
- Or you can do this yourself within 4 days and file a certificate of service (see http://www.familylaw.co.uk/system/uploads/attachments/0002/0941/FP6.pdf
- The Court will also tell you the date at which the first hearing will be held and this will be notified by the Court/you to the other side.

This application Form is called a Form A1
You can see a copy at http://www.familylaw.co.uk/system/uploads/attachments/0002/1193/Form_A1.pdf
You can't save this form but you can type on the form and print it

Issue your application at Court
- The cost is £200
- The proceedings officially 'start' when a Court Officer 'issues' the application i.e. processes it - there will be the date this has happened on the top of the application

Before the first hearing
- The first hearing will be between 12-16 weeks after the application was issued
- BEFORE that hearing both you and the Respondent to the application will need to have completed and exchanged Form E1 http://www.focus-mediation.co.uk/_webedit/uploaded-files/All%20Files/New%20Family%20Forms/Form%20E1%20Financial%20Statement%20(Co-Hab)%202013.pdf (together with the documents that form asks for). That should usually happen at least 35 days prior to the first hearing. You should also send that to the Court
- By 14 days before the first hearing you will need to prepare a concise chronology, schedule of issues and a financial questionnaire and send these to the Court

It is very important to remember that court proceedings are often seen as a big step particularly where children are involved; if there is any chance of reaching agreement either directly with the parent of your child or through mediation (see chapter 2, for more information) this is something to be encouraged. Your agreement can even be made into a court order. If you cannot don't worry, follow the steps above to make your application and read on.

> (i) **What is mediation?**
>
> This is a way of talking through your dispute without going to court. It will involve an independent third person who will help you both come to an agreement.

Three possible court hearings to determine the outcome of your case

STAGE 1	STAGE 2	STAGE 3
FIRST APPOINTMENT	FINANCIAL DISPUTE RESOLUTION (FDR)	FINAL HEARING
Sometimes the court combines these two stages where there is no need for any further directions		
Purpose: to make sure that the court has all the information necessary to progress to the next two stages.	**Purpose**: to negotiate an outcome between yourselves. Only two things can happen at an FDR – either the parties agree and the matter ends there or they disagree and the judge lists it for a trial.	The judge will make a decision about the outcome. You will need to give evidence to the court and make submissions about why the court should prefer your case.

STAGE 1	STAGE 2	STAGE 3
FIRST APPOINTMENT	FINANCIAL DISPUTE RESOLUTION (FDR)	FINAL HEARING
Focus: are the questions asked in the questionnaires appropriate questions? Do you need a valuation carried out of a property? Is there any other financial information that you require to effectively negotiate	**Focus**: both parties are encouraged to negotiate with help from the judge. The judge will not be the same judge as the judge at the final hearing. Parties make 'without prejudice' ie negotiating offers-these are a compromise and will not be shown to the court at a final hearing.	
Hearing: this is likely to be a short hearing just to deal with the directions the court should make in order for there to be an effective negotiation at the next stage.	**Hearing**: each side makes short submissions to support their cases and the judge will try and assist with, in their view, what may be a realistic outcome at trial. Parties will be strongly encouraged to compromise and think realistically about their cases.	

There is further, more detailed help in this book about the three different stages of court proceedings. If you are unclear about anything, it may be helpful to see a specialist family lawyer to talk things through or to see if they can assist you with the preparation of any paperwork.

What the court will take into account when deciding your case

As you may expect, each case has its own nuances. This section of the chapter intends to talk very generally about claims under

Schedule 1 of the Children Act 1989 before moving on to some more specific examples dependent on the type of application being made.

There are a wide range of factors that a court will take into consideration when looking at your case. Because of the way English law works, some of those factors are set out in the law that Parliament makes under Schedule 1 of the Children Act 1989. Other factors are set out in the precedents that the different courts in England make. General guidance is set out below, however there may be more specific law that applies to your particular circumstances. If in doubt, speak to a family law specialist.

Factors set out in Schedule 1 of the Children Act 1989

Factors applicable to you and the person that you are making the application against: the court will look at the following applicable to you and the person that you are making a claim against. The court has regard to these factors at the time of the application but also in the foreseeable future:

- Your income and their income.

- Both of your earning capacities. This is a matter which the court will make a decision about if there is dispute. The court will, within reason, expect both parties to be maximising their earning capacity. If you care full time for a small baby then the court may decide it is not reasonable for you to work now but that maybe you can do in the future; if your children are at school, it may be reasonable for you to work in school hours, or if older perhaps full time.

- Any property that you own or the other person owns.

- Any other financial assets that you or the other person owns.

Conversely, the court will also look at the 'financial needs, obligations and responsibilities' which each of you have. So, for example, if the person you are making a claim against is married with three other children then the court is not going to simply ignore the obligations and responsibilities which they will have to that family. They will be balanced by the court against the financial needs of the child in question.

Factors applicable to your child: The court will also look at:

- the financial needs of the child; and
- the income, earning capacity (if any), property and other financial resources of the child.

In most cases your child won't have any income or financial resources. This criterion may however apply to a child who is over the age of 18 and, say, trying to obtain some money to be assisted at university. It may be reasonable in those circumstances for them to get a part time job in the holidays to help with their university costs.

Where it is relevant the court will also look at:

- any physical or mental disability of the child; and
- the manner in which the child was being, or was expected to be, educated or trained.

In the case of the latter criteria this is only relevant where the court is going to be asked to make financial provision available for school fees, university fees or for other training.

Two factors applicable to lump sums only: in addition to the factor set out above, Schedule 1 of the Children Act 1989 also requires the court to address when considering making an order for a lump sum whether there are any capital expenses which have been incurred:

- in connection with the birth of a child or in maintaining a child; and

- reasonably incurred before the making of an order.

So items of capital expenditure may be a cot, pram or baby car seat for example.

Factors set out in the case-law

Standard of living: although the law in Schedule 1 of the Children Act 1989 does not set it out, the standard of living of the person you are seeking to make a claim against is important. The case-law sets out the following propositions:

- The child is entitled to be brought up in circumstances that bear some sort of relationship with the current resources and current standard of living of the person you are seeking to claim money from.

- As a matter of public policy and where resources allow, the obligation on parents to support their children should be respected in such a way so as to reduce or even eliminate the need for children to be supported by public funds.

The money has to be for the benefit of the child: and not for the benefit of the mother. The court has issued a specific warning against parents who seek to claim something for their child but which can only be said to be for their benefit. Asking for a Mercedes sports car with titanium alloy wheels for a child suffering from a physical disability is an example of an item of capital expenditure that could only be said to be for the benefit of the parent rather than the child.

BUT the child's welfare also includes the needs of the parent caring for the child: the court has said that it is important that the child is cared for by a person who is in a position, both financially and generally to provide that caring. The fact that a child needs a carer enables account to be taken of the caring parent's needs as well. In some cases this may mean that the ability of a parent to earn money is circumscribed by the need to care for the child. If you only have a young child, it may be realistic to not be working at all or only working part time and in an appropriate case for the other parent to make up the income shortfall. As the child gets older there will be more compelling arguments for the person caring for the child to work more hours.

Length of your relationship: it makes no difference if your child was conceived as a result of a long and settled relationship or as the result of one night of passion! It will make no difference to the financial outcome, however long or short the relationship is.

Some specific examples

The court, as you can see from the above examples, has a fairly broad discretion as to what can be ordered and what cannot. To help, there is some more advice on the likely approach a court may make adopt in specific types of application.

Settlement of property and lump sum orders

These are used if there is concern about the housing situation of you and the child or if there is a significant difference in the standard of living between the parents. The court will usually try:

- To provide accommodation for the primary carer and the

child. This will be held under a legal mechanism whereby the property will revert back to the paying party at the time that the child reaches the age of 18 or finishes full time tertiary education.

- A capital allowance for setting up the home (including, in the right circumstances for a car as well).

These types of order can be made by the court in cases where someone has a modest income as well as in 'big' money cases. This is because the type of orders a court can make does not depend on their income as a magnetic factor but the level of capital that they have. So, even in cases where there may be **just** enough money to re-house both parties (including with a mortgage), a court has the power to make orders to bring this into effect.

If you are responding to a claim of this type **beware**: there is case-law which supports the view that you may have to sell your house to ensure that the applicant and the child are housed. You may therefore have to move to more modest accommodation or take on a mortgage to satisfy the applicant's claim.

It is very important to get specialist accountancy advice, not just at the outset but on a periodic basis during the lifetime of a settlement of property order. This is especially so if you are responding to a claim. There are potentially three aspects of taxation that may need to be taken into account by a court in looking at these types of cases:

- *Stamp duty land tax* – the purchase of a property attracts stamp duty land tax on a sliding scale dependent on the value of the property.

To see current rates go to:

www.hmrc.gov.uk/sdlt/intro/rates-thresholds.htm

- *Inheritance tax* – if a trust is created as a way of settling the property and notwithstanding that this is done during the lifetime of the settlor it will still be potentially liable to inheritance tax as it potentially reduces the value of the settlor's estate.

> **More information on inheritance tax can be found on the HM Revenue and Customs website at:**
>
> www.hmrc.gov.uk/inheritancetax/index.htm

- *Capital gains tax* – even at the outset this could be payable in circumstances where a UK resident has transferred property into a trust and
    - it is already owned by the settlor;
    - it is not his main residence;
    - there is already a significant gain standing on the property.

There may also be capital gains tax charged at the end of the trust. HM Revenue and Customs has further information.

> **For further information about issues relating to tax go to the HM Revenue and Customs website at:**
>
> www.hmrc.gov.uk/cgt/

Remember that the court can only make one settlement of property order: the court could not make an order for there to be one house where the child and the primary carer both spend school term time and then another where they spend time in the holidays for example. The house for the child and the primary carer to live in may include a joint tenancy. The court can also only **make** a settlement of property order for a child who is under 18, although it can make a lump sum order for a child over the age of 18. However, the duration of a property settlement order can extend beyond a child's 18th birthday where there are special circumstances or the child is still undertaking full-time education. For example if your child was going to university and they were also taking a gap year, the court can ensure that the property they live in as a result of any orders made when they are still under 18 will not have to be sold until they complete that university education. If they are over 18 however and require a lump sum for books/computer whilst at university then the court could make those orders post-18.

Whatever the nature of the lump sum order you are seeking, **it is very important to set out in a specific schedule the individual capital items the child may need** eg a car, piano, one-off medical treatment etc. Lump sums are usually calculated by reference to any specific and planned expenditure.

Capital costs incurred in connection with the birth of the child or in maintaining the child and reasonably incurred before an order can be made

As with all lump sums it is very important to set out a specific schedule of costs of individual capital items incurred in connection with the birth or maintaining the child before you made the application to the court. It would be helpful to prepare a schedule of specific capital items claimed for with receipts and a price lists attached to support the case you are making.

Remember that this only applies to **capital** costs, eg prams, cots, baby car seats etc, rather than ongoing expenditure for example on nursery fees.

Income provision – generally

Please remember to look at the checklist in the beginning of this chapter to see whether your case allows you to make an application – this is only in limited circumstances.

If you do qualify then the income provision is going to be an income stream, usually paid each month to meet the needs of you and the child. In cases where there is more money and where the standard of living is greater, then it is acceptable for those needs to be quite generous.

If you are making the application because the non primary carer earns over £104,000 net pa then you will need to apply to the Child Maintenance Service for an assessment before the court can make any orders. This is because, for the court to be able to deal with the matter, rather than the Child Maintenance Service, the court has to have an assessment from them for the **maximum** amount. Details about the Child Maintenance Service are given at the beginning of this chapter.

In the first instance the court will be looking for payments to be made only until the child's 17th birthday, unless the court think it's right in the circumstances to specify a later date. The court cannot extend the payments beyond a child's 18th birthday unless:

- the child is in education or undergoing training for a trade, profession or vocation (whether or not in gainful employment), **OR**
- there are special circumstances which justify the making of the order beyond 18 years old.

'Special circumstances' includes a disability – more on this is set out below.

Finally, it is important to remember:

- An order for maintenance payments ceases on the death of the person making the payments.

- If the parent making the payments cohabits with the person who has received the payments for 6 months or more then any order for maintenance payments will cease to have effect.

- Either parent can go, after 12 months to the Child Maintenance Service to secure an assessment that will 'trump' any court order.

When looking at what a suitable income provision may be the court will, in certain circumstances, consider a carer's allowance for the person who may have had to give up work to look after the child or nanny's fees if the primary carer has to work.

Remember to draw up a realistic budget supported by examples (eg, if you usually shop at a specific supermarket tell the court this so that they understand where your figures come from). The court will scrutinise this budget and take a broad, common-sense assessment of what they think may be appropriate. The determining factor is going to be the needs of the individual child in light of the available resources. The aspirations of a primary carer for an enhanced lifestyle is not something that the court would consider as an appropriate benchmark from which to award maintenance payments.

Whether you are the person making the application or the person responding to an application, it is important to remember that where the person you are seeking to make the claim against has little by way of income but uses capital to maintain a certain lifestyle then maintenance payments can be made out of capital resources as well.

Income provision – where the child or non primary carer live abroad

In cases where the child or the parent who does not care for the child on a daily basis, lives abroad, but their income is less than £104,000 net pa the court, in calculating appropriate maintenance will normally use as their starting point the way that the Child Maintenance Service would make an assessment.

> For a helpful calculator to give you an estimate of what that amount may be visit:
>
> www.cmoptions.org/en/calculator/

School fees, university fees and training

There is no magic to a school fees award. If the parents have agreed that the child should be trained/educated in a particular way and the money is there to do this then there is generally little argument over applications of this type.

Disputes sometimes arise where one person wishes for the child to be privately educated and the other does not or the level of private education is disagreed: the costs of Harrow or Eton may be considerably more than other private schools. If there is disagreement then the court is not only going to pay consideration to Schedule 1 of the Children Act 1989 but also to section 1 and section 8 of the Children Act 1989. This is because as well as issuing an application under Schedule 1 of the Children Act 1989 you will also have to make an application for a 'specific issue order' ie, for the court to determine in light of all the evidence where the child should be educated. This will include consideration of all aspects of the child's welfare, any agreement between the parties as to how the child was to be educated as well as looking at the financial implications of the proposed education. There is more on making an application for a 'specific issue' order in chapter 8 of this book.

Disabled children

Where the subject of the application is a disabled child then maintenance payments and lump sum payments may be made beyond that child's 18th birthday and a settlement of property order may extend past the child's 18th birthday.

The disability can be physical or mental and the expenses arising as a result of that disability will be assessed by the court in the broadest sense.

Costs

You may wish to have some legal advice to assist you in some or all of your case. However, one of the biggest bars to obtaining satisfactory legal advice is the cost. In proceedings under Schedule 1 of the Children Act 1989 costs are something that the court can, in appropriate circumstances, help with. There are two things to consider:

- the costs of running your case (or 'interim' provision); and

- pursuing costs at the end of the case and whether the court can make costs orders against you.

The costs of running your case

In the past making an order for the respondent to pay for your legal fees was something that a court could not do. Helpfully, that position has now changed as it seemed unfair that the financially stronger person could be entitled to legal advice and representation whilst the financially weaker person was not.

One thing you should consider however is that the court will usually only make a lump sum order for your legal costs to be paid. An order for legal costs to be satisfied by an order for periodical payments would require the case to fall within the circumstances where 'income' orders are allowed. In the ordinary case therefore the initial factor to take into account is that the application will only have a chance of success if there are financial resources from which a lump sum could be paid.

The court will expect the person who is making an application for a legal costs allowance to:

- satisfy the court that they do not have assets of their own they can use or if they do;

- that they cannot reasonably deploy some of their assets (either directly or as the means of raising a loan) to fund legal costs;

- establish that they cannot enter into an agreement with a solicitor to take their costs at the end of the case, after the court has decided how much should be awarded; and

- show that they are unable to reasonably obtain funding from a company offering legal loans.

Procedure

If you do feel that there are no other options for funding legal advice or representation other than making an application to the court then the application form is an FP2 Application Notice under Part 18 of the Family Procedure Rules 2010.

> **For find the FP2 Application Notice go to:**
>
> http://www.familylaw.co.uk/system/uploads/attachments/0002/0937/FP2.pdf

Note that on this form you need to set out:

- What order you are seeking and why; and
- A draft order to the application

It may be helpful when you set out what order you are seeking to do a **short written statement** that you attach to your application form setting out:

- How much money you need and why (ie, that you have been to solicitors and they have told you their fees will be £x).
- That you have no assets that you could use to fund legal fees and cannot get help from your family or if you do that it is not reasonable to use those assets for your legal costs.
- That the solicitors you have spoken to are not prepared to enter into a financial arrangement with you that fees could be recovered at the end of the case.
- That you are not able to get litigation loan funding, or that the terms of such a funding arrangement are onerous.

> ⓘ **What is litigation loan funding?**
>
> Companies will offer a service whereby they will fund your legal costs and advance sums to you on the basis that this is paid back at the end of the court proceedings with interest.

Draft order: remember to include the name of the court and the case number, together with your name and the name of the person you are asking for money from. An example of a draft order is set out below:

In the [insert name] County Court   Case Number: [insert]

B E T W E E N:-

            MISS X   Applicant

            And

            MR Y   Respondent

Draft ORDER

BEFORE District Judge [leave blank] sitting at the [insert name of court] on [insert date]

IT IS ORDERED:

1. By [date] the Respondent shall pay or cause to be paid the sum of [insert amount] to the Applicant to obtain legal assistance in these proceedings.

2. Costs in the application [if you have incurred legal costs in making the application you may, in appropriate circumstances want to ask the other side to pay those costs. In that case you would want to put *'the Respondent do pay the costs of this application, to be summarily assessed as £[insert amount of costs expended].'*]

This type of application may seem a little daunting. Some solicitors firms are prepared to assist, advise and represent a client if such an application needs to be made, with the costs of that only payable afterwards. It may be helpful to speak to a solicitor about this. Consider also instructing a direct access barrister.

If you are responding to a claim of this type and do not have a legal representative to assist you, consider the following points:

- Lump sum interim costs allowances are only made in a handful of situations – why should your case be the exception? Do you have the funds to satisfy the claim the other side are making? What would be the impact on you if an interim costs award was made? Has the person applying sufficiently demonstrated that they cannot get funds in any other way?

- The legal costs given to the other side are not likely to be recovered – how does that affect your financial situation?

- What are the merits of the other side's case? Do they appear to be over-zealous to litigate so that you could say that the application is made other than for the benefit of the child? Can you show that they are a 'gold digger' perhaps looking at your lifestyle and trying to use the child to get as much for themselves as possible?

Costs orders at the end of proceedings

You will have seen earlier in this book that it is normally unusual for a court to order any costs to be paid by the 'losing' party to the 'winning' party at the end of court proceedings. This is the same in proceedings under Schedule 1 of the Children Act 1989, although there is perhaps a little more leeway for a costs order to be made. In particular, the factors that the court has to consider include:

- All the circumstances.

- The conduct of all the parties (see below).

- Whether the person applying for costs has succeeded in their case, even if they have not been wholly successful.

- <u>Any</u> offer to settle which was made previously.

Remember to always make sensible offers on costs. It is important to remember that you can preserve your position on costs by making sensible offers to settle the case. If you make these offers 'without prejudice save as to costs' the judge at a final hearing wouldn't be able to see the offer until discussing costs. For example imagine you were asking for a £250,000 house and a £50,000 capital fund for furnishings and a car. At trial the judge awards you £240,000 for a house and £30,000 for furnishings and a car. If you had written to the other side saying that you would settle for £200,000 plus a £30,000 capital fund seven months before the hearing, you may want to argue that the seven months of litigation post that offer should be taken into account by the court making a costs award against the other side.

It is important to remember to do this because there are cases where the person applying on behalf of the child has secured a 'win' in court but the court has not let them recover costs from the other side. The principle concern in recent cases has been the fact that there had not been any 'without prejudice save as to costs' offers which may have protected their position.

You may want to speak to a solicitor or barrister even if this is just to get advice about what a sensible offer may be.

What does the 'conduct' of the parties mean? This applies to the litigation conduct of the parties throughout the proceedings. The court is going to look at:

- Whether the parties have properly tried to speak about the case before resorting to court proceedings, including (but not limited to) setting out their case and what they are seeking properly in writing as well as seeing whether reasonable steps were taken to see if agreement can be reached.

- Whether it was reasonable for one party to pursue a particular allegation or issue.

- The manner in which one party has pursued or defended their case or a particular allegation or issue.

- If you are the person applying to the court, whether you have exaggerated your claim, even if you have been partly succeeded.

Checklist of things to think about if making or responding to a claim

If you are the person making the claim for the benefit of the child

Don't be put off if the person you are making the claim against is not a millionaire! Although a lot of cases in this area concern the wealthy few, where there is enough money to make a claim and a clear need for the child then it is perfectly possible to make a successful application.

This recent case study may be a helpful real life example of when an award was made in a more 'modest' money case.

> Miss X and her daughter Y (age 4) had to live with Mr Z, the father of the child, even though the relationship had broken down as they had not got the money to live elsewhere. Mr Z lived in a house (in London) which he owned in his sole name worth £650,000 but had no income other than his pension. He had no other savings. Although Miss X had savings of £250,000 and a potential lump sum due to her from a pension (of some £150,000) which she could draw on at the time, the effect of drawing this amount from her pension would render her incapable of meeting the income needs of herself and her daughter. She could not get a mortgage. This was not a case in which Mr Z fell into the category of Respondents against whom an award for maintenance could be made by the court (only the

Child Maintenance Service could do this). The court ordered that Mr Z should provide the mother with a lump sum of £150,000, together with £50,000 for furnishings. The effect of this was that Mr Z would have to sell his house which he had had since 1990. The relationship with Miss X had only been ongoing since 2007. He would also have to downsize to satisfy the claim as he could not secure a mortgage given his age. Although the property that Miss X and her daughter bought would revert back to Mr Z when Y reached the age of 18, this was going to be in 14 years time when Mr Z would be 75.

This example shows the real desire of the court to make orders for the benefit of the child, seemingly to the detriment of the respondent in the right circumstances.

- Consider whether you could claim a costs allowance (although be mindful of the limited circumstances when this would be appropriate and follow the advice given in the section on 'costs' above).

- When formulating the claim think laterally (particularly if there are special circumstances such as a disabled child) but as a minimum consider housing costs and a lump sum to cover costs of moving/refurbishment and other capital expenditure required. Provide detailed, realistic schedules to evidence the claim throughout the proceedings.

- When making your claim think carefully about the standard of living of the other parent and make your budget reflective of that. If you are one of the limited categories of people able to ask for an income award from the responding party, be careful to back this up with receipts/evidence. Don't forget that, so long as you can show it is 'for the benefit of the child' a carer's allowance is perfectly acceptable.

- Think realistically about the merits of the case at an early stage and make 'without prejudice save as to costs' offers to try and protect your position on costs.

- You should always take advice from a tax expert on the implications of, in particular, settlement of property awards.

If you are the person responding to a claim

- Think critically about the merits of the other side's case. Are the items they are asking for reasonable or are they more for their own benefit rather than for the child's benefit?

- Can the matter be settled or your position protected by a well-timed and realistic offer on a 'without prejudice, save as to costs' basis?

- So long as there is enough money there, in most small/medium asset cases there will be, probably as a minimum, a need to provide a suitable housing fund for the applicant/child. The case study in the above section is a true-life example – for the person responding to the claim this may have been a very difficult decision to swallow, despite the fact the money was coming back in 14 years time. The court does have the power to make some robust orders.

- If there is more money available then be aware that the housing fund for the child and the applicant may bear some resemblance to your own standard of living and may include other capital items such as a car for transporting the child.

- If you are responding to a claim where there is also a claim for income, make sure that the budget the applicant produces is realistic. Perhaps you want to produce your own budget with figures from suitable shops as to what a better figure may be.

- Check to see whether the applicant is applying for a costs allowance in circumstances where they have not explored other alternatives, or where the merits of the case do not justify such an award or where the impact on you is going to be profound.

- It is even more important for people responding to a claim to take tax advice than those making a claim. This is because settlement of property awards in particular can mean there are additional extras to be paid by way of tax that you should be aware of. Speak to a tax advisor if you are in any doubt.

Chapter 12

Enforcement of Court Orders

What you will learn

- What steps you can take when a person is not complying with the terms of a court order
- Specific enforcement action that you may consider where the court order relates to a Children Act 1989 case
- Specific enforcement action that you may consider where the court order relates to a financial case
- Some examples of the different forms of enforcement action
- Procedural hints and tips to assist you in making or defending an enforcement application

Introduction: what to do if the other side fails to comply with a court order – 'enforcement'

It important that you read court orders carefully and make sure that you understand what is required of you, and what the consequences are if you (or another person who is a party to/the subject of the court order) do not comply with the terms of the order.

In the vast majority of cases, orders made by the court are complied with. There are, however, occasions when it becomes necessary to return a case to court in an attempt to force the other party to comply with the court order. This is known as 'enforcement'.

It can also be necessary to enforce a formal undertaking (a solemn, binding promise given to the court and recorded appropriately on Form N117).

It should be said, at the outset, that enforcement is one of the more technical areas of law in which legal advice is particularly worthwhile.

If you find yourself in the position where a court order in your favour is not being complied with, or you find yourself on the receiving end of an enforcement application, it is useful to know that there there are a variety of penalties and sanctions that the court can use in an attempt to force a person to comply with a court order, or punish them for failing to do so.

Succeeding in an enforcement application is, in large part, about complying with the rules and getting the technicalities right. This chapter aims to provide you with some useful 'hints and tips' about how to make or defend yourself against an enforcement application.

Enforcement of orders relating to children (including child arrangements orders and other orders under the Children Act 1989)

There can be many reasons why a person feels that they have no choice but to apply for an order for enforcement of a court order which is not being complied with by another person.

The reasons can include the failure to make a child available on time or at all, to spend time with a person named in the court order, which is a breach of the court order. Or there may be some other breach of a specific term of the child arrangements order.

The starting point – the importance of the warning notice

The starting point before you consider the enforcement of a child arrangements order or other Children Act 1989 court order is to check whether a warning notice was attached to the court order in the first place.

The warning notice on the court order ought to state something like this:

WARNING NOTICE to: [   ]

Where a child arrangements order is in force: if you do not comply with this child arrangements order –

You may be held in contempt of court and be committed to prison or fined; and/or

The Court may make an order requiring you to undertake unpaid work ('an enforcement order') and/or an order that you pay financial compensation

> **What is contempt of court?**
>
> Contempt of court is an offence for being disobedient to a court of law. Examples of contempt of court are failing to comply with an order or request of the court, withholding evidence or being disruptive during court proceedings. If you are found to be in contempt of court you may be fined or sent to prison.

Where the court makes or varies (changes) for example, a child arrangements order, it must attach a notice warning of the consequences of failing to comply with the order.

What happens if you do not comply with a child arrangements order or other Children Act 1989 court order?

The court has a wide range of powers where a person has not complied with (and is therefore in breach of) the child arrangements order / Children Act 1989 court order without reasonable excuse. The range of the court's powers as a result of an application for enforcement proceedings includes the following (not an exhaustive list):

- Referral of the parents to a separated parents information program, or equivalent, or mediation (see Activity Directions and Activity Conditions below).

- Variation of the child arrangements order / court order (changing any of the terms of the order upon a consideration of the child's best interests).

- Enforcement order or suspended enforcement order.

- An order for compensation for financial loss.

- Committal to prison.

- A fine.

- An order transferring who the child lives with.

Before getting to the stage of making an application for enforcement proceedings, the court is likely to try and make orders to persuade the relevant person to comply with the court order first. These orders include:

- Activity directions (under section 11A, CA 1989).

- Activity conditions (under section 11C, CA 1989).

> **(i) What is an activity direction?**
>
> It is a direction requiring a person who is a party to the proceedings to take part in an activity that would in the court's opinion help to establish, maintain or improve the involvement in the life of the child of that person or another party to the proceedings.
>
> The direction sets out which activity the person is to undertake and which service will provide that activity. The aim is to help the person to understand the importance of complying with the court order and making it work.

What factors does the court consider when deciding whether or not to make an activity direction?

The welfare of the child is the court's paramount (most important) consideration.

Are there any limits on making an activity direction?

Yes. An activity direction cannot require a person to:

- Undergo medical or psychiatric treatment, examination or assessment.

- Take part in mediation.

> **(i) What is an activity condition?**
>
> An activity condition is a condition imposed by the child arrangements order which requires a person to take part in

> an activity that would in the court's opinion help to establish, maintain or improve the involvement in the life of the child concerned of that person or another party to the proceedings.
>
> The activity condition must specify the activity and the service providing the activity.
>
> The aim is also to help the person to understand the importance of complying with the court order and making it work.

What types of activities may be included?

There are a variety of activities, but broadly they fall within the following categories of programmes, classes and counselling or guidance sessions in order to:

- Assist a person to establish, maintain or improve contact with the child; or

- Address violent behaviour; or

- Enable or facilitate involvement in a child's life; or

- Attend information sessions or advice about making arrangements for involvement in the child's life, including by mediation.

- Essentially there are three primary examples activity directions:

    (1) Information meetings about mediation – provided by the Legal Aid Agency approved providers on a one-off basis, free of charge to both parties if either party is publicly funded. The parties will be required to participate, but can initially be seen separately.

(2) Separated parents information programmes – provided by Cafcass commissioned providers, typically involving group sessions lasting for a total of four hours, free of charge to all. Generally both parties are required to participate. Any programmes will be delivered to them separately.

(3) Domestic violence prevention programs – run by Cafcass commissioned providers, involving an intensive program of 60 hours of intervention.

Cafcass are likely to recommend the activity that they think is suitable to address the issues/problem that has arisen or is likely to arise in the case.

> (i) **What is Cafcass?**
>
> This is an organisation known as the Children and Family Court Advisory and Support Service. Every year Cafcass helps over 140,000 children and young people who are going through care or adoption proceedings, or whose parents have separated and are unable to agree about future arrangements for their children. Cafcass is the voice of children in the family courts and helps to ensure that children's welfare is put first during proceedings. http://www.cafcass.gov.uk/

Who can have an activity direction or an activity condition imposed upon them?

There are three types of people:

- A person with whom the child lives or is to live.

- A person who's contact with the child is provided for in the child arrangements order.

- A person upon whom an activity condition has already been imposed.

When can the court make an activity direction or activity condition regarding enforcement?

There are two primary situations:

- Where a person has failed to comply with a provision of the child arrangements order, or
- Where the court is considering what steps to take because of a person's failure to comply with a provision of a child arrangements order (enforcement proceedings).

When can the court make an activity direction or activity condition?

Before making an activity direction or imposing an activity condition the court must be satisfied of the following four matters:

(1) That the proposed activity is appropriate in the circumstances of the case.

(2) That the service provider for the activity is suitable.

(3) That the location of the proposed activity is in a place where the person can reasonably be expected to travel to.

(4) The court must consider the likely effects of the direction upon the subject person in particular to include: potential conflict with a person's religious beliefs, any interference with working hours or studying hours.

The court can ask a Cafcass officer to provide information about the four matters above.

The court can ask a Cafcass officer to monitor compliance with an activity direction or an activity condition and to provide a report back to the court if there is any failure to comply.

Where activity conditions and activity directions are either not appropriate, or do not have the desired effect, the court will consider other enforcement measures.

When is the court prevented from making an activity direction or activity condition?

There are three general circumstances namely:

- The court cannot impose an activity condition or direction on a person who is a child unless the person who is the child is also the parent of the subject child.

- The court cannot impose an activity condition or direction on a person where the child arrangements order is an excepted order (which usually involves orders related to adoption orders).

- The court cannot impose an activity condition or direction unless the person is habitually resident in England and Wales, and if the court does make a contact activity direction it will cease to have any effect if the person is no longer habitually resident in England and Wales.

What if your ex partner is breaching the terms of the child arrangements order (or the previous contact order) and there is no warning notice attached?

In those circumstances you would be wise to apply for a warning notice to be attached to the order.

The application is made using Form C78.

The procedure is set out in the Family Procedure Rules 2010, Rule 12.33. In summary:

- The application shall be made without notice (without the need to inform the other party that you are making the application, just make the application to the court).

- The court may deal with the application without having a court hearing.

- The court may decide to deal with the application at a court hearing, in which case steps will be taken to ensure that the other party is properly given notice of the application and the forthcoming court hearing.

You will make this application to the Family Court.

If you are faced with receiving a Form C78 application, then you should ensure that you obtain a copy of the original court order.

Enforcement orders

What must the court be satisfied about in order to grant an enforcement order?

Here are seven important factors to consider (there may be other/different relevant factors depending upon the particular circumstances of the case):

(1) The court cannot make an enforcement order unless the person concerned has received a warning notice, or if the person has been otherwise informed of the terms of the warning notice.

(2) The court must be satisfied beyond reasonable doubt that a person has failed to comply with the provision of the child arrangements order. If that is proven, then the court may make an enforcement order imposing on the person an unpaid work requirement.

(3) The court must be satisfied that making an enforcement order is necessary to secure the person's compliance with the child arrangements order.

(4) The court must be satisfied that the likely effect on the person of the enforcement order being made, is proportionate to the seriousness of the breach of the child arrangements order.

(5) Before making an enforcement order, the court must be satisfied that provision for the person to undertake unpaid work can be made in the local justice area that the person lives within.

(6) The court must be satisfied that regarding the breach, it has considered information about the person and the likely effect of the enforcement order upon him.

(7) When making an enforcement order in relation to a child arrangements order, the court must take into account the welfare of the child who is the subject of the child arrangements order. However, the welfare of the child is not the court's paramount consideration for an enforcement order application.

The court does have the power to suspend an enforcement order for as long as it thinks fit. Sometimes this course of action can secure compliance with a court order without the need for the suspended sentence to be activated.

The court may also make more than one enforcement order in relation to the same person on the same occasion.

Is there a defence to an enforcement order application?

Yes. If you have a reasonable excuse for failing to comply with a provision in the child arrangements order, and that reason is accepted by the court, then the court is unlikely to make an enforcement order.

Who has to prove 'reasonable excuse'?

The person who is claiming to have a reasonable excuse must prove that to the court. Usually this information is provided in writing in the form a witness statement and then by giving oral evidence at a court hearing.

The court must be satisfied on the balance of probabilities (that is, the court must be satisfied that the reasonable excuse is more likely than not to be the truth).

Some important facts about enforcement orders

There are points to remember about enforcement orders including:

- The maximum number of hours of unpaid work that a court can impose is currently 200 hours. The minimum number of hours of unpaid work is currently 14 hours.

- The court may ask a Cafcass officer to monitor, or arrange for the monitoring of a person's compliance with an enforcement order, and to report to the court about any failure to comply or about any unsuitability to undertake the unpaid work.

- Where the court makes an enforcement order, the court

Enforcement of Court Orders 329

must attach a warning notice setting out the consequences of breaching the order, for example the imposition of a further enforcement order, enhancement of the existing enforcement order or use of contempt of court sanctions.

- If the terms of the enforcement order are breached (not complied with once the order is made), then the matter can be brought back to court and the court may amend the original order to make it more onerous or impose another enforcement order.

It is useful to refer to the Children Act 1989, Schedule A1: Enforcement Orders for further reading on this matter.

Committal to prison for contempt

It is extremely important to ensure that the evidence and procedure rules are followed strictly regarding contempt proceedings (see below under the Contempt of Court and Enforcement of finances section for a discussion of this).

Are there any limitations on the court's ability to make an enforcement order?

Yes. There are three primary situations:

- A court cannot make an enforcement order against the person who has failed to comply with the provision of a child arrangements order unless that person is at least 18 years old.

- The court cannot make an enforcement order where the child arrangements order is an excepted order (which usually involves orders related to adoption orders).

- The court cannot make an enforcement order unless the

person is habitually resident in England and Wales, and if the court does make an enforcement order it will cease to have any effect if the person is no longer habitually resident in England and Wales.

Compensation for financial loss

If the court is satisfied that:

- a person who is subject to a child arrangements order has failed to comply with the provisions of a child arrangements order; and

- failure to comply has caused another person to suffer financial loss as a result.

Then the court can make an order requiring the person in breach to pay the affected person compensation for his financial loss.

Is there a defence to an application for compensation for financial loss?

Yes. If the person has a reasonable excuse for failing to comply with the provision of the child arrangements order, and that is accepted by the court, then the court is unlikely to make an order of compensation for financial loss.

Who has to prove reasonable excuse?

The person who is claiming to have a reasonable excuse must prove that to the court.

The court must be satisfied on the balance of probabilities (that is, court must be satisfied that the reasonable excuse is more likely than not to be the truth).

If the application is successful, how much compensation will be received?

The amount of compensation cannot be more than the amount of the applicant's financial loss. The actual figure will be determined by the court.

How will the court determine how much compensation should be paid?

The court must take into account two primary factors:

- the person's financial circumstances, and
- the welfare of the child.

How to make an application for an enforcement order or an application for an order for financial compensation

The application for an enforcement order or for an order for financial compensation must be made on Form C79 by a person who falls in the following criteria:

- A person who the child lives with.
- A person who spends time with/has indirect contact with the child pursuant to a child arrangements order.
- An individual who is already subject to an activity direction or activity condition or the child himself.

Costs

You must never forget that the court has the power to make a costs order against another party, that is an order requiring one party to pay the other party's legal costs. Reference ought to be made to chapter 8 for further discussion about costs.

Contempt of court (including the powers to impose a fine / committal to prison)

The current scheme for enforcement orders sits alongside the court's general power to impose sanctions for contempt of court, therefore it remains open to a court to consider imposing a fine or a custodial sentence for any breach of a child arrangements order relating to contact that may be proved in committal or family proceedings.

> **What is contempt of court?**
>
> Contempt of court is an offence for being disobedient to a court of law. Examples of contempt of court are failing to comply with an order or request of the court, withholding evidence or being disruptive during court proceedings. If you are found to be in contempt of court you may be fined or sent to prison.

Similarly to the other forms of enforcement, it must be proven that a person has been given advance notice of the consequences of a breach of the court order.

For cases where a warning notice was not attached to an enforcement order, this is normally achieved by the attachment of a penal notice to the order. Breach of such an order may then give rise to committal proceedings.

The courts have jurisdiction to punish a breach of any order by way of a fine of up to £2,500 or by committal to prison for up to two years in contempt proceedings. It is a matter for the court which is the most appropriate form of sanction.

Contempt of court sanctions are seen as remedies of last resort.

Order transferring who the child lives with

Transfer of residence is often remedy of last resort, where the court concludes that often (although not always) the resident parent is intent on frustrating the order which seeks to provide a child with the chance to spend time with the person specified within the order. The case of *Re S (Transfer of Residence)* [2010] 1 FLR 1785 is a useful one to consider if this method is under consideration.

Useful resources

If you do need further information, here is a list of resources that will be helpful:

- Children Act 1989 in particular: section 1, section 8 and section 11, Schedule A1

- Contempt of Court Act 1981, section 14(2)

- European Convention on Human Rights, in particular Articles 6 and 8

- Family Procedure Rules 2010, in particular Rules 12 and 37 and their associated Practice Directions

- Practice Direction 12B – Child Arrangements Programme, paragraph 21 – Enforcement of Child Arrangements

- Practice Direction 12N – Enforcement of Children

Act 1989 Child Arrangements Orders: Disclosure of information to officers of the National Probation Service (High Court and county court)

- Useful case-law includes: *Hale v Tanner* [2000] 1 WLR 2377; *Hammerton v Hammerton* [2007] EWCA Civ 248; *Re L-W (Enforcement & Committal: Contact)* [2010] EWCA Civ 1253; *Re Jones (Alleged Contempt of Court)* [2013] EWHC 2579 (Fam)

- Guidance to Cafcass practitioners on their roles in supporting the courts in their use of the section 11 A-P provisions: http://www.norfolkfamilyjusticeboard.org/publications/cafcass_guidance_on_the_operation_of_contact_enforcement_provisions_dec_2008.pdf

Enforcement of orders relating to finances

Methods of enforcement

Of the many methods of enforcement in this area, it is useful to break them down into the following groups (not an exhaustive list):

- methods that remove an uncooperative party from the equation;
- raising money by selling or transferring the other party's assets;
- imposing a fine or imprisonment, ie those that seek to 'punish' or threaten the liberty of the other party.

Starting point – essential words

Understanding how enforcement works is made difficult because of the number of technical terms that continue to be used. These include the following:

- 'Arrears' – an amount that has already fallen due and is therefore owing.

- 'Contemnor' – someone who has breached an order or direction made by the court and is therefore in 'contempt of court'.

- 'Judgment creditor' – this is the person who the order says should receive money.

- 'Judgment debtor' – this is the person who the order says should pay money.

Does the person in breach of the order have any assets? – Obtaining information from judgment debtors

Whichever method of enforcement is going to be appropriate, it is usually a good idea to start out by gaining an impression of the financial position of the party against whom you wish to enforce.

This can be done by requiring the other party to attend court to provide information about their finances for the purposes of enforcement.

In order to obtain the information the following applications can be made:

- Make an application under Part 33.3 of the Family

Procedure Rules 2010 for enforcement by 'such method as the court considers appropriate'.

- Or make an application in Form N316, which details the information required.

Both of which will have the effect that the debtor attend the court for questioning.

Which enforcement method should I use and how do I make my application?

A freestanding application to obtain information from a judgment debtor is only necessary if you are intending to apply for a specific method of enforcement. This is because Part 33.3 of the Family Procedure Rules 2010 gives the party who is owed money the option of either specifying the method of enforcement they seek, or applying in general terms for 'such method of enforcement as the court may consider appropriate'. That application will *automatically* result in an order being made for the party owing the money to attend court to provide information. For the non-lawyer, this form of application is usually the most sensible.

If a general application is to be made it should be made in Form D50K. Part 33.3 of the Family Procedure Rules 2010 specifies what should be included in the application.

Can I claim interest?

Yes. If you are making a claim for interest to be paid on the debt, then you must set out the total amount of the interest you are claiming and set out how you have calculated that amount.

It is also worth noting at the outset that, in the event that you are seeking to enforce arrears that were incurred more than a year ago, you will need the permission of the court before an enforcement application can be made in respect of those arrears. Such an application must be made in advance and in accordance with Part 18 of the Family Procedure Rules 2010 using Form D11. A statement setting out the amount of the arrears and when they were incurred must accompany the application.

How can I remove an uncooperative party from the equation?

If a person will not sign the paperwork required to put the court order into effect, for example, to sell or transfer a property, then the court can nominate another person to do so, usually a judge.

The application should be made in accordance with Part 18 of the Family Procedure Rules 2010. In advance of making the application, the court will expect to following to have occured:

- You have attempted to get the other party to comply.

- You detail within the application all efforts that have been made to get the other party to comply.

Can you raise money by selling or transferring the other party's assets or income?

Yes. You can consider a charging order in these circumstances:

- You are seeking to enforce a fixed sum (usually a lump sum order, but also potentially a costs order, interest or arrears of maintenance *but not* a settlement order under Schedule 1 of the Children Act 1989).

- You want to secure a charge against an asset belonging to the other person.

This form of enforcement is commonly used against land or property owned or co-owned by the person owing the money but can also be used where that person holds certain stock or unit trusts (although charging orders cannot usually be made against personal pensions). If there is any doubt as to whether a certain asset can be charged, it is advisable to have reference to the Charging Orders Act 1979 and/or to take legal advice.

How do you make an application?

The procedure in an application for charging orders is set out in three important documents:

- The Charging Orders Act 1979.
- Part 73 of the Civil Procedure Rules 1998 (and the associated Practice Direction).
- Part 18 of the Family Procedure Rules 2010 (and the associated Practice Direction).

It is important to read these sections in full to appreciate the procedure to be followed.

Make the application to the Family Court on Form N379 if the application relates to land, or Form N380 in other circumstances.

Remember to give notice to anyone who might have an interest in the asset that is to be charged.

What action will the court take?

There will usually be a minimum of three distinct steps:

Enforcement of Court Orders

(1) The court will usually make an 'interim' charging order without a hearing. This imposes a charge over the other party's interest in the chosen asset.

(2) Another hearing will then be listed and the interim charging order must be served on the other party (and anyone else named in Part 73.5 of the Civil Procedure Rules 1998 where relevant, or anyone directed by the court) at least 21 days before the hearing. Anyone served with the interim charging order is not permitted to allow a transfer of the relevant asset.

(3) There will then be a final hearing, at which the court will either decide the application or list a trial of any issues (including as to ownership of any asset if that is disputed). When considering whether to make a final order, the court must consider all the circumstances of the case, including not only the circumstances of the person owing the money but also whether anyone else that the person owes money to would be 'unduly prejudiced'. Usually however, the first party to obtain a charging order takes priority. It is incumbent on any third party with notice who objects to the charging order to file and serve written evidence setting out their objections at least 7 days before the hearing.

A charging order made against land can be registered at the Land Registry. This is advisable in order to prevent dealings with the property. It is usually worth obtaining the assistance of a conveyancer for this task, although a Land Registry Practice Guide (No. 76) is available on the Land Registry website for the more intrepid.

What about the costs of the application?

You can apply to claim your costs back under the County Court Rules Order 27, Rule 9. The costs are fixed in accordance with Part 45 of the Civil Procedure Rules 1998, Part 45.

It is advisable to read these provisions before incurring any legal costs. Land registry costs are also usually allowed.

Strictly speaking, a charging order is not really a method of enforcement. It is a means of obtaining security, because the charging order does not itself result in payment of the debt. Instead it is a route to obtaining an order for sale of the property, which you can apply for once the charging order is made final. This can be done using the procedure set out in Part 8 of the Civil Procedure Rules 1998 and Practice Direction 73 and upon sale the proceeds can be used to settle the debt, either in full or part. Any additional proceeds will be returned to the party owing the money.

Attachment of earnings order

What is an attachment of earnings order?

If the other party receives income as an employed person (including any fees, bonus, commission, overtime etc), or receives statutory sick pay, it is possible to obtain an 'attachment of earnings order', which requires the employer to deduct a certain amount from the other party's salary on a weekly, monthly or other basis (which can include the principal amount due under the order, as well as any arrears and costs).

Attachment of earnings orders can also be made against certain pensions, ie those that relate to past service or for loss of employment but not social security pensions or those that relate to disablement or disability. If there is any disagreement about what constitutes 'earnings', the court is able to determine the issue.

If money is received via an attachment of earnings order, where does it go?

When paid, the monies are sent to the court (via an intermediary known as 'CAPS', ie the Central Attachment of Earnings Payment System) and forwarded on to the person to whom the money is due.

The court has another option, the attachment of earnings order can be suspended with a view to making the other party comply; if they do not, then suspension is lifted and the attachment of earnings order comes into force.

How does an attachment of earnings order work in practice?

If made, the order will specify the rate of deduction and also a 'protected earnings rate', which represents the amount, having regard to the payer's resources and needs, which the payer should retain as a minimum from their income, in order to meet their basic needs.

The court will usually have reference to the amount that the person would receive by way of social security benefits (including income support, housing benefit and tax credits) when deciding what the protected rate should be. Unfortunately, such orders lapse when the person owing the money ceases employment with a particular employer. In those circumstances the order can be directed to any new employer, although this can be a sluggish process. This method of enforcement is available for periodical payments and some other orders, including for the payment of lump sums.

Most armed forces personnel and seamen (other than fishermen) are not eligible for attachment of earnings orders. If the other party is a serving member of the armed forces, an application can be made to that person's commanding officer or the defence council for deduction from the pay of the serviceman concerned. Such applications are unusual and legal advice is recommended.

How to make an application for an attachment of earnings order

The procedural code for attachment of earnings orders is comprehensively set out in the County Court Rules, Order 27, which can be found in Schedule 1 to the Civil Procedure Rules. This section should be read and followed in full.

An application should be made to the Family Court.

You should use application Form N337 (Form N64A for a suspended order) and follow the procedure set out in rule 33.3(1) of the Family Procedure Rules 2010.

You will need to apply for permission to enforce arrears that are more than 12 months old if necessary (see Part 18 of the Family Procedure Rules 2010). The other party is then required to complete a reply and statement of means on Form N56 within 8 days of service, following which there will be a hearing (at least 21 days after the application).

If you have difficulty finding the other party, you can apply to the court for assistance. Where there is difficulty finding and serving armed forces personnel, again an application can be made. The court has additional power to order the party owing the money to provide further information about any employer and his earnings, resources and needs and if necessary to attend court for this purpose; failure to attend is punishable by imprisonment.

The costs

You can apply to claim back the costs you incurred in seeking this order if successful, under the County Court Rules Order 27 rule 9, and these are fixed in accordance with Part 45 of the Civil Procedure Rules 1998. It is advisable to read these provisions before incurring any legal costs.

It is worth noting that the court's power to make committal or execution orders is limited where an attachment of earnings order has been made.

Third party debt orders

> (i) **What is a third party debt order?**
>
> A third party debt order transfers a debt that is owed to the other party to you, so that instead of the third party owing *the other party* money, they now owe *you* money.
>
> This is most helpful where the other party has bank accounts with sufficient balances to meet the debt (as, technically speaking, the bank 'owes' the account holder that money).

How to make an application for a third party debt order

The procedure is set out in three primary documents:

- Part 72 of the Civil Procedure Rules 1998.

- Part 72 is subject to the modifications made by rule 33.24 of the Family Procedure Rules 2010.

- Practice Direction 33 Family Procedure Rules 2010 (and the associated Practice Direction).

Firstly, an application is made for an interim order.

The application should be made in the same Family Court where the original order was made, unless proceedings have been transferred, and the application form is Form N349, which sets out the details required.

To obtain an interim order in relation to a bank account, it is usually enough to demonstrate that the other party holds a bank account with a specific institution and evidence of a recent balance.

What action will the court take?

These orders are made without a hearing and the court will fix an amount below which the third party should not reduce the debt (usually the amount due plus costs). The interim order will also specify the amount that the person applying may recover my way of costs.

The order must be served first on the third party (at least 21 days before the hearing) and then on the other party within 7 days. If the third party is a building society or bank it is required to report to the court as to the balance on the relevant account(s) and whether it asserts any right to the monies (if for example the person owes the bank money on an overdraft or loan), or if it is unable to comply with the order for any reason. The bank account holder is entitled to apply to the court for a sum to be released to meet their living expenses and prevent hardship.

At the final hearing, the court will decide whether or not to make a final third party debt order. The court can determine any dispute as to whether the money is in fact owed by the third party at that hearing or set a later date. The court will then decide whether to make the final order, having particular regard to the circumstances of the person owing you money and any prejudice to third parties to whom that person owes money.

Execution against goods

> **(i) What is an order for execution against goods?**
>
> This order is best explained as follows:
>
> - This method of enforcement can be used where a specific sum is due under a lump sum order, a periodical payments order or a costs order.
>
> - The order provides for the seizure and sale of goods or possessions belong to the party owing the money in order to satisfy the amount owing.
>
> - The terminology involved with this method of enforcement is old fashioned; the process is referred to as issuing 'a writ of fieri facias' (in the High Court) or 'a warrant of execution' in the county court. In everyday language, it is often referred to as 'getting the bailiffs in'!
>
> - If the application is successful, the High Court enforcement officer or county court bailiff will deal with both seizure and sale.

How to make an application for an order for execution against goods

The application should be issued in the same Family Court that made the original order.

In the High Court, Form PF86 should be used (called a *'praecipe'*); the procedure is set out in the following documents:

- Rules of the Supreme Court, Order 46.

- Rule 18 of the Family Procedure Rules 2010 (and the associated Practice Direction).

- Rule 33.3 of the Family Procedure Rules 2010 requires a statement to be filed along with the application and a writ in Form numbers 53 to 63.

The procedure in the county court is governed by Order 26 of the County Court Rules. Form N323 should be used, together with the statement required by rule 33.3 of the Family Procedure Rules 2010.

In the county court, a warning notice is issued 7 days before any attempts are made to enforce. It is possible then to apply to suspend the execution of the warrant, the procedure for which is governed by Order 25, rule 8 of the County Court Rules.

In either case, if the order relied upon is more than six years old, permission must be applied for in advance. In addition, permission of the court is required to enforce if the other party has applied to vary the order relied upon. As is the case with other forms of enforcement, permission is required to enforce arrears more than 12 months old. Rule 18 of the Family Procedure rules governs the procedure for an application for permission.

Before engaging with this method of enforcement it is worth considering what valuable items the other party may own that are worth seizing. Orders cannot be enforced against certain items, such as tools of the trade (including vehicles) and other essential equipment or possessions of the other party or their family, such as clothing, furniture, books, bed linen etc. If you do not believe that the other party has any items of value, this method of enforcement is probably not worth pursuing.

The costs

The costs relating to such applications are fixed. The details can be found in Part 45 to the Civil Procedure Rules.

Fines and imprisonment (punitive / coercive)

If you are in a position where none of the above methods of enforcement appear likely to succeed, you may wish to consider slightly more forceful methods, including those which involve a punitive element such as a fine or imprisonment. If you are seeking to enforce an order which does not involve payment of a sum of money then this will be your only choice.

Before going down this route it is advisable to seek legal advice and probably representation.

What must the court be satisfied about in order to grant an order for a fine or imprisonment?

There are a number of essential factors to consider namely:

- Proving your case to the required standard to have someone imprisoned or fined can be difficult. This is because the courts impose a higher burden on the applicant where someone's liberty is at stake, or punitive measures are being considered.

- The test to be applied is the same as in the criminal courts, ie the case must be proved 'beyond a reasonable doubt'. To be satisfied 'beyond a reasonable doubt', the judge is essentially required to be 'sure', or firmly convinced of the evidence. This is a different test than that ordinarily applied in the family courts, which is referred to as a 'balance of probabilities', simply meaning that in order to find a fact proven the judge must believe that it is probably true (ie, more likely than not).

- The court is also required to take a 'proportionate' approach to enforcement.

There are two main forms of punitive/coercive enforcement, 'judgment summons' and 'committal for contempt of court'.

In addition, the Family Court has the power to disqualify a person from holding or obtaining a driving licence in circumstances where child support is unpaid.

Judgment summons

> (i) **What is a judgment summons?**
>
> This is a method of enforcement dating back to the Debtors Act 1869 and can be used to enforce orders for the payment of specified amounts of money (including lump sum and periodical payments orders).
>
> The person owing the money will be required to attend court and, if the court is satisfied beyond a reasonable doubt that the individual had the means to pay and willfully refused or neglected to do so, that person can be sent to prison for up to six weeks.

How to make an application for an order for judgment summons

There are some important key facts to consider when making this application:

- Before applying for such an order, it is important to ensure that the person owing the money has been 'personally served' (ie, by a process server) with the original order; and that the original order contained a penal notice warning the person about the consequences of breaching the terms of the order.

- The application is made in Form D62 to a 'convenient' Family Court, bearing in mind where the party owing the money lives and works.

- A 'judgment summons' will then be issued by the court and must also be personally served at least 14 days before the hearing date.

- Further procedural rules are contained within Part 33 of the Family Procedure Rules 2010 and must be carefully observed.

What action will the court take?

- If the person owing the money does not attend the first hearing, the matter will be adjourned and the papers served again.

- If no attendance is made at the second hearing, the court has power to have the individual arrested and brought before the court, or sent to prison for up to 14 days.

- If the party owing money does attend, the court will consider whether it has been proven, beyond a reasonable doubt, that the party owing the money has, or has had since the date of the order the means to pay, and has deliberately refused or neglected to do so.

- The person owing the money cannot be required to give

- evidence (either themselves or by producing documents) if they do not wish to do so (due to the privilege against self-incrimination).

- If the case is proved, the party owing the money can be sent to prison (known as 'committal').

- More commonly, the sentence is suspended to give the party owing the money time to pay the amounts outstanding (as well as the costs and any further sums becoming due) before being committed.

Remember that if a court subsequently makes an attachment of earnings order, a suspended committal order lapses and cannot then be relied upon.

The court will generally expect that applications for committal to prison are brought only as a last resort where other methods have failed. Furthermore, when considering a judgment summons application regarding a periodical payments order, the court is required to consider whether the order should be varied or suspended *even if* the party owing the money has not applied for variation.

With such applications, it is absolutely vital to ensure that the rules set down in Part 33 of the Family Procedure Rules 2010 are observed in order to ensure that the application does not fail due to interference with the human rights of the party owing the money. Also expect that the court will take care to ensure that the party owing the money has had the opportunity to take legal advice and prepare a defence. As stated previously, in applications that threaten the liberty of the other party legal advice and representation is strongly advised.

Committal for contempt of court

In addition to the judgment summons procedure, the courts have jurisdiction to commit persons to prison for up to two years

Enforcement of Court Orders

for contempt of court, which includes refusal to, or neglect in, complying with a court order or undertaking. Any alleged breach must be proven to the standard 'beyond reasonable doubt'.

It is important to remember that except for in the circumstances below a person shall not be arrested or imprisoned for failing to pay a sum of money.

The exceptions are:

- Default in payment of a penalty, or sum in the nature of a penalty, other than a penalty in respect of any contract.

- Default in payment of any sum recoverable summarily before a justice or justices of the peace.

- Default by a trustee or person acting in a fiduciary capacity and ordered to pay by a court of equity any sum in his possession or under his control.

- Default by a solicitor in payment of costs when ordered to pay costs for misconduct as such, or in payment of a sum of money when ordered to pay the same in his character of an officer of the court making the order.

- Default in payment for the benefit of creditors of any portion of a salary or other income in respect of the payment of which any court having jurisdiction in bankruptcy is authorised to make an order.

- Default in payment of sums in respect of the payment of which orders are in the Debtors Act 1869 authorised to be made.

Provided, first, that no person shall be imprisoned in any case excepted from the operation of this section for a longer period than one year; and, secondly, that nothing in this section shall alter the effect of any judgment or order of any court for payment of money except as regards the arrest and imprisonment of the person making default in paying such money.

How to make an application for an order for committal to prison

The procedure is set out in to following primary documents:

- Contempt of Court Act 1981.

- Rules 18 and 37 of the Family Procedure Rules 2010 (and the associated Practice Directions).

- Family Court (Contempt of Court) (Powers) Regulations 2014.

Again, it is very important that the procedure is observed to the letter to ensure that the application does not fail due to breaching the human rights of the other party.

The standard procedure for beginning proceedings for committal for enforcement of an injunction or an undertaking is by way of the procedure set out in rule 18, Family Procedure Rules 2010. The application must identify, separately, numbered each alleged act of contempt.

The affidavit or statement in support should narrate the facts relied on, but the list of alleged breaches must be given in the application notice.

The committal procedure is available for the breach of an order (but not an order to pay money or an undertaking to do so except in limited situations set out below) or direction of the court. As such, a committal application can be brought for eg the failure to comply with an order for disclosure. As stated previously, the litigant must think carefully before invoking this procedure for a minor breach of case management directions.

It is unlikely that the court will not impose a committal for failure to comply with an order that has been remedied before the hearing. Furthermore, as with any method of enforcement threatening the liberty of a party, the committal process is a remedy of last resort and will not be entertained by the court where other less serious sanctions are available.

As with the judgment summons procedure, the person who is alleged to have breached the order cannot be required to give evidence and the breach must be proven beyond a reasonable doubt. In the first instance orders are usually suspended to give the individual the opportunity to comply. Even if a person is sent to prison for the breach, they can secure their release by applying to 'purge their contempt' by complying with the order.

Due to the complexity of the law and rules, and the need to observe procedure very carefully, it is strongly advisable to take legal advice and obtain representation in cases where committal is likely to be pursued.

Less common methods of enforcement

Depending on the circumstances of the case, other forms of enforcement may be required instead of those already mentioned above including, for example (not a full list):

- More complex methods such as applying for receivership (appointment of an independent party, usually an accountant, to manage property or assets belong to a party in order to obtain funds to pay a debt) or sequestration (impoundment of assets) may also be available, along with the option of petitioning for bankruptcy. Due to the complexity and risks involved with such procedures, it is generally-speaking advisable to seek specialist legal advice before proceeding with any court application.

- In addition, it is possible to seek an order for the impoundment of an individual's passport in order to aid an enforcement application, although such applications are unusual and orders rarely made. Such methods of enforcement fall outside the scope of this work and legal advice is recommended if such avenues are to be pursued.

- Equally enforcement abroad of orders made in England or Wales, or enforcement of orders made abroad in this jurisdiction, is outside the scope of this work. In such circumstances it is advisable to contact the governmental Reciprocal Enforcement of Maintenance (REMO) Unit helpline for assistance, and/or to take legal advice.

> **For information about the Reciprocal Enforcement of Maintenance Order (REMO) Unit go to:**
>
> **https://www.gov.uk/remo-unit-helpline**

Enforcement of undertakings

Practice Direction 33A of the Family Procedure Rules 2010 makes specific provision for the enforcement of undertakings.

The court will consider the following important matters:

- Where an undertaking of a financial nature has been given, paragraph 2.1 provides that such an undertaking can be enforced as if it were an order of the court (using one of the methods referred to above).

- Paragraphs 2.2–2.3 set out the requirements that must be met for an undertaking to be enforceable, although it has

- also been established that an undertaking is enforceable where it forms an integral part of a court order.

- If you are in any doubt as to whether an undertaking is enforceable, take legal advice.

Enforcement and variation

You should always remember that an application to enforce an order may be met by the other party making an application to change the order anyway. In circumstances where one party has applied to enforce and the other party has applied to vary, you should be aware that courts tend to investigate whether there should be a variation *first*, and then look at enforcement *second*, even where the enforcement proceedings were issued first. This can cause considerable frustration for those who get some way down the route of enforcing an order, just to find that the process is stalled or even derailed by a variation application.

Further research

- The Family Procedure Rules can be found at http://www.justice.gov.uk/courts/procedure-rules/family. In particular Rules 18, 33 and 37 (and their associated Practice Directions).

- The text of 'Acts' (known as 'legislation') can be found by searching at www.legislation.gov.uk. In particular the Charging Order Act 1979, the Contempt of Court Act 1981.

- Some case reports can be found at www.bailii.org or via a general search on the internet.

- Forms and official guidance leaflets can be found by using the search facility at http://www.justice.gov.uk/forms/ or from your local court.

- In addition, the Family Court Practice (known to judges and lawyers as 'The Red Book'), is an invaluable source of advice and guidance on enforcement procedures and rules. This should be available at any good law library.

- The Civil Procedure Rules can be found at http://www.justice.gov.uk/courts/procedure-rules/civil/rules.

Dos and don'ts

DOS

✔ **DO** read carefully, and comply with, the rules

✔ **DO** ensure that the other party is fully aware of the terms of the court order and the consequences of failing to comply with those terms

✔ **DO** ensure that the other party has sufficient time to comply with their obligations, in particular if he or she is the person owing the money, as otherwise you may be faced with a hearing being adjourned

✔ **DO** be patient – the court process can often be slow, which is particularly frustrating if you are owed money

DON'TS

✘ **DON'T** waste time or money in enforcing an order against someone who is unable to pay. It is very important to carefully consider the merits of enforcement at an early stage, particularly where it appears the other party has no or very little money. The court is not likely to send the other party to prison for breaching an order he or she is unable to comply with, and you may end up wasting both time and money

✘ **DON'T** be afraid to seek legal advice where necessary.

Enforcement applications can be daunting and technically difficult, and a little outlay on lawyers at the outset can be well worth it in the long run

✗ **DON'T** attempt to avoid the court process if someone is applying to enforce an order against you. The court is likely to catch up with you and the consequences could be very serious

✗ **DON'T** allow emotion or frustration to get the better of you at court – the judge is much more likely to be helpful if you are able to communicate your position calmly and clearly

Appendix

Glossary

Abduction	Where one parent or relative takes a child usually overseas without the permission of the other parent or the court
Acknowledgement of service	Document sent to the respondent to a divorce along with the divorce petition. Respondent completes to acknowledge receipt of petition, whether agrees or disagrees with contents of petition and the position on costs
Adultery	Having a sexual relationship outside of your marriage. A ground for divorce
Alternative dispute resolution (ADR)	Resolving your disputes other than through the courts
Annulment	When a divorce is set aside
Answer	A statement from a Respondent saying why they object to the divorce petition
Appeal	Legal process to overturn an earlier decision of a judge on the basis that it was wrong
Assets	Anything that you own
Attachment of earnings orders	A method of enforcement in a financial case where an employer is directed to pay wages of one spouse directly to another to meet an outstanding court order

Barrister	A lawyer specialising in advocacy and advice in a particular area of law. Wears wig and gown in non-family cases
Cafcass officer	Cafcass is a government agency called Child And Family Court Advisory and Support Service. Officers of Cafcass are appointed by the court to advise on child welfare and safeguarding issues
Capital Gains Tax	A tax on the sale or transfer of some assets
Cash equivalent transfer value (now know as Cash Equivalent)	The value of a pension for the purpose of transfer between different pension schemes
Chambers	A barrister's office
Charging order	A method of enforcement in a financial case leading eventually to the sale of an asset to meet a sum due under a court order
Child arrangements order	The order made by the Family Court that determines with whom a child will live and who the children will spend time with
Child Arrangements Programme	The procedure adopted in the Family Court when the court is asked to make a Child Arrangements Order
Child support/child maintenance	Usually a monthly sum paid by one parent to another in respect of a child's income needs
Children's guardian	Generally an officer of CAFCASS appointed by the court to represent the interests of the children in court when the issues in the proceedings are complex and the child's interests cannot be advanced fully by the other parties to the proceedings or by the court asking for a section 7 welfare report

Civil partnership	A same sex relationship which has been legally formalised giving rise to legal rights and obligations
Clean break	Not having to pay monthly payments to an ex-spouse. All financial obligations are brought to an end if there is a clean break
Committal for contempt of court	Sending to prison for not complying with a court order
Common law wife/husband	There is no such thing!
Contact (or access)	The time that a child will spend with the parent who they do not live with
Contact order	Contact orders no longer exist and are now called Child Arrangements Orders
Contempt of court	An offence of disobeying a court order
Co-respondent	Someone other than a husband and wife who has a claim brought against them
Court order	An order made by a judge
Cross-examination	Questions asked in court by a barrister to challenge the evidence of a witness
Custody	No longer used in the Family Court. A Child Arrangements Order will determine where the child lives. It does not grant 'custody'
Decree absolute	The final decree which formally brings the marriage to an end
Decree nisi	A preliminary decree which is required before the marriage can be brought to an end
Deed	A formal legal document that is executed in a particular way
Defendant	A person defending a claim being brought against them

Desertion	A ground for divorce when a husband or wife has left the other without their consent for more than 2 years in the last 2.5 years
Directions	A court order usually requiring a particular step to be taken
Disbursements	A payment that is made usually by a solicitor and then claimed back from their client
Disclosure	Formal legal process for revealing the existence of relevant documents
Dissolution	Bringing the marriage to an end
Domestic abuse or violence	Any incident or pattern of controlling, coercive, threatening, violent or abusive behaviour between those aged 16 or over who are or have been intimate partners
Domicile	Normally the country where your main home is
Evidence	Something that is used to prove a fact
Ex parte	Without telling the other side that you are about to make an application to the court. Now called 'without notice'
Examination in chief	Initial questions asked in court to a witness by the barrister of the party calling the witness
Family Procedure Rules 2010 (FPR)	Rules which provide an essential code of procedure for family proceedings in the High Court, County Court and Family Court
Financial dispute resolution hearing (FDR)	A settlement hearing in financial remedy cases
First directions appointment (FDA)	The first time a financial remedy case comes before the court and where the court makes directions to advance the progression of the case

Glossary

First hearing dispute resolution appointment (FHDRA)	The first hearing in the Family Court to consider an application for a child arrangements order
Form E	A sworn financial statement in standard format that parties to financial remedy claims are required to complete
Former Matrimonial home	In financial remedy proceedings this refers to the home last lived in as a family. Abbreviated by lawyers to FMH
Freezing injunction	An injunction preventing the disposal or use of assets including money
Garnishee order	An enforcement process now called a third party debt order. Where A owes money to B and B owes money to C under a court order; a court order can be made requiring A to pay the money owed to B directly to C
Gender recognition certificate	A formal document evidencing a change of gender
Ground	The basis for bringing an application or case
Inheritance tax	Tax paid by a person's estates on their death
Injunction	A court order usually preventing a particular course of action
Interim hearing	A hearing to deal with matters that arise before a final hearing
Joint tenancy	An equal and undivided share in property
Judgment in default	A judgment ordered against a party who has failed to respond to service of a claim

Judgment summons	A summons to appear in court to face examination under oath as to whether a judgment debt can be paid, if it can the sum must be paid or there is a risk of imprisonment
Judicial separation	Formal separation allowing you to live apart without divorcing but still obtain financial remedies
Jurisdiction	The ability of a court to hear a case
Land Registry	Government body that holds records of land ownership
Legal aid	Government funding to lawyers for legal advice and representation
Lump Sum orders	A financial remedy requiring a certain or ascertainable sum of money to be paid by one party to another
Maintenance	The old term for periodical payments
Maintenance pending suit	Periodical payments before decree absolute
McKenzie friend	A non-legally qualified person who helps a litigant in person at court by providing support
Mediation	A form of alternative dispute resolution where a third party (a mediator) assists a couple to reach agreement about children and financial issues
Mediation Information and Assessment Meeting (MIAM)	A meeting with a mediator that is required to take place before applications can be issued. Meeting explains the benefits of mediation.
Memorandum of understanding	The without prejudice document setting out any agreement made at a mediation
Non-molestation order	A court injunction seeking to prevent domestic violence

Non-resident parent	The parent with whom a child does not live with 50% or more of the time
Occupation order	An order preventing a home owner from living in their home
Order	A direction of the court to perform or not to perform an identified act
Parental responsibility	The legal term used to describe the rights and responsibilities held by parents of children. All mothers have parental responsibility. Fathers also have parental responsibility if married to the mother at the time of the child's birth, if named on the birth certificate, if the court has made a parental responsibility order or the parents have registered a parental responsibility agreement
Pension sharing	A financial remedy splitting a pension and transferring a % of the pension to the other party
Periodical payments orders	A financial remedy requiring one party to a marriage to pay usually monthly sums of money to an other
Petition	Formal document that starts the process of divorce, judicial separation or nullity
Petitioner	The person who starts the process of divorce, judicial separation or nullity
Pleading	An old word to describe a statement of case
Power of arrest	A power that can be attached to an occupation order which means that the police will deal with any breach of the order
Practice Direction	A protocol issued to provide supplemental or further information to rules of procedure in the courts

Privilege	You don't have to disclose this category of evidence to the other side.
Prohibited steps order	An order made in the Family Court to prevent a parent from taking specific steps concerning a child, such as taking the child out of the country or changing the child's name
Property adjustment order	A financial remedy where the court orders one party to the marriage to transfer property to the other
Property transfer orders	A colloquialism for a property adjustment order
Redemption	When a mortgage is settled
Re-examination	Questions asked by the barrister for the party calling a witness following cross-examination
Residence order	No longer in use. The Family Court will determine where a child will live by making a child arrangements order
Respondent	The party defending an application or claim
Rights of audience	The legal right to address the court
Secured creditor	A person who is owed money and who has a charge or mortgage over property owned by the person owing him money
Self-incrimination	Where a witness or party reveals that they have committed a crime whilst giving evidence. There is a privilege against self-incrimination
Service	The formal process by which legal proceedings or applications are obtained by a respondent
Settlement	An agreement bringing the end to an application or a case

Specific issue order	An order made by the Family Court to require a parent to exercise parental responsibility in a specific way, such as requiring the child to attend a specific school
Stamp duty land tax	A tax on the purchase of residential land (homes) and stocks and shares
Statement of arrangements	No longer in use. It was a form that was required when filing for divorce but this was abolished in July 2014
Statement of case	A formal legal document usually drafted by a barrister that sets out the basis for a claim or a defence
Stay	A court authorised halt to proceedings
Tenancy in common	Joint ownership of property but each owner is entitled to a specific proportion of the property
Transcript	A written record of court proceedings
Trial	The hearing at which a judge decides for the first time the final outcome of a case
Trust	A legal relationship where property is held by one party subject to obligations to another
Undertakings	A solemn promise to the court which if broken is a contempt of court (see above)
Unreasonable behaviour	A ground for divorce
Urgent interim application	An urgent application made prior to the trial
Without notice	An urgent application made without letting the other side know
Without prejudice	An off the record discussion or correspondence

INDEX

References are to page numbers.

Activity conditions	321
breach of terms	325
types of activities	322
when they can be made	324
when they cannot be made	325
who can they be made against	323
Activity directions	321
breach of terms	325
examples	322
limits	321
types of activities	322
welfare of child	321
when they can be made	324
when they cannot be made	325
who can they be made against	323
Alternative dispute resolution (ADR)	15, 280
Arrest	166
Assets	
matrimonial assets	214
non-matrimonial assets	214
Attachment of earnings order	340
armed forces	341
costs	343
making an application	342
rate of deduction	341
where money is sent	341
Barrister	22
free advice from	26
public or direct access barrister	25
Breakdown of relationship	5, 7
emotions	7
practical considerations	10
Budgets	
schedule of assets/debts	222, 242
Charging order	337

Child arrangements order	98, 198
enforcement	318
warning notice	319
non-compliance	320
Child arrangements programme	174
dispute resolution appointment	181
fact finding hearing	185
final hearing	185
first hearing dispute resolution appointment	174
position statement	176
example of	178
review hearing	181
Child maintenance	14
Child Maintenance Service	211, 267, 290
Children	
applications for orders	98
responding to	103
urgent applications	102
best interests of	34
child arrangements order	198
delay in court proceedings	35, 200
disputes about	33, 50, 171, 197
appeals	188
costs	187
fact finding hearing	129, 185
final hearing	129, 185
first hearing dispute resolution appointment	128, 174
gathering information	52
interim/directions hearing	128
letters before action	96
principles	200
enforcement of orders	318
warning notice	319
financial provision from the court	289
who qualifies	290

Children—continued

harm suffered by	36, 201, 202
maintenance for	266
no order principle	37, 204
parents' ability to meet child's needs	36, 201, 203
periodical payments	
order/maintenance	211
child in further education	211
child reaching 18	211
disabled child	211
non-biological parent	211
physical, educational and emotional needs	36, 200, 201
prohibited steps order	198, 199
specific issue order	198, 199
welfare checklist	35, 116, 200
welfare of	10, 34, 35, 39, 40, 188, 198, 200, 213, 216, 300, 306
wishes and feelings of	36, 200

Children and Family Court Advisory and Support Service (Cafcass) 121, 175, 323

Civil partnership

annulment	84
conditional order	79
considerations on relationship breakdown	47
dissolution	79
defended	83
desertion	80
five years' separation	80
grounds	80
process	80
two years' separation with consent	80
undefended	81
unreasonable behaviour	80
final order	80
petition	79

Clean break 214

Cohabitation

financial disputes	45
financial provision for children	266, 267
meaning	266
property disputes	273
appeals	286
case management	283
costs	285
joint ownership	274
procedure	279, 281
sole ownership	274, 276

Cohabitation—continued

property disputes—continued	
statements of case	282
trial	284

Collaboration 14, 15
Contact after separation 89
Contempt of court, committal

for	350
application	352

Couple therapy 9
Court bundle 249

contents	249
copies	252

Court orders

attachment of earnings order	340
child arrangements order	98, 198
lump sum order	39
non-molestation order	142
occupation order	142, 145
order for execution of goods	345
parental responsibility order	99
pension sharing order	39
periodical payments order	39
prohibited steps order	98, 198, 199
property adjustment order	39
special guardianship order	99
specific issue order	98, 198, 199
third party debt orders	343

Court proceedings 21, 97

applications for financial help	104
responding to	105
applications for non-molestation/occupation orders	105
responding to	106
applications involving children	98
responding to	103
urgent applications	102
issuing an application	97
without prejudice, meaning	238

Directions order 246

disclosure of information	246
witness statement (s 25 narrative statement)	246

Disbursements 22
Dispute resolution appointment 181
Divorce

acknowledgement of service	73, 74
adultery	63, 65
decree absolute	63
decree nisi	63

Index

Divorce—*continued*
- defended — 76
  - time limits — 77
- desertion — 64
- five years' separation — 64
- grounds — 63
- no fault system — 65
- petition — 63, 68
  - accompanying documents — 70
  - contents — 69
  - delivery or service of — 71
  - fee for issue — 71
  - financial application on — 70
  - prayer — 69
  - responding to — 73
- process — 62, 68
- two years' separation with consent — 64
- undefended — 74
- unreasonable behaviour — 63, 65, 68
- who can apply — 62

Domestic violence — 141
- appeals — 165
- directions — 158
- duration of orders — 159
- enforcement of orders — 166
- evidence — 160
  - respondent's statement — 162
  - schedule of allegations — 161
  - statement in support — 160
- hearing where violence is contested — 163
- non-molestation/occupation orders
  - application — 146
    - responding to — 151
  - service — 150
  - factors for issuing — 154
- undertaking — 156
- urgent cases — 155

Enforcement — 117, 317
- compensation for financial loss — 330
  - amount — 331
  - application — 331
  - costs — 332
  - defence against application — 330
    - reasonable excuse — 330
- domestic violence — 166
- foreign orders — 354
- meaning — 318
- orders — 326
  - application — 331
  - breach of terms — 329

Enforcement—*continued*
- orders—*continued*
  - contempt of court — 329, 332
  - costs — 332
  - defence against application — 328
    - reasonable excuse — 328
  - monitoring compliance — 328
  - relating to children — 187, 318
    - activity conditions — 321
    - activity directions — 321
    - transfer of residence — 333
    - warning notice — 319
    - welfare of child — 327
  - relating to finances — 334
    - action taken by court — 338
    - application — 336, 338
    - attachment of earnings — 340, 341, 342, 343
    - charging order — 337
    - claiming interest — 336
    - contempt of court — 350, 352
    - costs — 339
    - definitions — 335
    - execution against goods — 345, 347
    - fines/imprisonment — 347
    - judgment summons — 348, 349
    - methods of enforcement — 334
    - obtaining information — 335
    - third party debt orders — 343, 344
    - uncooperative party — 337
    - variation — 355
    - warning notice attached — 328
    - when can they be made — 326
  - undertakings — 354

Essential dos and don'ts
- case preparation — 117
- civil partnership, dissolution — 85
- disputes involving children — 204
- disputes relating to property — 287
- divorce proceedings — 85
- domestic violence — 169
- enforcement of court orders — 356
- financial remedy applications — 263
- preparing to go to court — 139

Execution against goods, order for — 345
- costs — 347
- making an application — 345

Expert evidence — 186, 230

Family arbitration — 14, 20
- finding an arbitrator — 20

Family Court applications
  stages of 88
Family home
  beneficial interest in 272
  financial orders
    notice to mortgagee 230
  occupation order 145
    application 146
  ownership 210
  sale of 210
Finances
  applications for financial help 39, 104
    case preparation 113
    compensation principle 43
    contributions made during
      relationship 42
    dividing assets 41
    full disclosure of finances 44
    letters before action 96
    needs of parties 41
    partner not earning 42, 43
    responding to 105
    sharing assets 42
    unmarried couple/cohabitants 45
  disputes about 38
  relationship breakdown, after 12
    gathering information 53
Financial dispute resolution
  hearing (FDR) 129, 233, 236
  directions order 246
  financial provision for child 295
  hearing 244
  no agreement at 246
  preparation before 240
    family law rules 240
    making offers/proposals 240
  reaching an agreement 239, 245
  schedule of assets/debts 242
  types of order made at 238
  what happens at 236
  without prejudice proceedings 238
Financial provision (children) 289
  applications 292, 313
    process 293
    unmarried parents 292
  capital expenses paid in
    connection with child's
      birth 291, 303
  child living abroad 291, 306
  child under 18 292
  costs 307, 308, 311
  disabled child 290, 306, 307

Financial provision (children)—*continued*
  factors considered by court 297
    disability of child 298
    earning capacity 297
    financial assets 298
    income of parties 297
    length of relationship
      irrelevant 300
    needs of child 298
    property owned 297
    standard of living 299
  final hearing 295
  financial dispute resolution
    hearing (FDR) 295
  first appointment 295
  responding to a claim 315
  school fees 290, 306
  settlement of property 291, 300
  tax issues 301
  university fees 291
  who qualifies 290
Financial remedy proceedings 207
  appeals 255
    court bundle 257
    new evidence 258
    permission to appeal 255, 256
    respondent's notice 258
    stay of proceedings 258
    time limits 256, 257
  capital orders 210
  clean break principle 214
  compensation 213
  complying with final order 255
  costs 254
  disclosing information about
    finances 220
  documents needed for 221
  example of case summary 223
  factors to consider 212, 215
  final hearing 130, 247, 252
    court bundle 249
    evidence 252
    judge's decision (judgment) 254
    open proposals 248
    preparation for 247
  financial dispute resolution
    hearing (FDR) 129, 233, 236, 238, 240, 244, 245, 246
  first appointment 129, 221, 225, 230, 233, 234, 235
  Form A (application form) 217
  Form E (financial information
    form) 218
  income orders 210

Index

Financial remedy proceedings—*continued*
   lump sum order   210
   maintenance pending suit   260, 261
   pension sharing   39, 210, 242
   periodical payments order   210
   sale of property   210
   schedule of assets/debts   222, 242
   sharing principle   214
   types of court orders   210
   variation of orders   259
   welfare of child   213
First appointment   221, 225
   documents needed   226
      chronology   227
      questionnaire   227
      statement of issues   226
   expert evidence   230
   financial applications   129
   financial provision for child   295
   hearing   230
   preparation before   233
   questionnaires   232
   steps taken after   234
First directions appointment (FDA)   104
   notice of   105
First hearing dispute resolution appointment (FHDRA)   128, 174
Former matrimonial home   210

Going to court   97, 119
   addressing the judge   130
   appeals   139
   applications for financial help   104
      responding to   105
   applications for non-molestation/occupation orders   105
      responding to   106
   applications involving children   98
      responding to   103
      urgent applications   102
   case management documents   121
      case summary   122
      chronology   124
      position statement   122
      skeleton argument   122
   closing submission   138
   hearing
      day of   126
      preparation before   125
      types of   128

Going to court—*continued*
   issuing an application   97, 98
   judgment   139
   oral evidence   133
   preparation before   120
   witness questioning   135
      cross-examination   136
      examination-in-chief   135
      preparing for   137
      re-examination   137

Internet divorce   28
Internet resources
   child maintenance   15, 267, 290, 306
   Children and Family Court Advisory and Support Service (Cafcass)   121, 175, 323
   Citizens' Advice Bureau   151
   court forms   29, 68, 81, 98, 105, 117, 144, 147, 218, 308
   court procedure   96
   domestic violence   168
   family arbitration   20
   instructing a barrister   23
   instructing a solicitor   23
   judge, addressing in court   131
   legal aid   27
   legislation   33, 142, 172, 210, 268
   local family court   71, 97, 146
   managing finances   13
   mediators   95
   Reciprocal Enforcement of Maintenance (REMO) Unit   354
   Relate   10
   Resolution   23, 92
   support in relationship breakdown   10
   taxation advice   13, 301, 302

Judge
   addressing in court   131
Judgment summons   348
   action taken by court   349
   making an application   348
Judicial separation   85

Law, family
   case law   54
   Child Support Act 1991   32

Law, family—*continued*
    Children Act 1989   32, 34, 35, 36,
        37, 51, 113, 190, 192, 197, 198,
        200, 267, 289, 290, 291, 292,
        293, 297, 298, 306, 307, 311, 318
    Civil Partnership Act 2004   32, 39
    Family Act 1996   106
    Family Law Act 1996   114, 116, 141,
        142, 144, 167
    Family Procedure Rules 2010   142, 171
    Human Fertilisation and
        Embryology Act 2008   172
    Matrimonial Causes Act 1973   32,
        39, 40, 42, 62, 116, 212, 213, 261
    Trusts of Land and Appointment
        of Trustees Act 1996   49, 268

Lawyer
    charging rates   22
    choosing   22
    fees   22

Legal advice
    obtaining   21

Legal terminology/definitions
    advocacy   119
    alternative dispute resolution
        (ADR)   15
    arrears   335
    barrister   22
    beneficial interest   272
    beneficial ownership   46
    claimant   283
    clean break   214
    contemnor   335
    contempt of court   166, 319, 332
    court bundle   90, 126, 249
    cross-examination   252
    defendant   283
    directions   158
    disbursements   22
    enforcement   318
    evidence-in-chief   252
    family based arrangement   267
    interim order   13
    judgment creditor   335
    judgment debtor   335
    judgment summons   348
    legal ownership   46
    litigant in person   23
    maintenance pending suit   261
    McKenzie friend   24, 149

Legal terminology/definitions—*continued*
    Mediation Information and
        Assessment Meeting
        (MIAM)   19, 94, 174
    non-matrimonial assets   214
    order for an account   272
    parental responsibility   190
    pension sharing   39, 242
    Practice Direction   142, 172
    re-examination   253
    return date hearing   153
    s 25 narrative statement   247
    Sears Tooth agreement   28
    service   72
    statement of truth   162
    stay of proceedings   258
    submissions   164
    undertaking   156
    without prejudice   90, 238

Letters before action   95
    cases involving children   96
    financial claims   96

Litigant in person   23
Litigation   21
Lump sum order   39, 210
    variation   259

Maintenance pending suit   260, 261
Marriage
    annulment   84
Married couple
    considerations on relationship
        breakdown   47
McKenzie friend   24, 149
    role of   24
Mediation   14, 17, 93, 295
Mediation Information and
    Assessment Meeting
    (MIAM)   19, 94, 174

Negotiations before court
    proceedings   89
    keeping records   92
    letters before action   95
    without prejudice correspondence   89
Non-molestation order   141, 142
    acts prohibited by   143
    applications   105, 146
        responding to   106, 151
        service   150
    case preparation   113
    enforcement   167

Index

Non-molestation order—*continued*
    factors for issuing   154
    without notice hearing   149, 155

Occupation order   141, 145
    applications   105, 146
        responding to   106, 151
        service   150
    balance of harm test   154
    case preparation   113
    enforcement   168
    without notice hearing   149, 155

Parent
    alcohol or drug abuse   203
    mental health of   203
Parental responsibility   190
    acquiring   192
    agreement between parents   194
    birth mother   191
    contact with child   196
    error on birth certificate   193
    married parents   191
    meaning   190
    more than one person having   191
    no power to impose   197
    step-parent   197
    unmarried father acquiring   195, 196
        birth registration   192
    unmarried parents   191
Parental responsibility order   99
Penal notice   166
Pension benefit
    sharing   39, 210, 242, 259
Periodical payments order   39, 210
    agreement between parties   211
    amount   212
    child for   211
    duration   212
    former spouse/civil partner   211
    variation   259
Preparing a court case
    fact-finding hearing   110
        Scott-Schedule   110
    final hearing   112
    financial cases   113
    interim hearing   107
        bundle   110
        case summary   109
        court papers   107
        position statement   109
        statement for court   114
Prohibited steps order   98, 198, 199

Property
    beneficial interest in   272
    joint tenancy   273
    legal interest   273
    sale of   210, 259
    tenants in common   273
Property adjustment order   39
Property transfer order
    variation   259

Reaching a settlement   89
    keeping records   92
    letters before action   95
    without prejudice correspondence   89
Relate   9
Relationship counselling   8
Relationship therapy   7, 8
Relationship, breakdown of   5, 7
    cohabitating couple   265
    emotions   7
    information gathering
        children, about   52
        finances, about   53
    practical considerations   10
    resolving issues   47
        children   50
        married/civil partnership   47
        unmarried couple   49
Resolution   23

Schedule of assets/debts   222, 242
Separated parents information
        programme   323
Separation
    contact after   89
Special guardianship order   99
Specific issue order   98, 198, 199
Spouse
    maintenance payments   211

Third party debt orders   343
    action taken by court   344
    making an application   343

Unmarried couples
    considerations on relationship
        breakdown   49
    financial disputes   45
Unmarried parents
    financial provision for child   292